What People are saying about the works of James R. Fisher, Jr., Ph.D.

Work Without Managers: A View from the Trenches (1991)

One of the ten best business books of 1991! Fisher opens angrily by declaring, "Any large company today is 20 to 30 divisions in search of a corporation." He asserts that *silent killers* afflict corporate progress. A *Dallas Morning News* columnist called it "the most insightful, perceptive examination of the American workplace today." I wouldn't go that far, but read it and you'll blush, beam, or bark.

—*Industry Week* (December 2, 1991, p. 42)

Work Without Managers is a major work of 1991. It is our opinion that **Work** promises to foster a controversy that will be instrumental in affecting a fundamental change in the American workplace. It is a work making a significant contribution to American management and business enterprise.

—*Business Book Review Journal*
(Volume 8, Number 1)

T0265687

Confident Selling for the 90s **(1992)**
(Pulitzer Prize nominee)

"Yes, the book is focused on selling. But then all encounters in life are selling. Fisher claims in the future work will center on *cells* rather than individuals, and credit will be shared according to contribution to the team's success. It could turn out to be as prophetic as John Naisbitt's Megatrends."

—*New Awareness Magazine* (June 1992)

The Worker, Alone! Going Against the Grain **(1995)**

"It is indeed a book alone, in a category all by itself. In it Fisher calls for an awakening of America's work force as fundamentally profound as Emerson's **Self-Reliance** essay was to the 19th century.

—Charles D. Hayes, author of
Beyond the American Dream (1998)

I have just surmised what constitutes an important book: one written by Dr. Fisher, which proves embarrassing because it makes us think about things we would otherwise prefer to ignore.

—Gary Herrity, Principal
Horace Mann Elementary
Clinton, Iowa

The Taboo Against Being Your Own Best Friend
(1996)

"Churchill once had a great line about nothing being as powerful as the simple declarative English sentence. Dr. Fisher is one of the few folks writing in this genre who knows what he meant. *The Taboo* is full of these simple looking, but profound, and from a marketing angle, readable sentences, such as 'We are not happy campers. We have lost our moral compass.'"

—James W. Wright, Senior Columnist
The Dallas Morning News
Dallas, Texas

Fisher bares his soul in this book, and in doing so, exposes mine to me. The message here is not to celebrate self-indulgence, but to provide a strategy for penetrating it in order to arrive at self-acceptance. That compound word is so easy to say, "self-acceptance," yet so difficult to realize. Be advised, Fisher offers no detours on this important journey.

—Dr. Billy G. Gunter, Professor of Sociology
University of South Florida
Tampa, Florida

Six Silent Killers:
Management's Greatest Challenge (1998)

Invest the time, really read the book, and you'll probably agree that the central reasons for an unhappy workplace are some well-defined "killers." And, ever so handily, Fisher will lead you to one more conclusion: that there's a seventh killer somewhere here. It's a management profession failing to move forward with the times, that talks endlessly about "vision" and "empowerment" while refusing to loosen "the command-and-control screws" even one turn.

—Dr. Thomas Brown, Associate Editor
Across the Board:
The Conference Board Magazine (June 1998)

Fisher doesn't pull any punches in this book, and I like that. His brilliant and succinct writing style makes this book an absolute must for anyone who: (a) makes decisions about employees (hiring, firing, performance assessments); (b) can't put their finger on employee challenges; and (c) for those looking to improve productivity and well being in their workplace. I wish I had this book 30 years ago, but grateful that I have it now! Thank you James R. Fisher, Jr.!!!

—**Glenn V. Wilson,** Restaurateur
Zelienople, Pennsylvania
(Comment appeared on **Amazon.com**)

WORK WITHOUT MANAGERS

SECOND EDITION

DR. JAMES R. FISHER, JR.

WORK SECOND EDITION
WITHOUT
MANAGERS

A VIEW FROM THE TRENCHES

TATE PUBLISHING
AND ENTERPRISES, LLC

Published by Tate Publishing & Enterprises, LLC
127 E. Trade Center Terrace | Mustang, Oklahoma 73064 USA
1.888.361.9473 | www.tatepublishing.com

Tate Publishing is committed to excellence in the publishing industry. The company reflects the philosophy established by the founders, based on Psalm 68:11,
"The Lord gave the word and great was the company of those who published it."

Book design copyright © 2014 by Tate Publishing, LLC. All rights reserved.
Cover design by Jim Villaflores
Interior design by Jimmy Sevilleno

Published in the United States of America

ISBN: 978-1-62902-714-2
1. Psychology / Industrial & Organizational Psychology
2. Psychology / Social Psychology
14.07.28

ALSO BY JAMES R. FISHER, JR.

- Confident Selling
- Confident Selling for the 90s
- Purposeful Selling
- The Worker, Alone!
- The Taboo Against Being Your Own Best Friend
- Meet Your New Best Friend
- Six Silent Killers
- Corporate Sin
- In the Shadow of the Courthouse (novel)
- A Look Back to See Ahead
- Time Out for Sanity!
- Confident Thinking
- A Green Island in a Black Sea (novel)

"We live today in a globally interconnected world, in which biological, psychological, social, and environmental phenomena are all interdependent. To describe this world appropriately we need an ecological perspective which the Cartesian world view does not offer... What we need, then, is a new paradigm—a new vision of reality; a fundamental change in thoughts, perceptions and values."

—Fritjof Capra,
Austrian-born American physicist

"The man who embraces a new paradigm at an early stage must often do so in defiance of the evidence provided by the problem solving. He must, that is, have faith that the new paradigm will succeed with the many large problems that confront it knowing only that the older paradigm has failed with a few. A decision of that kind can only be made on faith."

—Thomas S. Kuhn,
American physicist and philosopher

DEDICATION

I N MEMORY OF my mother, Dorothy Cecilia Fisher and my father, James R. Fisher, Sr., my wife, Betty Ann; the memory of my uncle, Dr. Leonard M. Ekland, my cousin Robert Ekland, and the memory of Rachel Carson and Gregory Bateson, she for her concern for the ecology of our planet, and he for the ecology of the interior landscape of our mind.

With a special thanks to George Edward Daly, Calgary, Alberta, Canada

ACKNOWLEDGMENTS

T HE FIRST AND most important acknowledgment is to my wife, Betty. She created the climate conducive to this long and demanding project. Additionally, she was influential in the format and presentation of ideas. And of course, she was much involved in the many drafts before this manuscript reached its final form.

A special thanks to George Edward Daly of Calgary, Alberta, Canada. Without his tireless effort, understanding, expertise, patience and electronic savvy, Work Without Managers would not have come to fruition in this second edition. This is also true of eight other works that are part of this second edition collection. He has helped to craft my ideas in a form and format to resonate with working professionals today. This includes editing my original introductory essays.

Also, I would like to acknowledge the support of Dr. Christa Kirby, who read the original manuscript and supplied useful editorial comments. I would like to thank Don Maxam, who gave the manuscript a "sanity check"; Jim Lange, who cared desperately that the book reach its intended audience of professional workers and managers; and Jackson Fulbright and Betty Fisher, who turned some of my visualizations into comprehensible graphics.

Next, I would like to acknowledge my employers over the years (Standard Brands, Inc., U. S. Navy, Nalco Chemical Company, Honeywell, Inc., Honeywell Europe, Ltd., and The Professional Institute of The American Management Association), who have provided me with a wonderful laboratory and fertile opportunity for research. Were it not for that experience 'in the trenches,' this effort would have been but a hollow voice. It would be remiss not to also include the many years in academia from elementary through graduate and postgraduate education, as these, too, are jobs. All of them are part of the same laboratory, the same whole cloth. We get a report card every day whatever the endeavor.

For five summers while attending the University of Iowa, I was employed by Standard Brands, Inc., working in virtually every department of this chemical processing company. Upon graduation, I assumed a position with this same company as a chemist in R&D Research.

After returning from active duty in the US Navy, I joined Nalco Chemical Company as a chemical sales engineer in Nalco's Industrial Division. I was promoted to the position of a corporate executive in Nalco's International Division, working in South America, Europe and South Africa.

On my return from South Africa, I spent the next six years in graduate school at the University of South Florida and Walden University, earning a Ph.D. in social, industrial and organizational psychology, consulting on the side to Fortune 500 companies.

Upon graduation, I continued consulting and then joined one of my clients, Honeywell, Inc. as a management and organizational development psychologist in Honeywell's Avionics Division. I was promoted to director of human resources planning & development to Honeywell Europe Ltd.

After that assignment, taking the history of this diverse experience to heart, I turned to writing books to capture the essence of what I had learned.

Acknowledging the words of the late Senator Barry Goldwater that "America is the best idea in the history of man," I consider myself blessed having been born and bred in the United States of America. Were I to have been born in Europe, for instance, it is doubtful that someone like myself would have had the experiences to conceive much less write Work Without Managers.

Finally, I would like to acknowledge my mother, who, like Romain Gary's mother in his autobiography, *Promise At Dawn* (1966), put the fire of adventure into me, while insisting that I had 'appointments to keep.' Thank God for such mothers!

TABLE OF CONTENTS

AUTHOR'S NOTE

MANAGERS!
WHO NEEDS THEM?

LIKELY IT SEEMS far-fetched at first glance, a workplace absent of managers. After all, who among us has experienced a workplace without this all-important class of working professionals? And they seem to be multiplying, not diminishing in numbers. Everyone wants to be a manager, and the B-Schools are flourishing. We're sold on management. Yet, the more management is emphasized and the more managers we have, the less successful and fulfilled we seem to be as a society and as individuals. Our institutions and corporations are teetering on the brink of ruin.

Something doesn't add up. Could it be that management as a field is not the panacea we have been led to believe? Perhaps managers do not have the answers we thought.

Why Work Is Not Working Like It Ought To

We've all experienced it. Our employers seem to expect something quite different from us than what we expect of ourselves; that we know we are capable of doing. Their expectations are quite modest to what we expect of ourselves.

Our performance is constantly judged, micro-measured in fact, but what is judged and measured seems to have little to do with what we are capable of doing, and what we feel ought to be important to our employer. While we may have as much or more education and experience than our managers, we are treated like adolescents. And therein resides the problem.

We are no longer dependent on adults as we once were for guidance, discipline and ideas. We are adults. We like our work and we're full of ideas and energy. We are ready to be tapped, to be activated, but with trust and acceptance.

Evidently, managers do not know this; do not understand the huge potential sitting right under their noses. How do we tell them? Well, we don't because we think they should already know this. We're the audience. Remember, that is our dutiful programmed role. And we have passively accepted this role for a long time; too long. In fairness, the threat of termination, rarely stated, is always inferred in every exchange between managers and the managed. Speaking up is death, as it were. Call it bullying if you wish.

Further, the culture in which we work is hard to fathom. It is designed for another time and another work force. We're told our job is one thing, but the culture conspires against our doing the job properly. Our work does not seem that important to our managers. It would appear it is more important to behave, to fit in, to be submissive and comply than challenge work assignments that seem ill advised or counterproductive. Yet, we know our work is important; our managers tell us it is. When we inform our manager about inconsistencies between our objective and what is accepted upon delivery, we find ourselves treated as if we are the problem. We shut up. The organization continues chaotically along, while conflict and political maneuvering steadily siphons off our energy, good will, and our trust. We inadvertently find ourselves drifting into skepticism and passivity.

So, let's recap. What do we have? We have a highly trained and motivated workforce of professionals who are assumed by their employers and managers to be unmotivated, undisciplined and even unintelligent. We have managers who believe their job is to train, direct, correct, manipulate and motivate these professional employees, when these workers know as much or more about the business climate and company challenges, and what needs to be done, now.

To compound the problem, the workplace environment is structured, unintentionally to frustrate the efforts of professional workers to create and deliver their work. As problems arise, they are dealt with as localized disturbances or dismissed as the misunderstandings of simple-minded workers. What could be more absurd?

To state this unequivocally, I am serious about a workplace without managers. We need not be constrained by the past, as we now are. We are free to discard our outdated and unexamined assumptions about work, workers and workplace. And, most excitingly, we're ready to release the potential of this work force unencumbered with artificial barriers such as anachronistic management and atavistic managers.

The Bigger Picture

We have been flummoxed. The present became the future, without warning. A spate of books, not long ago, sought to ease our discomfort by 'explaining away' the apparent contradictions. We've read Alvin Toffler's "Future Shock" (1970) and Dennis Gabor's "Inventing a Future" (1963) and Barbara Ward's "Lopsided

World (1968)," as well as C. P. Snow's "Two Cultures" (1959). They were all reasonable books, but changed nothing.

To be fair, these books thoroughly described the fundamental dislocations of society and the broad trends. What they failed to do was to explain why we haven't gotten where we thought we were going, and have ended up in the place that we are.

Work Without Managers: A View from the Trenches attempted to answer this important question, not philosophically, but in practical empirical terms from the trenches. Some reviewers found the book "angry" others found it provocative, still others found it insightful, all agreed it challenged the status quo, the infallible authority of management and "business as usual practices." *Industry Week* (named *WWMs* one of the ten best business books of 1991*), The Business Book Review Journal* (one of the four major works of 1991 in its genre), and NPR radio's *All Things Considered* said:

This is not casual corporate bashing; Work Without Managers is premeditated capital punishment of standard managerial systems that Fisher thinks have outlived their prime, and may not have been useful even then. (December 20, 1990).

Tellingly, it touched a nerve in certain quarters. That nerve has spread as if the organization had the shingles. Among other things, Work Without Managers argued that the First Industrial Revolution was over in 1945:

"A shocking look at American business; why it operates in '1945 nostalgia,' as six silent killers threaten to destroy it; and how only American Leadership can still save the day!"

About the same time this was being published, control theorist Russell L. Ackoff proposed that the world was going through a Second Industrial Revolution. He wrote:

"Since World War II, we have entered into a period, which will be to the future what the Renaissance was to the past. We have moved into a new age that is fundamentally different from the age, which we have come, an age that began with the Renaissance and ended essentially with World War II."

Ackoff's ideas align with sociologist Pitrim Sorokin's hypothesis. He published *Social and Cultural Dynamics* (1937), scores of years before the Ackoff thesis. Sorokin postulated the theory that we are at the end of a 600-year "Sensate Day." His "Sensate Day" commenced with the high Renaissance of 1500 A.D. in Italy, and ended with the First Industrial Revolution. Thus, we are living in Ackoff's Second Industrial Revolution, and are entering Sorokin's 600-year "Ideational Day" of the glorious tomorrow.

Remarkably, two theorists, generations apart, envisioned the same phenomenon, the end of one historic era and the dawn of another, differing only in their descriptive nomenclature.

The Paradox

We have departed the Old Machine Age and have entered the New Machine Age, characterized by microprocessors, satellites, software, robotics, and cyberspace. You may know it as the Information Age. Regardless, it's all very new and exciting, liberating in fact. Yet this New Machine Age is encumbered with some troublesome remnants of the past, principally a devotion to *reductionism*.

Reductionism is a method that seeks to reduce complex systems, to collections of parts, in order to understand and manage them efficiently. Each part is then small enough to be understood and managed independently. The disciples of reductionism, who are legion, fervently believe it to be the one and only way to understand and manage complex systems. For the most part, no one even questions this methodology. In truth, it is not often spoken of as reductionism.

It's ironic that reductionism is so ubiquitous in the computer age that it is taken for granted and unrecognized as a possible impediment. As a method of analysis and control, it has been popular for well over a century. It pervades virtually every field of sciences and the humanities: atoms in physics, cells in biology, indices in economics, Freudian elements of personality (id, ego and superego), Skinner's behavior conditioning psychology, as well as reductionism in sociology, philosophy, literature and linguistics.

Societal Reflex Thinking

Although some disciplines have moved away from reductionism, our cultural reflex is still to default to reductionism. It is evident in our susceptibility to simplistic solutions, particularly to stubborn complex problems. It is also the strongest indication that management in general is "out of sync" with the workplace of our times. Management loves simplifications; in fact it runs from complexity, while it vociferously denies the practice.

Although narrow logic dominated Machine Age Thinking, and the limits of linear logic in this non-linear age are increasingly apparent, these limits have not been sufficient to discourage their dominance. Like the limits of linear logic in this non-linear age, causation has not always proven reliable.

During the First Machine Age, the concept of environmental stewardship was unimaginable. People lived in "closed systems" obedient and unquestioning of dogmas that drove the workings of industrial society; a world of discrete parts with no explanation provided to workers about how these parts coalesced into a whole, or why. They were paid to do, not to understand.

People came to accept the notion that the whole could never be greater than the sum of its parts. Today, we know that is not true, but oddly, we do not usually act on that knowledge.

Mistaken Certainties

Machine Age thinking also relied on a process called "analysis," which was similarly governed by reductionism. To explain something, such as the workings of a large organization, it was first reduced to its elemental parts, figuratively and then actually. These parts were analyzed, optimized and then given their own goals. Consistent with the linear logic of Socratic thinking, these components were explained in the context of a particular problem. Management called it "cutting the problem down to size." Meanwhile, in the world of psychology, the structure of behavior was reduced to the phenomena of discrete syndromes.

Realistically, most problems don't respond to this breakdown because Machine Age thinking is not meant to deal with complexity, per se, but to impose synthetic systemic controls as if people were parts of a machine and reacted identical to each other. As history has shown, people as persons have been known to prove clinkers to this machine. The result is that the problems solved are generally not the problems faced. "Paralysis of Analysis" is the term given to this absurd occurrence, where the original problem is lost in the process.

Human Resources Reductionism

Reductionism among professional knowledge workers has been a disaster. How can you break down knowledge work into independent specialized functions and then reassemble the work performed, expecting reasonable "results"? Incredibly, managers have operated with this expectation. On paper, the *expected* vs. *achieved results* appear to correlate, but in reality there is only too frequently a large gap.

This is because professionals are not programmed robots. Consequently, there is a good chance that the correlation between workers and the work and each other could introduce spuriousness, which finds them not related to the work at hand. The controller (manager) and the controlled (workers) are not always on the same page, and therefore are not likely to get off on the same dime. With professionals, imposing a draconian chain-of-command methodology only compounds the problem. What is the answer? See that the controller and the controlled emanate from the same person. How do you do this? You do this by creating the suitable workplace culture.

Consider the Machine Age concept of "Management by Objectives" (MBOs) championed by Peter Drucker, a master of reductionism. He introduced MBOs as a rationally ordering way to achieve corporate goals. His intentions were sound, but the concept was not. Widely adopted by corporations, it soon became ritualistic practice with little downside when the work force was largely blue-collar. It has been ineffective and counterproductive, however, with professional workers, who have essentially replaced blue-collar workers, and yet the practice persists.

A factory mentality is a holdover from the 20th century when workers were treated as things to be managed rather than persons to be led, when profits came before people and no one saw the immorality of this. Performance Appraisal System (PAS) was meant to be a coaching, counseling, guiding and directing mechanism to improve workers' competence and performance. Instead, it reinforced management chain-of-command control of professionals indicating who was in charge, as these professionals were confined to a labyrinth of open cubicles, while managers had closed offices where they could regally dispense modest pay increases and, for the effort, stifle professional development. Scott Adams's "Dilbert" cartoon has had much fun penetrating this absurdity.

From the mid-twentieth century on, fad theories continued to percolate as to how to assess this changing work force and gauge its problem solving contributions. These fads included charismatic management, cosmetic interventions, communication schemes, leadership style paradigms and finally, engineering cybernetics.

The workplace became recognized as a "system" consistent with control theory, which provided a template for evaluating and accepting or rejecting these previous theories.

Unconscious Incompetence

Today, unconsciously, most organizations, de facto, are still committed to Machine Age thinking, and reductionism, but ironically, in a rather more vigorous way.

These organizations, private and public, for profit and non-profit practice reductionism by reducing the system to discrete autonomous elements: that is, departments, divisions, functions, and technologies. Ackoff cautions this divisional pursuit is a self-defeating strategy if this is not understood:

The performance as a whole is affected by every one of its parts. That is a basic characteristic of a system. If you think of a corporation as a system, this means that every department (division, technology, function) can affect the performance of the corporation. That is the first condition of a system. If you have a department, which has no effect on the performance of the corporation, the one thing you can be sure of is that it is not a part of the corporation.

A second characteristic of a system is that the way that any part affects the whole depends on what one other part is doing. No part of the system has an independent effect on the whole. What this says is that the way marketing affects corporate behavior depends on what other departments do, and visa versa.

Now the third condition is the most complex. If you take these elements (components) and group them in any way, they form subgroups. These subgroups will be subject to the same first and second conditions as the original elements were, that is, each subgroup will affect the performance as a whole and no subgroup will have an independent effect of the performance of the whole.

Ackoff argues this is the difference between an indivisible part and an indivisible whole and the roots of the current Intellectual Revolution.

Standing Back

Systems Thinking is the new approach to the problem solving and organizational effectiveness. It means moving from a preoccupation with parts of things to a new concentration on the whole and on the wholes of which there are these parts, or a shift from analysis to synthesis.

With *analysis*, if you wanted to explain a problem, you took it apart, explained the parts, then put it back together again, explaining the problem in terms of the parts.

In *synthesis*, if you wanted to explain a problem, you did exactly the opposite. You didn't look at the problem to be explained as a whole to be taken apart, but as a part of a greater whole. You explain the whole of which it is a part, and then extract an explanation of the thing you started with from an explanation of the whole.

If this sounds confusing, it is because of our conditioning. It may seem to be counterintuitive thinking, which often comes into play in organizational development (OD) work. Ackoff comes to our aid:

If you consider a system and take it apart to identify its components, and then operate those components in such a way that every component behaves as well as it possibly can, there is one thing of which you can be sure.

The system as a whole will not behave as well as it can.

The corollary is this, if you have a system that is behaving as well as it can, none of its parts will be.

Consider some advantages of counterintuitive thinking:

It nullifies the practice of interdepartmental competition and validates the synergistic power of cooperation.

System Thinking abhors the idea of "comparing and competing" as this fosters imitation. A company doesn't search for excellence. A comapny creates excellence. Unequivocally, with a central focus, people in the company realize they are sitting on acres of diamonds.

Work Without Managers acknowledges the workplace isn't working like it used to work. Counterintuitive thinking may not have been critical to Machine Age thinking, but is essential to *Systems Thinking* in the Information Age.

The Cure Is Known

Ackoff's theorems, as you see, have special significance to *Work Without Managers*. In my more than forty years working in corporations at every level of organization on four continents, I have found the absence of control theory to be of devastating consequences. In this original work (1991) I wrote:

> *Take Corporate America. Any large company today is 20 to 30 divisions in search of a corporation. The pendulum of centralization-decentralization is more a yo-yo contest with no clear winners, only painfully confused losers. Trauma is written on the face of American enterprise. Meanwhile, this once powerful and energetic nation doesn't seem to know what is happening.*

I wish it were possible to declare that Corporate America has changed, but as you read this book, you will see it has changed little. While work has evolved from brawn power to brainpower, from blue to white collar, from managers to professionals, from assembly lines to software manufactured products, from brick, mortar and steel institutions to online universities at a fraction of the cost of higher education, from distinctive technological disciplines to complex hybrids, and from hierarchies and position power to Skunk Works and knowledge power, managerial approaches have not changed.

The failure to embrace the unique requirements of a professional work force continues to throw Corporate America off its stride, and thus every worker. Think of how you can apply the lessons learned here to your job, and by extension to operations in general. The first step is to take charge of your work, which is the best way to take charge of your life. Damn the torpedoes. You don't need managers. They need you!

—James R. Fisher, Jr., Ph.D. © April 29, 2014
Edited by George Edward Daly, Calgary, Alberta Canada,

THE AMERICAN DILEMMA AND THE PHANTOM CHALLENGE

Amerikas Krankheit: The Trauma of the Modern Organization

THE ERA OF the *free lunch* has ended. The 20th century, which began with such paternal control and obedience for America, has run amuck. Now, nothing (and no one) is in control.

Take Corporate America.

An *undeclared psychological war is* being waged within most major enterprises today, with bodies falling on all sides, and nobody's paying attention. The principle players are worrying about *what's* 'in,' *what's* 'out'; *who's* 'in,' *who's* 'out'; *who's* making points, *who* isn't… while the marketplace is disappearing into the sunset. [1]

Chaos masquerades as *business as usual.* Friedrich Nietzsche (1844-1900) asserted chaos is the ultimate route to discovery—but what we are experiencing in America is absurd.

As wont is our American Way, the *paralysis of analysis is* substituted for a quiet appraisal of what is happening. A new frame of reference appcals little to the American *mind of the time.* The American appetite is for the quick-and-dirty solution, with the stamp of *corpocracy.*

Amerikas Krankheit ("The American Disease"), as the Germans put it, is running rampant, out of control. Formerly confined to government bureaucracies, it is now a rash affecting American business, education, and industry. *The American Disease of Corpocracy* has these common characteristics:

- Management is insensitive to its employees.

- Management supports company politics at the expense of productivity.

- Secretiveness is the measure of communication.

- The principal product is paperwork (now metadata).

- Endless meetings are the 'way' (when in doubt, hold a meeting).

- An internal focus is maintained, so potential markets are ignored.

- Short-term planning and thinking is preferred to embracing challenges ("Plan, plan and plan some more!").

- Individual initiative is never supported ("You never know where it might lead.").
- Management has isolated itself from employees by building mahogany towers between them.
- A 'covert' hostility to innovation is maintained while it is overtly praised. [2]

No organization of any size is above suspicion of such a charade. Not long ago, I was part of a United States multinational corporation's European headquarters in Brussels, Belgium. In that cozy setting Human Resources operation, alone, had a vice president, two directors and two managers, and a supporting staff of nine professionals. Productive work was as 'foreign' as catsup is to French cuisine. We were a corporate resource with symbiotic connection to the corporation's confederation of divisions. We operated with:

- A perceptible lack of organizational control and focus;
- A cadre of non-thinking-thinkers organizing non-doing-doers around non-thing-things.

Take a closer look at your own operation. Do you see any of these same distressing features? If you do, it's time to ask, "What shape are we in?"

I've watched this scenario for many years, even participated in it, but have always waited for someone to shout, "Enough already!" Instead, I've been treated to a confection of bromides, and outright con jobs… with the latter seemingly winning the day.

In this book, I tell what I think needs to be done. It is one man's view from the trenches by a *practicing social scientist* who attempts to cut through the special interests that hold most of us in *economic, social, and psychological bondage.*

Toward an Ecology of Mind

Rachel Carson's *Silent Spring* (1962) alerted the world to another kind of pollution, the use of synthetic chemicals as insecticides. Scientists of the day rebuked her for her lack of cool scientific objectivity, her anecdotal evidence, and her passages of purple prose laced with innuendoes of doom. She was stepping on an industry's pocketbook, and it felt the pinch.

In Ms. Carson's book, the chemical insecticide *DDT* was king, and empires were built on the spine of this complex, synthetic chemical's success. Much as microelectronics and cybernetics are the gods of today, *chemistry*, some sixty years ago held the world in its sway. *DDT* had saved millions from the suffering of such insect-borne diseases as malaria. Small wonder it was elevated to public idolatry, for it carried the promise of an insect-free age.

This spirited woman's mission was not that of the iconoclast. On the contrary, she readily admitted the benefits of chemical pesticides. Nor did she advocate the complete end to their use. Her advocacy was for moderation and a more realistic limitation in the use of these chemicals.

Similarly, my advocacy is for moderation in the use of hyperbole in the world of organization, and realistic appreciation of the modern work force in the world of work. Simultaneously, I condemn the *free lunch* brigade and the soft-bellied optimists who seek 'gain without pain,' and 'having it both ways.'

Rachel Carson's aim was condemnation of the trigger-happy, indiscriminate use of insecticides of which science knew so little in terms of ultimate ecological effect versus possible benefits. She warned that tragedy may await us *over the horizon* if we continue our cavalier disregard for our planet's *ecology*. Melodramatic? Perhaps. But she, in an almost mystical presage, envisioned the shrinking of our Earth's bounty. Her work was a biological warning, a social commentary, and a moral reminder of our limited capacities. I consider my message in that same vein.

Our lagging response to this foreboding is painfully remembered with the nuclear fiasco at Three Mile Island and the nuclear meltdown tragedy at Chernobyl. In the wake of these events, I wonder if Ms. Carson's message was forceful enough.

Pollution continues as our planet's most pervasive problem. But pollution has taken on a more ominous dimension—psychological pollution; what I call *mind pollution*, or the '*free lunch*' mentality.

Rachel Carson was given to such provocative, emotive phrases as *elixirs of death* and *irreversible chains of reactions*. Her obvious aim was to penetrate a complacent public conscience. So is mine. She saw public ignorance as a communicable disease. So do I. She foresaw an impending biological time bomb. I foresee an impending psychological time bomb.

Ms. Carson observed her planet and was horrified by the terrible waste; by the public's flagrant disregard for ecological prudence and economy. My concern is focused on our *internal environment;* on our flagrant disregard for the *ecology of mind*. She envisioned a threat to our well-being from 'outside,' while I see a psychological threat to our *collective will to survive*.

The *pollution of mind* rides on the *free lunch* mentality; the mentality that believes there are acts without consequences, growth without pain, something for nothing, television as reality… luck. Now we have texting and tweeting, and living nearly every waking hour with our heads down operating the latest electronic gadget.

It is the world of the *spoiled-brat generation* and the *Jacuzzi economy*, where what you have is more important than what you are… where becoming has more attraction than being… where personality and performance are used as synonyms… where the artificial is more splendid than the real… and where *real work* has been given a bad name.

The American Dream—and all that it entails—is an illusion. Yet, the *free lunch* mentality persists as if this dream were real.

My hypothesis is that the *free lunch* mentality increasingly pollutes our very will and challenges our ability to see, much less deal with the real problems of our diminishing capacity to perform productive work.

Rather than deal with these hard questions, it would seem we prefer to be entertained with palatable solutions. Give us dessert with our *free lunch*.

So, we move into the 21st Century no longer innocent, but not yet worldly, and neither especially cruel nor corrupt. We leave the 20th Century no longer youthfully ignorant, but not yet wise and civilized. We are a *nation* that aspires to greatness while forever celebrating mediocrity. Illusion and self-destruction have shielded us from the reality of our actions because *we are Americans,* and, so are not expected to act otherwise. No longer. Excess has caught up with us. The *free lunch* is over.

EndNotes

(1) Such books as Lisa Birnbach's *Going to Work* (New York: Villard Books, 1988) provide a complete guide to the *best* neighborhoods in which to live, which schools to attend, stores to shop; and where to get *power* haircuts, *power* shirts, *power* watches, etc. It is 'bonding and belonging' brought to the point of hedonistic excess.

(2) *Wirtschaft Woche,* January 16, 1987.

INTRODUCTION

Work Without Managers is for and about the professional/technical worker in America. During the past thirty years I have observed and studied the American work force and witnessed the explosion of this new, burgeoning class onto the American scene.

I am now thoroughly convinced that the key to America's revitalization efforts is to be found in the professional/technical worker. Regrettably, American management has been unable or unwilling to integrate this fresh, collective, decision-making intelligence into its business strategy. Instead, the professional/technical worker has been essentially force-fitted into a management system designed and maintained for an earlier time.

Work Without Managers is directed at professional/ technical workers, who seem to have little sense of their *real power* and *influence* to enact change. But it is also written for managers who want to know what their professional employees are thinking and feeling about work, management, the organization, and themselves.

Since World War II, five significant transformations have reshaped patterns in the American workplace:

The blue-collar worker, once constituting eighty percent of the work force, now represents less than twenty percent.

Over fifty percent of all workers are minorities and women, with less than fifty percent being white males.

Mind has become the 'cutting edge' over matter. The ability to think is far more critical than the willingness to take orders.

Symbolic interaction lies at the core of performance and hard work ('blood, sweat and tears') is all but irrelevant.

As Peter Drucker so succinctly puts it, the symbolic economy drives the real economy. The industrial economy has therefore become uncoupled from production, resulting in capital movement, as opposed to trade, driving the world economy. [1]

On balance, therefore, nothing is as it was more than a half century ago… yet you couldn't tell this from the way business is conducted in the organization. Everything around the organization has changed, while it remains resolutely fixed in the nostalgia of 1945.

In recent years, American workers have watched in astonishment as traditional support systems disappeared. They can't count on the company as they once did, nor can the government ensure their safety and security. Nothing is certain anymore, and rumors carry the day. This is a new and chilling ordeal for a work force which had been shielded from the rest of the working world. In the good old days, all American workers had to do was show up for work and behave, and their standard of living was ensured. Now, they must take charge of their lives or they won't even own the clothes on their backs.

Wake-Up Call Towards a Little Understanding

The main purpose of this book is to wake Americans up to what is happening in their workplace where professionals, the ever-increasing majority, fail to take command. In sheer numbers, the professional class has edged out the middle class as the dominant group in American society. Its legitimacy and claim to power comes through formal education, and not through pluck and luck as with the majority of the middle class. But, in any case, professionals have yet to be heard, and with few exceptions, they are selected, trained, measured and rewarded as if they were no different than blue-collar workers. They have accepted this treatment begrudgingly until now, but as time runs out for America, so does professional workers' patience.

Consider this against the consensus opinion that the workplace is in the midst of a transforming revolution. Professionals are the critical mass which makes the difference between success and failure, not management. Management, as we know it, belongs to another era. Yet, the truly transforming revolution needed by this country must render modern management as an integral part of the professional class, not above or in command of it, but intrinsic to it.

Put differently, professional-technical workers and managers belong to the same *Post-Industrial Revolution* guild, similar in many ways to the craftsmen of old. Still, we seem obsessed with management as the key, giving only passing attention to professional workers. The message has apparently not gotten through that the organization 'sinks or swims' on the basis of the assimilation of this guild into an effective leadership entity... which, clearly, we do not have today. No wonder clarity slips through our grasp. Management, as the custodial power of the organization, in any case, is anachronistic.

This discussion covers a broad range of ideas and phenomena. It represents someone who has stopped, looked and listened to the patterns and relationships in his world of experience. Obviously, a presentation of many aspects of this revolution will occasionally be superficial, given the limitations of space, time and knowledge. Nonetheless, a systems or holistic view is advocated in which all subsystems are part of the same whole.

The existence of 'separate realities' implies that each person sees things differently. Even within the same family or cultural system, such as the organization, a wide variance in beliefs, concepts, and values is inevitable. Most of us overlook this variance because our biases tell us that what we personally perceive is not only accurate, but absolute. Our thinking tells us that the reality we perceive is the only reality that exists. [2]

Actually, there are many levels of reality implicit in any observation... as there are levels of consciousness in viewing them. In order to see another person's 'separate reality,' it is prudent to realize that ours is only one view of many possibilities. With this realization, we are able to accept others as we find them, and to see with some objectivity, their realities. I have made a very concerted effort to accept others as I've found them; I hope you find my observations helpful within the context of your own reality.

Organization of the Book

This book is organized around six themes and chapters:

Chapter One—The Need For A New Organizational Paradigm

The present structure of the organization does not support the requirements of its charter. This fact is explored in terms most readers know only too well from their own experience.

Chapter Two—Incipient Catastrophe

Continuity, discontinuity and catastrophe are the themes of this discussion. Using René Thom's model of *Catastrophe Theory,* the remarkable and inevitable shift in organization power and influence is depicted. It is also suggested that time is running out on 'things as they are,' and that it is time 'to fish or cut bait.' There is a choice to be made—panic and let events dictate the future of the organization, or embrace reality and predict the future by creating it.

Chapter Three—Echoing Footsteps

The 'game of business,' invented by America and the corporate society created to conduct that business, is now being used against us. Europeans and Orientals are 'eating our lunch,' playing America's game. And there is little evidence that we know what to do about it other than panic. The corporate calm, which is profiled in the business quarterlies, has been replaced by a madhouse.

Chapter Four—The Mad Monarchs of the Madhouse

A profile of six silent killers of the organization is proffered. These silent killers now contaminate organizational life, primarily because of the organization's stubborn resistance to treating professional workers with the freedom, trust, and respect that they deserve.

Chapter Five—The Three Dominant Cultures of The Organization, Or Why We Can't Get From Here To There

Human Resources was presented with an incredible opportunity, but blew it. This eclectic discipline had the chance to tell management what it needed to hear, yet chose instead to tell it what it wanted to hear. In this ill-fated manner, it became 'management's union' and the 'goat' of the organization's decline.

Chapter Six—So What!

The theme here is the simple process which can make a miracle of a mess, if we have but the will, understanding and courage to 'make it happen.' What makes the process complex is the *American Dilemma and Phantom Challenge.*

When America's survival was threatened (WWII) and its pride bruised (Russia's launching of Sputnik), it mobilized resources and regained the advantage. Both cases were reactions to external stimuli by an essentially passive constituency. The shock woke America up if only briefly.

America won WWII because of its capacity to work. It placed the first man on the moon because of its capacity to meet a palpable challenge. Now that its economic foundation and standard of living are threatened, it doesn't sense the threat and thus the challenge remains a *phantom* to it. Each chapter attempts to get inside this *Phantom Challenge* and reveal the apparent nature of it and America's options for dealing with it. This phantom challenge is seen as having a cultural base which has grown out of a desire to solve a problem *(worker productivity)* with the same type of tired strategy that caused the problem in the first place.

The *Culture of Comfort* grew out of a splendid opportunity, post WWII world markets. When Western Europe and Japan challenged this dominance in the 1960s, ill-conceived attempts to meet this challenge only drove us deeper into insulation and isolation, or the *Culture of Complacency.* Now we are struggling to find our way back to the *Culture of Contribution.*

Such a return demands radical rethinking about employees, work, management and the organization. It also demands courage to face the reality of the *American Dilemma.*

Scope of this Assessment

This book is about *performance.* Americans are not performing and the American mythical edge is all but committed to legend. It is also about *leadership.* Management appears lost in its own set of confused priorities, valiantly attempting to play the role of leader without recognizing its essential partner, the professional worker, in the enterprise. Leadership, as practiced by most American managers, consequently, is a maintenance function maladapted to growth challenges. Management still operates with infallible authority stubbornly maintaining "business as usual" practices even when that authority and those practices nearly led to a second Great Depression in 2008.

This book is also about the *intellectual* and *consulting communities* which have made a fast coin telling myopic management what would get the quickest results. While management has been struggling for help at every turn, the help given has actually reinforced the illusion of management's power and the worker's obsequious dependence. Intellectual capital and the power of people now supersedes financial capital, something that has yet to be acknowledged much less fathomed.

Authentic influence has shifted imperceptibly to professional workers with them seemingly the last to know. Therefore, not surprisingly, they watch from the sidelines waiting for management to solve *The Dilemma* that can be solved only through their creative participation.

This finds most workers essentially *management dependent (Culture of Comfort)*. Meanwhile, worker power 'falls between the chairs' as everyone seems braced for a miracle.

In essence, then, this is a book about the *culture of organization*. [3]

Karl Marx once said, "We know who we are by what we do." That is less obvious today. Identity is now more likely defined in terms of organization and profession. We have moved from a society of sacred institutions (e.g., home, family, church and school) to a psychedelic collage of formal and informal connections. The advent of the social media and the Internet finds billions, not millions on such instruments as Facebook. We crave connection, paradoxically, as technology increasingly isolates us from each other.

If management is primitive, the *organization* is more so. Even though it is a recent development, many Americans have cultivated a counter dependency upon it (*Culture of Complacency*). Yet, the organization has proven to be a fragile support system for such dependent workers. As a result, erratic behavior has become the norm rather than the exception with the rumor mill an inverse function of morale.

Some may charge, with good reason, that several elements within these representative cultures embody over-simplifications or that they are expressed in somewhat simplistic terms. If so, I plead 'guilty.' It is hoped, however, that this does not distract you from seeing your own organization with greater clarity and understanding.

Given this construction, the point being made here is that no organization can exist without a *Culture of Contribution*. Even with such a culture, the organization could still be moving in the direction of *comfort* or *complacency* with almost imperceptible swiftness. Chances are all three cultures exist in even the best of organizations. What about yours?

The American Mind of the Time!

American workers, over the course of the last century, have become self-critical to a fault. Self-contempt more than selfishness would appear to rule the mind of many contemporary workers. From the *Tyranny of Technology*, to the abandonment of the sacred, from the *Culture of Narcissism* to the banal greed of the *Yuppies* (or currently "Millennials" as they are now called), there seems a pervasive cynicism clinging to the American conscience. Still, cut through the facade of Ivan F. Boesky and Boyd L. Jeffries, who led a gang of Wall Street traders with inside information, and you are likely to discover this naked cynicism... riding on a free lunch mentality. [4]

Should the reader think this was a 20th century phenomenon, think again. This is as old as time only it has become more sophisticated and therefore economically more threatening to society. Charles Ponzi brought his scheme to the United States in the early 1920s, and it was perfected by Allen Stanford and Bernard Madoff, among others, in the early 21th century. Both men will spend the rest of their lives in prison for bilking investors of millions of dollars. Stanford ran a high profile investment company, while Madoff was once the chairman of the NASDAQ stock market.

If these characters were really bad, it would be easier to accept. But they appear too much like ourselves. Regrettably, we live in a time when most of our sins are venial sins and most of our sinners lack imagination and daring. This is the most grievous of indictments. No prior age had giant saints without giant sinners. We have neither.

So, this book is also about the *Outsider*. Since the first human beings took it upon themselves to step out of the cold and into the warmth of mystic fire, life has been guided by leaders who were *Outsiders.* The tribal side of mankind has always responded to the *Outsider* who understood the insider; to the person who could step back and outside the warmth of limited reason to embrace the coldness of the arational [5]; who could construct and rearrange but not judge; who could escape the rigid patterns of experience and belief and not be afraid to lead.

Finally, this book is about *you* and *me.* The paradox of our time is that we say all the right words but seldom live them. Words have become surrogates for thinking, feeling and behaving. We have become a passive people with a horrible waste of energy and light. So, it is written to feel the *discomfort* of that fact. The future is not out there. It is here. It begins and ends... with you and me.

We no longer have the luxury of externalizing our pain or projecting our guilt. We cannot wait for a miracle. We cannot wait for someone else to 'harness our fire.' Time has run out. It is the fourth quarter of the ultimate game... which is our American destiny.

Endnotes

(1)   Drucker, Peter F., "The Changed World Economy," *Foreign Affairs,* Spring, 1986, pp. 768-791.

(2)   Suarez, Rick, Roger C. Mills, and Darlene Stewart, *Sanity, Insanity, and Common Sense* (New York: Fawcett Columbine, 1987), pp. 32-38.

(3)   The workplace and organization are used interchangeably. This includes the formal organization: a highly organized group having explicit objectives, formally stated rules, and a system of defined roles, with designated rights and duties; and the informal organization: the system of personal relationships that develop spontaneously as individuals interact within the formal organization. The informal social norms, rites, rituals, traditions and sentiments register a dominant influence on the formal organization in

DR. JAMES R. FISHER, JR.

the form of a pervading culture, a culture which is either supportive or not of productive work.

(4) Lasch, Christopher, *The Culture of Narcissism: American Life in an Age of Diminishing Expectations* (New York: W. W. Norton & Company, Inc., 1978).

(5) Edward Debono introduced this term with his concept of *Lateral Thinking* (1970). DeBono sees three fallacies to our conventional method of thinking: (1) that the established way of looking at a situation is the 'only way, because it is right;'(2) that through logic, alone, you can arrive at the 'best' perception; and (3) that no matter where you start with your inquiry, if your logic is correct, then you will eventually reach the 'right' answer. Of course, this is the rational approach, which DeBono sees as horribly in error and, therefore, why he advocates the arational. You will see that Debono has had little influence, even with the massive push for quality. Companies took this to mean "doing everything right" the first time was the answer to the quality problem. Yet, a focus on the critical 20 percent would likely resolve 80 percent of the quality issues. Stated another way, "doing everything right," could conceivably make only 20 percent of the difference.

CHAPTER ONE

A NEED FOR A NEW ORGANIZATIONAL PARADIGM

"It was the best of times, it was the worst of times, it was the age of wisdom, it was the age of foolishness, it was the epoch of belief, it was the epoch of incredulity, it was the season of Light, it was the season of Darkness, it was the spring of hope, it was the winter of despair, we had everything before us, we had nothing before us, we were all going direct to Heaven, we were all going direct the other way—in short, the period was so far like the present period..."

—Charles Dickens, British novelist

S O BEGINS CHARLES Dickens in *A Tale of Two Cities* (1859), writing about the French Revolution and its impact on society—especially the societies of London and Paris. Dickens goes far beyond this and suggests the basic difference between changing society and changing oneself. All change starts with the individual, he said. The most dramatic change occurs when the individual voluntarily chooses to act differently.

In every period of history there has been a gulf between revolutionary ideas and traditional values. This is embodied in the conflict between personal honesty and expediency, rational calm and panic. It characterizes the American character and culture in today's troubled times.

Dickens could have been writing about late 20th century America and the persistent struggle between workers and managers, over organizational control and worker involvement. And the organization's attempts to mask this struggle tend only to intensify it.

Make no mistake. We're in the middle of a revolution. Ironically, the focus continues to be on management. Workers remain outside the equation, due largely to the determined, albeit faulty belief that if you fix management, everything else falls into place. The focus must be shifted to workers, or continuous change will cause an eruption into discontinuity and catastrophe.

Real power has shifted dramatically from management's domain to the dominion of workers, but workers behave as if management still possesses the power. The organization waffles like a rag doll in the wind, struggling against this reality. Uncertainty reigns supreme and power is falling between the chairs.

Several factors have contributed to this dilemma:

- America's values have changed.
- The changes have affected the way Americans relate to one another, both in the workplace and the home.

- The knowledge explosion has produced a very distinct type of worker, with a perspective and style different than we have known in the past.

- Moreover, the critical mass of the organization has shifted from activity to information; from doing to thinking; from producing to serving; from working to symbolic interaction.

- The information edge no longer resides with management, but is well distributed throughout the work force. Consequently, management is not only at the mercy of *expert systems*, but of experts who design and control those systems.

Finally, as a result of the shift from 'doing' to 'thinking,' there is a veritable struggle to determine what constitutes *real work*. With the product as likely to be 'software' as 'hardware,' there is mass confusion as to what to do, let alone who is in charge.

Because vested management is *results oriented*, and real work has shifted to being primarily *process driven*, there is a strong need to re-examine work in terms of process and outcome:

- When work is measured in terms of 'results,' management perceives workers as *costs*. This is reflected by cost cutting practices aimed solely at reducing headcount.

- *Making an impression* and keeping one's job thus become more important than *making a difference.*

Conversely, when work is viewed as a 'process,' attention focuses on *doing the right things*, rather than doing everything right the first time. Doing the right things fosters teamwork, whereas being obsessed with doing everything right the first time, leads to chronic errors being ignored or denied, that is, until there is no recourse but to face them. This results invariably in finger pointing and dissension in the ranks.

Where the focus resides is more a matter of *personal values* than of management style. Yet, most discussion in past years has centered on management style. Today, quality is the focus of discussion, and the same absurdity that possessed those bent on the *right style* has American organizations scrambling to do everything right instead of focusing on the right things. The current focus on quality tends to be a *stylistic overlay*, superimposed on workers by management. It will disappoint because the organization has not thought through the crippling impact of *cultural biases*.

The quick, cosmetic fix will no longer do. If this continues to be the only approach accessible, then America will not survive the 21st century as a first-rate nation.

America is not Europe, nor is it Japan. What works in Europe and Japan fits neither the American culture nor the American value system. America's essence is unique to America. This is where the problem lies, and where the answer will be found.

Meanwhile, America's dilemma is that it perceives this challenge as a phantom. When America's physical survival was threatened with the Japanese bombing of Pearl Harbor, we mobilized our resources quickly and won World War II.

Figure 1-1: The American Dilemma and the Phantom Challenge, or 'When you don't feel it, you don't react to it.'

When Russia launched Sputnik in 1957, our pride was on the line, and we consolidated our technology and put a man on the moon in another decade. But most of us look past the column in the morning newspaper citing the 40 million homeless or hungry, and look up across the breakfast table, and say, "pass the sugar."

World War III has, in reality, been raging since 1960, as an economic war. Are we concerned? No, not if it has not touched us. The landscape in our mind remains the same, despite the pending earthquake of changing values reverberating beneath our troubled surface.

A Look at Old Values

Not unlike Dickens' *A Tale of Two Cities,* subtle but massive changes in American society and the individual have led to a cultural breakdown. The main cause of this breakdown is denial. A secondary cause is attempting to make traditional approaches work in the face of transformational cultural changes.

The established culture of American society, the *common good,* has failed to support the society that it would define. Yet, many of its advocates, often located in American think tanks, stubbornly insist it is the only way. Against this reality, the culture of *personhood* now struggles to establish itself. The Millennials are simply the latest rendition of this trend (see "The Me, Me, Me Generation," Time, May 9, 2013).

[Millennials are lazy, entitled, narcisistic and live with their parents, although past college. They epitomize personhood to the extreme.]

Americans of World War II vintage generally think in terms of "what is good for the country, state, church, school, family, and company is good enough for me!" Americans of the post-Vietnam War era think more in terms of "the right to know, the right to an opinion, the right to be wrong, the right to fail, the right to work, civil rights, and civil disobedience." In a word, they think in terms of controlling their own destiny, rather than having it dictated to them. Millennials, critics are apt to point out, allow parents to carry their baggage now, but not being locked into tradition may be our salvation later.

Blue-collar workers continue to value the *common good*, while modern professional workers increasingly value *personhood*. This is becoming a distinct difference.

	Common Good	Personhood
Authority	Position Power	Popularity/knowledge
Loyalty	To the organization	To self/peers
Discipline	Reward/punishment	Caring/respect
Motivation	Fear	Challenge/contribution

Figure 1-2 Shifting American Values

This difference has already had pivotal ramifications across America, from the home to the workplace. Adversaries have been made of parents and children, teachers and students, the clergy and laity, managers and workers… leaders and followers in all walks of life. It has also produced a perceptible gap between expectations and achievements in the organization.

So traumatic has the situation become that many parents, educators, executives, clergy and leaders are abandoning the conflict. They have abdicated in frustration, proclaiming that they are *powerless* which has been elevated to a new level of distinction with the arrival of the so-called "Millennials."

Meanwhile, the few who are still hopeful remain convinced that the answer lies in the *common good*. They invariably turn to quick-fix fads and techniques involving 'change' in the way we train, work, and manage. What is missing is looking at the person that is the worker differently.

In the organization, the myth persists that if workers are managed and trained differently, and if work is defined differently, problems will dissolve and workers will automatically change. But the myth proves to be a lie. Results of these efforts have demonstrated little or no significant change.

In the Defense Industry, billions of dollars are being spent in the name of *Total Quality Management (TQM)* to redefine work and train managers and workers in the workplace. This represents a panic attempt at appearing to be in control, when everything is running out of control. It has the illusion of dealing with the problem, without embracing it (which has become an American pastime).

This approach is consistent with our American history: "It hasn't been fatal in the past, so it won't be fatal in the future." Consequently, there seems little inclination to understand and respect the changing values, beliefs, and expectations of the dominant new breed of American workers.

From a cultural perspective, management is no closer to understanding modern professionals than modern professionals are to submitting to the edicts of management.

This failure in understanding is the reason nonfunctional or reactive thinking dominates the organization's every activity. This is painfully displayed in the prominence of the 'rumor mill,' where backstabbing, duplicity, chicanery, Cover Your Ass (CYA) and Show Your Ass (SYA) games are part of 'standard operating procedure.' It is also where *six silent killers* of the organization feast on the organization's preoccupation with the negative... and with itself.

These crippling propensities are discussed later as the *Six Mad Monarchs of the Madhouse*: passive aggressive, passive responsive, passive defensive, malicious obedience, approach avoidance, and obsessive compulsive behaviors. These behaviors epitomize the effect (not the cause) of organizational instability and fatigue precipitated by management's failure first to acknowledge, and then to deal with, the cultural shift from *common good* to *personhood*.

Workers of a Different Mind

Average American workers who were formerly tied to their jobs by fear, lack of skill, and ignorance have become educated and mobile, discovering new horizons of opportunity. Reared largely in latchkey or single-parent homes, these workers were left mainly to their own devices while growing up and, by default, became essentially their own parents.

In the absence of external control and paternal regulation, they developed their own internal self-monitoring systems. Parental absenteeism denied them the security of traditional values, leaving many of them bruised or scarred by life experiences for which they were not adequately prepared. But it also produced individuals who, in an effort to survive, had to find their *own centers*; had to think for themselves. [1]

These individuals respond quite differently than their parents to external control; to conventional motivation and wisdom. They are more inclined to intrinsic interests (what they want to do) than extrinsic interests (what they have to do); more stimulated by challenge than external manipulation.

These new American workers learned to make choices. Attempts to manage, manipulate, and motivate them with traditional reward and punishment fail miserably. They actually find these attempts amusing.

Giving professional workers time off as a punishment and more money as a reward, consequently, hasn't been successful in changing their behavior. Work is not the center of their lives, so time off is neither an embarrassment nor a concern. As for money, they will take it, "thank you very much," and go on behaving as before. Indeed, attempts to preserve the 'traditional' American value system with them have only quickened its demise.

Control, known in the organization as power and influence, now belongs to them. And, because it emanates from within, if they don't know this, they certainly sense it. Even if not consciously aware of it, by refusing to submit to management's dominance they demonstrate their sense of power in their behavior. Questioning the system, the role of management, and the requirements of work itself are manifestations, as is a failure to respond to conventional management practices. Professional workers are gradually discovering that they are both the controller and the controlled.

Empowerment—a word that has become associated with all workers—first gained legitimacy with *Women's Rights*. When women started to insist on being treated as persons and not merely as chattel, they made a break through. Now, empowerment is a gift that workers give to the organization only when it meets their professional, emotional, and psychological needs.

Ironically, these needs are well known to the organization, but rarely understood. The sheer dint of publicity and executive 'psychobabble' makes them well known (thanks largely to the 'script' written by Human Resources).

Human Resources is a profession that has grown out of what I call *The Prison of Panic Called NOW!* or 'Why Johnny Won't Work,' which is covered in some detail later. Paradoxically, Human Resources has grown exponentially with the decline in the health and stability of our American economy. Rather than examining American workers and developing a strategy to take full advantage of their potential, Human Resources has elected to deny the essence of the problem (the changing values of American workers), and to deal with its symptoms (declining productivity).

Human Resources has created processes and programs that deal with this decline by rewarding conforming behavior. This conforming behavior develops a 'machine age mind' that is unresponsive to innovative activity or sudden change—both 'givens' in the modern organization. It creates a reactionary constituency, with the machine mind distorting the reality of its experience. More energy is spent, as a consequence, in dysfunctional behavior than is devoted to actual work.

Alan Valentine puts it succinctly, "Whatever else may be made mechanical, human values cannot." [2]

Yet, safely ensconced in executive intrigue, far removed from the trenches, Human Resources has had a splendid opportunity to make a difference, and has elected instead to 'make an impression.' It has become more enamored of presenting, packaging, and promoting illusive ideas, than spearheading breakthrough actions.

With CEOs of most American Fortune 500 companies educated in science and engineering, Human Resources has promoted what will sell, not what is needed. It has appealed to the rationally ordering, mechanistic minds of these executives with *Quality of Work, Quality of Work Life, Quality of Management, Total Quality Management, Total Employee Involvement,* and *Participative Management,* so that their respective acronyms have become burned into their psyches.

With so much time, energy, and expense spent on this attractive packaging, little remains for implementation. So, each of the initiatives listed above, with few exceptions, has sputtered to irrelevance—only to be replaced by yet another. And so it goes.

These imperfect attempts have come to be far better known than understood; more a conversation piece than a better way of doing business. There isn't a CEO in American industry, commerce, education, religion, government, or the military whose staff cannot produce an impressive Power Point presentation to document their organization's commitment to these initiatives. Yet, American management and Human Resources are grasping at straws, and building cathedrals out of them.

Unfortunately, the only employees who respond consistently to these initiatives are from the disappearing rank-and-file of blue-collar workers. They have been led and conditioned regimentally and take these types of exhortations in stride. Still, there is nothing more damning to society than conforming children who become uninspired, unimaginative, conforming adults. More than that—reminiscent of the *Hawthorne Effect*—these workers are flattered by the attention given to them and moved to please. [3] Accustomed to being treated as interchangeable parts in a machine, the slightest display of humanism was bound to elicit a positive response from these workers.

Meanwhile, professionals, who are much less responsive to such manipulation, play their sly game of 'smoke and mirrors' (or, what you see is not necessarily what you get). They are 'on' to the game, and want no part of it.

In essence the dichotomy between professionals and blue-collar workers is as sharply defined as that between the *common good* and *personhood*. But the nuances of these differences are neither acknowledged nor understood by management, let alone the workers. For convenience, and consistent with a rationally ordering, mechanistic mindset, management stubbornly insists on interpreting motivation as if all workers respond to the same values and beliefs. This, of course, is far from the case.

Given this propensity, management seeks to magnify its effectiveness by saluting the achievements of blue-collar workers, while remaining self-blinded to the almost total apathy, on the part of professionals to its leadership. Blue-collar workers may be the last bastion of the *common good*, but they are also a shrinking constituency.

In any case, blue-collar workers are not the problem. On the contrary, thanks to a good assist from automation, hands-on labor costs are dropping precipitously, making American blue-collar workers among the most productive workers in the world. But hands-on labor represents only 10 to 15 percent of the cost of a product or service. True cost savings and operating efficiency are found in indirect labor costs—the costs of services of professionals.

In the face of this, what does management do when it feels the crunch? It initiates cost cutting redundancy exercises by laying off those who have the least political leverage in the organization—blue-collar workers, janitors, secretaries, technicians and yes, professionals who don't conform. It is incredible when you think about it. To wit:

Management prunes the organizational tree by cutting at the roots. Meanwhile, those who have spent much of their time managing their careers and little of their time doing real work keep their jobs, thus precariously weakening the organization.

Is it any wonder we're in trouble? Each time management engages in such activity, it makes the organization less resilient. Like a rubber band that can be stretched only so many times before it loses its elasticity, the organization ultimately experiences a nervous collapse, a cultural breakdown. It no longer can respond to accelerating demands.

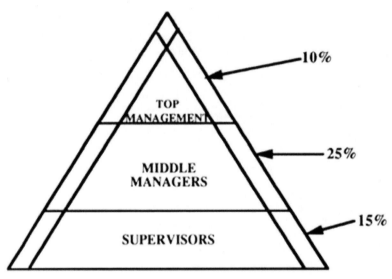

Figure 1-3: Pruning the Management Pyramid for
Organizational Effectiveness.

Judicious pruning of the management pyramid is a noble mission. Speaking conservatively, top management can be cut by 10 percent, middle management by 25 percent, and first-line supervision by 15 percent without cutting a single blue-collar worker, janitor, secretary, technician, or professional, and most organizations would almost immediately become twice as effective. This represents true tree pruning. Like the trees of nature, it will stimulate growth, and give a new zest and color to the organization's foliage.

The idea of a "leaner organization" was introduced to the world by Toyota in the 1970s. This fueled changes across the globe in manufacturing and product development, especially in South East Asia Rim countries, and in Germany in Europe. The United States watched this happen with Detroit losing its world dominance in automotive manufacturing, and still did not act until Toyota plants laced their way across the American continent. Now, in the 21st century, academics and consultants are promoting the "lean enterprise model" for all organizations.

That said it is encouraging to note that here in 2014 pruning of the organizational tree is not only taking place, but the very idea of a hierarchical pyramid as the corporate paradigm is undergoing serious rethinking. Unhappily, however, redundancy exercises continue with the least able to seek comparable employment elsewhere are the first to go.

The "reaction syndrome," which is indigenous to American enterprise remains still in vogue. Staples, the nation's largest office-supply company, has announced, as this is being written, the closing of 225 stores as part of a plan to save $500 million. Nearly half of the chain's sales are now generated on line. This retail retrenchment will shed more than 10,000 employees, many of whom will find it difficult to acquire other employment in this present economic climate.

Enter Management's Union

Initially, instead of confronting this problem *(management creep)*. Human Resources concentrated on using acronyms to play 'Quality Monopoly.' Ironically, the game of quality, which has been so effective with blue-collar workers, actually arises out of the value system of *personhood.*

While organizations are reducing their raw numbers of people, there is a deceptive *management creep.* Staff engineers and other designated specialists are sharing in the executive bounty as the ratio between managers and workers grows perilously narrow. Soon it will be a one-to-one ratio, with as many managers as workers. Who, then, will delegate to whom?

Take a high-tech division of one Fortune 100 company, with 4200 employed. It had 250 managers, supervisors, and staff engineers. Several iterative reductions found the same division with 3200 employees, but now 400 managers, supervisors, and staff engineers. Over the same period, the operation had doubled its sales. Initially, Human Resources had 65 employees and seven managers. After a series of redundancy exercises, the staff had been reduced to 34 employees, but still with seven managers. Meanwhile, most professionals had to do the work of two or more people.

Human Resources professionals—supposedly the employee's advocate—have had the opportunity to educate management to the cultural shadings of *personhood* and the relationship of those shadings to professionals. They have also been in a position to create a psychological climate to facilitate this educational process. But, due to a lack of comprehension or courage, they have contributed instead to organizational strife and dysfunction.

Is it any wonder, then, that nonfunctional behavior dominates the organization, and that those so disposed rule with a contemptuous disregard for the organization's mission? Professionals have learned how to appear busy without being gainfully employed; how to please the boss without doing productive work. This behavior clearly results from telling management what it wants to hear, rather than what it needs to do.

Human Resources has been at the center of this deception and in the process has become, by default, *management's union*. It has lost its identity and its role.

Human Resources has become more inclined to be management's advocate than *to serve* employees; more comfortable playing management's tune than discovering its own music. It has had the responsibility of the 'inside outsider' from the start, but has elected to play the role of the sycophant. Consequently, it has declined the function of the provocateur—the role of the consultant—choosing instead that of the consoler; the role of the 'yes man.' And so Human Resources has gravitated to being what the organization didn't need—a union for management. As a result, it has put the organization in jeopardy; perhaps not by design, but certainly by dereliction of duty. This was at a time when the organization urgently needed a leader and a healer. With the organization in such infirmity, a tremendous opportunity was lost.

This was considered a subjective expression of anger when WWMs was published in 1990. Many corporate scandals in the subsequent 25 years have confirmed the legitimacy of this premise. Management regaled with its infallible authority and business as usual practices despite the consequences of its actions. Human Resources, which had access to management, chose not to confront the arbitrary nature of this authority or of these practices. The economic meltdown of 2008 being only one of the consequences of the described condition.

By being in a reactive, obsequious mode, Human Resources has denied the reality of the situation—the need for radical restructuring to serve the organization's *first customer*, its people. It serves no useful purpose to point fingers, or hold Congressional Hearings after-the-fact, as everyone knows, once some time has elapsed, it is back to business-as-usual practices as if no learning has taken place.

Individual Success and Organization Values

The structure of the American organization is at war with what is going on inside the American worker. The structure does not fit the behavior required.

Why? If you treat people with respect and dignity, accepting their values and beliefs, you get one type of worker. If you take people for granted, imposing your values and expectations on them, you get another. These variables imply different structures. Too many American organizations are still imposing their values irrespective of what may be those of their workers.

Consequently, an amazing amount of energy and individual/ organizational health are put at risk daily. And because work does not take place in a vacuum, inappropriate or irrelevant activity will fill the void if the climate is not right for productive effort. The organization culture follows this structure whatever the organization: (1) the structure of work determines the function of work; (2) the function of work creates the workplace culture; (3) the workplace culture dictates organizational behavior; (4) organizational behavior establishes whether the organization will thrive and survive, or vegetate and expire.

The *collision of values* can easily be illustrated by what success means to today's professional and to the traditional manager. You may well discover from the following, which side your personal values lie.

Dirk Edwards, a corporate director of international operations for an American multinational corporation, lived in Brussels, Belgium. He had accepted the assignment because he wanted to learn why the *European Economic Community* was so successful against American companies. He also felt he could make a contribution, given his specialty in organizational development. Neither money nor career enhancement entered into his decision to accept this assignment.

The entire thrust of Dirk's discipline was *enabling*, not manipulation. He was trained to help people do what they wanted to do, not what he thought they should do. But, because organizational structure seldom permitted this, he was well acquainted with irrational behavior.

Recognizing that behavior follows structure, Dirk created self-management work teams, and watched 'irresponsible' workers become responsible and productive. To him, success meant contributing to the success of others. "If we serve well our first customers—our peers and the users of our services," he would say, "we will be successful, and so will our customers." This belief found him more inclined to pay attention to what those below him thought than what those above him demanded.

He was not into 'correct behavior'; nor was he into making workers perform to someone else's standards. Everyone likes to be measured, he believed, but only if they can have input into the design of the standards by which they are to be measured. Dirk schooled his people in processes that permitted them to make such determinations.

Dirk also fulfilled his role as servant to his people by providing them with the tools, resources, training, and conditions they felt would allow them to do their best work. Once they had a clear view of what needed to be done, he stayed out of their way.

This supportive behavior made Dirk popular with his people. His people got results. Within the company, he gained a reputation for effectiveness. Management saw the results, but demonstrated little curiosity as to how they were obtained, assuming Dirk managed much as they did. In any case, he was seen as perfect for the European assignment.

Given these circumstances, perhaps naively, he moved to Europe, and continued his quest to serve.

And then, about six months into his European assignment, the following conversation took place between Dirk and his boss during a three-hour train trip from Brussels to Amsterdam:

Boss: "I get the feeling I want you to be more successful than you want to be."

Dirk: "Define success for me."

Boss: "Well, making an impression on the (European) affiliate general managers, keeping our corporate fathers happy in the United States, keeping me out of trouble."

Dirk: "What about the operations?"

Boss: "What about them?"

Dirk: "What if doing something significant requires making some people uncomfortable, making you unhappy? What then?"

Boss: "You don't do it. You're only over here a few years. Don't try to be a hero. Remember, all I want is to make you successful. That's my point."

Dirk: "What do you think motivates me?"

Boss: "What motivates you? What motivates us all: pleasing the boss, promotions, belonging to the club, making the bucks, getting the perks, being able to provide comfort for the family? Right?"

Dirk: "What motivates me is challenging work, the freedom and control to do it in my way, and your trust, respect, and support when I fall short of the mark. Money has little to do with my motivation; nor do promotions, perks or status."

Boss: "Bullshit!"

This exchange illustrates both a strained relationship and a deep breach in values between the two men. They clearly operated in 'separate realities,' and neither understood the other. There was little trust; little feeling that they were on the same team. Dirk had no sense that his boss was on his side, let alone that he would be there for him if he was in trouble. The boss failed to realize that true leadership calls for his people to respect him; to believe in him. That only then will they follow him.

Curiously, because he did not respond to the expected motivators, Dirk intimidated his boss. The fact that Dirk's authority came from within was incomprehensible to his manager. Meanwhile, Dirk sought his manager's trust in order to enhance his own *self-trust*—so that he could act more responsibly. Ironically, this is what his boss desired as well. But the boss believed he could best accomplish this by weakening Dirk's will to be his own person; by making Dirk more dependent on him for success. Not surprisingly, this growing gap in value orientation ultimately ended in Dirk's being sent home early.

The Need to Please Others

To the traditional manager, success is commonly measured in terms of status, money, promotions, and perks. These are external factors that affect a person who is motivated by a 'High Need to Please Others.' They also arise out of the culture of the *common good*.

A Need to Please Others should not be confused with the need to *serve others*. On the contrary, the *Need to Please Others* is actually self-serving and reactive. It promotes the inclination to be tentative. Such a person doesn't cast a single corporate vote until he is sure which side will prevail. It is the abode of indecisiveness.

Paradoxically, a Need to Please Others is likely to exhibit a preoccupation with *position power* at the expense of *purposeful performance*. Purposeful performance is chiefly driven by accurate, relevant information. Timely and appropriate information, not frenetic activity, is the basis of organizational success. Unfortunately, given the current bias toward appearance (style) rather than substance, the person with position power is often the last to know. Why? Because information must pass through layer upon layer of managers who all have a *High Need to Please* with each tailoring their information accordingly.

Consequently, relevant information seldom gets beyond the functional group or operating floor. And, because relevant information represents the 'candle power' necessary to see through the fog, this has critical repercussions in the modern organization. The bureaucratic lens of formal authority can then be likened to an organizational cataract adding to the murky condition, rather than improving the vision.

Organizational climbers, commonly known as "pyramid climbers," are much more adept at serving those above them than serving the organization. To the climbers, those above *are* the organization. They display an uncanny ability to anticipate their superior's needs and react to them. Doubtlessly, this skill is of some merit in the traditional organization, but it represents a colossal handicap to today's mainstream organization.

This handicap goes beyond the problem of the promotion of disinformation, debilitating as that is, to a dearth of leadership. Because their chief talent is bureaucratic tact, rather than strategic engagement, *organizational climbers* are incapable of leading. They have been schooled to react to situations, not to anticipate them.

One of the most mundane indicators of this behavior is an obsession with extraneous information. They have a soap opera mentality wanting to understand where all the bodies are buried. Organizational climbers show an amazing facility for reacting to rumors, or indeed, even spreading them. Panic sets in when the expected plot of engagement fails to follow its anticipated design.

Speaking parenthetically, this is one reason for the advent of consultants and the promulgation of fads. The organizational climbers are the buyers of these services and techniques. They don't know what they want because they have never thought through their problems to an original need basis. What is worse, they don't even know what they don't want.

Given this—the present state of most American organizations—the value system of the *common good,* which such behavior identifies, resolutely holds on. It is not that the 'common good' is an undesirable ideal. It is simply that the organization is not served well by those who now practice it.

In Choosing a Different Path— a Need to Please Self

Question: In an age of mediocrity, where are the pathfinders?

Answer: They are everywhere, but unlikely to be found in complex organizations. The irony is that they start their own, such as Bill Gates, Steve Jobs, and now those cut from the same cloth as Mark Zuckerberg of Facebook.

To the new breed of professionals, success is measured in terms of challenging work… in doing something significant, in having freedom and control of what they do, in being trusted and treated with respect and dignity. Regrettably, most organizations are not structured to abide, much less promote this climate. Meanwhile, professionals grow tired of bureaucratic constraints that sponsor *non-thinking thinking and non-doing doing of non-thing things.*

Make no mistake, the society of the *common good* was, and is, a different society than the society of today. What's more, we can't go back to the way it was.

Yesterday, a family meant a man, woman, and child—not two or more members of the same sex in an intimate relationship. Religion meant 'faith,' not a Church of Scientology. School meant a building dedicated to education, not a class tutorial on a student's iPad in a coffee shop. Government meant a national entity, not an international marketplace. And work meant making a product, not creating and distributing information. It meant a place away from home, whereas now more and more it means working at or near one's home.

Remember, the structure and infrastructure of the society of the *common good* were designed by autocratic, authoritarian minds who envisioned a static bureaucratic world forever.

These designers, many of whom are still actively among us, hold nostalgically to divine rule, infallible authority and business as usual practices, where a state of control, order, and a sense of position and place in dependent obedience are manifestly the norm.

These values of the 18th century, and earlier, served American society well up to, and through World War II. But with that war, *the entire world changed.* One of the most remarkable changes was the arrival of American professionals—a post WWII phenomenon. These workers have evolved over the past 70 years to differ radically from other American workers in terms of education and experience, attitude and disposition, motivation and perspective, discipline and outlook. Spiritually and materially, they are more authentic because they embody the conflict in our society.

Of every five American workers today, four belong to this class of professional workers in this new century. Yet, the organization behaves as if its people are sealed in a 1950s time capsule.

Wherever they look, *comfort* is embraced; there is a preoccupation with safety. Caution is sponsored at the expense of courage; dependency at the expense of initiative; maintaining the status quo at the expense of embracing the challenging demands of change.

Greatness, which Walt Whitman celebrated without embarrassment, is throbbing in every professional's heart. But to reach for it remains threatening to the status quo of a maintenance-driven culture.

Perhaps the best index of today's aversion to greatness is the venality of our times. It is reflected in the quality of our sinners. Periods of historical significance are punctuated by extremes in human behavior. To wit, to have great saints, you need great sinners. Neither are to be found in the American firmament today. Our sinners are wimpishly venial. There's not a mortal sinner in sight.

Contemplative professionals are motivated mainly by internal factors, or what they think; they have a *High Need to Please Themselves*. Pleasure comes from being committed to, and involved in, something of consequence. They are appalled by 'busy work,' by people without opinions, by people who have a high need 'to be liked,' by people who are secretive, by people who are terrified of somebody 'losing control' or 'showing their ass,' by people who are afraid to disobey, by people who are afraid to fail, by people who avoid those who think differently than they do.

In the traditional sense, this motivation could easily be read as selfish and calloused. Nothing could be further from the truth. On the contrary, what motivates professionals with this mind-set is *enlightened self-interest*, with the principle drive being *to serve*. Robert Greenleaf captures this essence in his description of the *servant as leader*.

"A new moral principle is emerging which holds that the only authority deserving one's allegiance is that which is freely and knowingly granted by the led to the leader in response to, and in proportion to, the clearly evident servant stature of the leader." [4]

Greenleaf goes on to say that those who choose to follow this principle will not casually accept the authority of existing organizations. On the contrary, professionals will only respond to those chosen as leaders who are trusted as servants to the organization. Greenleaf concludes that, in the future, the only viable organizations will be those that are predominantly servant-led.

Be aware that this is consistent with the common drive of professionals. They desire to be useful, to do something worthwhile, and to make a significant contribution to the well being of others. This also epitomizes the expression of greatness.

Further, as opposed to bureaucratic certainty, professionals thrive in a chaotic atmosphere, where diverse control emanates, and surprise is routine fare. *Role identity* is important, but authority over that identity is blurred.

With *role identity*, you know your capabilities and limitations, and the contributions you are expected to make. In other words, *role identity* is skill or performance-based.

Responsibility and authority, traditionally, are derived from the formal mandate of organization, which now appear in rather meaningless job descriptions and formal organizational charts.

As quickly as these descriptions and charts are made, they become obsolete. Scant attention is paid to them because they discourage cooperation and teamwork, and are a hindrance to performance and contribution. Therefore, when *role identity* is well understood, responsibility and authority move necessarily with the dynamics of routine—from interdependence to autonomy, and back again.

On balance, work brings professionals pleasure when it is focused on the people with whom they work (their peers), and on the people they serve (the user community). It is this propensity to serve that drives them toward greatness. With it, they have a *sense of role;* a sense that involves the *courage to serve,* to take risks, to sometimes embrace failure in that service. Unfortunately, the organization too often is fixed on maintenance, caution, and success.

What is perhaps surprising about professionals is that they have more the *mind of the artist* than the analyst. They appreciate the limits of technology, and the greater possibilities in serving humanity through expressions of humility and love. They see society's dependence on hard science becoming a veritable entrapment. And, like Alice in Lewis Carroll's *Through the Looking Glass* (1946), they have looked deeply into the mirror and seen how we have become nearly helpless to extricate ourselves from it.

- Question: Are professionals different from the rest of us?
- Answer: No. They only accept what we have refused to see—'ourselves as we are.'

Boldly confronting their limitations, they see the world as it is. Beyond that, they embrace the challenge to create dangerously; to surpass the limits of 'pleasing others' to the pleasure in 'pleasing self,' by embracing the greatness that resides beyond the horizon of self in the land of serving and leading others. Here, greatness demands risk and possible failure in the belief that there is a will to create a more relevant culture.

With so much mind power, professionals are choosing a different path. They prefer an atmosphere of diverse control, collegiality, surprise, and autonomy to the culture of bureaucratic certitude. The latter drives them toward maintenance and mediocrity preoccupied with safety, fostering the belief that progress means 'not making mistakes.' Caution, rather than courage, is the byword, for mistakes are punished more vigorously than achievements are rewarded.

The punishing reality is that confidence decreases, as does risk taking, as professionals move up the hierarchy. This creates an imprisoning climate for professionals, and makes the organization tantamount to a madhouse.

Professionals suffer vainly in this managed world, which is mismanaged to the extreme. They are managed as if they are *things* doing things, the way blue-collar workers have always been managed. But professionals have been trained to think, not to 'do' in the sense of things. By treating them as "things to be managed," professionals become activity centered, fawning and reactive rather than creatively engaged in the work at hand.

Because management can do only what it knows, *learned helplessness* is nurtured and promoted. This is destroying the will to survive, much less prevail.

When management forces professionals to become routine doers, it denies the psychological shift from external to internal motivational control; from the *management-centered* to the *worker-centered* organization. Moreover, by this denial management makes the organization ripe for rebellion or suicide. Peter Drucker is correct when he warns, "For the rest of this century and far into the next, the competitive battle will be won or lost by white-collar productivity." [5]

We are losing the battle. And we are heading for catastrophe by our refusal to acknowledge the shift in power, and to embrace a new organizational paradigm.

Endnotes

(1)   Karl Zinsmeister of American Enterprise Institute puts this in perspective: "While only five percent of the children in Japan live in something other than an intact two-parent home, in the U.S. the figure is currently 27 percent and rising... about two-thirds of all American children will spend some time in a single-parent household" before they leave their teens (*The Tampa Tribune*, April 10, 1990). A quarter century later (2014), these statistics have gotten beyond alarming: The percentage of births to unmarried women by race: 72.1% African American; 53.4% Hispanic; and 35.9% white (Eduardo Porter, Tampa Bay Times, March 6, 2014).

(2)   Valentine, Alan, *The Age of Conformity* (Chicago: Henry Regnery Company, 1954) p. 81.

(3)   In the famous Hawthorne Study at Western Electric in 1927-1932, no matter how the conditions were altered, the workers responded positively. It was the attention and desire to please that was uncovered as the motivator. See Homans, George C., *The Human Group* (New York Harcourt, Brace & World, Inc., 1959) Chapters 3-6.

(4)   Greenleaf, Robert K., *Servant Leadership: A Journey Into the Nature of Legitimate Power and Greatness* (New York: Paulist Press, 1077) p. 10.

(5)   Elizabeth Whitney, "The Real Laggards: White-Collar Workers," *St. Petersburg Times*, January 17, 1988.

CHAPTER TWO

INCIPIENT CATASTROPHE

"Traditionally, one party identifies itself with the establishment's power structure, while the other is the people's advocate. Prosperous times, when the political pie is big enough to satisfy everyone, favour the establishment because popular involvement declines into sentiments such as 'you never had it so good' and don't rock the boat.' Hard times, on the other hand, lead people to adopt more militant political stances, and the dominant slogan is 'it's time for a change.'"

—**Alexander Woodcock and Monte Davis,**
Catastrophe theorist and writer respectfully

"I have noticed when visiting the West, a certain illness, and I call this the illness of stabilization."

—**Lech Walesa**, founder of Poland's Solidarity Union, on visiting the United States in November, 1989.

W E ARE EXPERIENCING an unfolding of continuous, almost imperceptible change in the workplace that could—at any time bring about an abrupt, discontinuous change in the behavior of masses of people. It is a process that has gradually been gaining momentum since World War II and is now straining the economic, emotional, and intellectual fabric of American society.

A *Rational Ordering Society*, such as ours, has great difficulty admitting this fact, much less grasping it, because the reality is unresponsive to quantitative methodology, cause-and-effect analysis, or linear logic. That is why this discussion is proffered in a different context.

René Thom, a theoretical mathematician, accepts the limitations of conventional wisdom, developing what he refers to as *Catastrophe Theory*. This theory is an attempt to understand the subtleties of the *change process*, and to deal with them accordingly. In that sense, then, catastrophe theory is a predictive concept. In mapping such trends, Thom uses differential mathematical topology—a sophisticated form of geometry—to avoid the restrictions of linear curves and regular solids of Greek geometry. Not being a mathematician, my intention here is to use the model for descriptive purposes, in an explanatory framework.

Due to its foundation in topology, catastrophe theory is *qualitative*, not quantitative. This is an important distinction. It describes and predicts the shapes of processes like maps without scales. On the other hand, it does not indicate how far away these processes are from occurring, how large they are, or even when they might occur. It is, rather, a consciousness/enlightening mechanism to alert us to impending change so that we can deal with it appropriately. Change can be of such proportions as to set off a chain-reaction of catastrophes.

According to Thom, all phenomena continuously seek, and then struggle to maintain, a *stable state*. Stable states, in terms of topology, represent sets of points, lines or surfaces, in a behavioral space. *Catastrophe, then, is any discontinuous transition that occurs when a system can have more than one stable state.* The *catastrophe* occurs when one stable state 'jumps' to the other stable state.

That would, in the organizational sense, be moving from the stable state of the *management-centered* to the adaptable state of the *professional worker-centered organization*. Because there are no intervening states between the two that are stable, the transition here is *discontinuous*. Therefore, the ultimate passage from the initial state of *management control* to the final state of *professional worker control* is likely to be precipitously brief in comparison to the time spent in the previous stable states. Indeed, one day soon, in the blinking of an eye, the organization will be transformed from authoritative control to egalitarian consensus. And with this, management, as we know it, will disappear as if it had never existed.

[To put this in the proper context, in 1990, or before the explosion of instant electronic communication via the Internet across the globe, movement was already apparent away from the infallible authority of corporate management. Yet, there was little evidence of adjustment to the rushing dominance of an elite (i.e., from blue-collar to white-collar) work force, or in the command and control practices of management vis-a-vis work in the workplace, except cosmetically. For the corporate hierarchy held fast and remained bloated, as business as usual practices persisted. Everything was changing and yet nothing was changing. A quarter century later it gives us pause to wonder why.]

Understandably, the 'stable state' of organization is resisting this change, as are most observers and writers on organization.

Either they would preserve the stable state of management control by formulating 'how to' prescriptions, or they would deny the radical transformation that now seems inevitable. Continuous change in the landscape of organization is clearly apparent and is fostering a discontinuous change in the behavior of management and the work force—especially professionals.

[Academics and consultants in 2014 are echoing many of the ideas here, but their collective focus is still with corporate management as if it is the answer. These consultants and academics are saying the right words—leaner hierarchy, eliminate "non-work work," define workplace values, etc.—but clearly with corpocracy stirring the drink. This has been the problem. Professionals are still responding to this programming euphemistically called "leadership." It has nothing to do with leadership. Consequently, the challenge is to energize professionals to breakdown the barriers between disciplines, and launch a customer-friendly approach to work that will be more competitive in the marketplace. They have the answers! Today, they have access to corporate intelligence, and understand the competitive climate from the trenches. Response today emanates from the trenches, not from mahogany row.]

It is difficult to 'see things differently.' By definition, the most complex system imaginable is the human mind, which must be one degree more complex than whatever it imagines. *Catastrophe theory* proposes that qualitative stability is a necessary characteristic of thought. We think on the basis of how we are trained to think. We deal with our problems on the basis of what we know. And we see what we expect to see. Without this *qualitative stability*, recognition and memory would be impossible. Yet, that stability finds us not venturing too far from the expected.

Regardless, Thom holds the evolutionary view that, just as our bodies are adapted for crawling, walking, and running, and just as our hands are adapted for grasping objects and shaping tools, so our minds are adapted for modeling topologically the world in which our bodies, hands, and minds evolve. [1]

Everywhere—in thought, language, and perception—discontinuity and qualitative change occur continuously. The transition from one way of seeing something to another way of seeing it is discontinuous. You cannot stop it halfway. Catastrophe theory offers an alternative way of looking at the world; perhaps not more correct, but certainly more complete, and surely radically different than what one's cultural conditioning (bias) has afforded.

Consider Figure 2-1. When you look at this optical illusion steadily, the transition from seeing the little circle in the center of one face to seeing it in the corner of the other is discontinuous. Some may see it in the corner first, and the center second. There is no way of predicting which way one will see it. Whatever the perceptual mechanism at work, the change itself is stable. Both visual interpretations are coherent. Both make sense of the pattern.

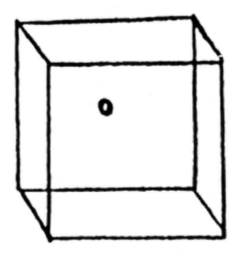

Figure 2-1: Where is the circle in the cube?

We obviously see what we want to see. Yet, perhaps one of the reasons this concept of incipient organizational catastrophe is difficult to grasp is because any *stable discontinuity* (e.g., professional worker control) does not depend on the specific potential for the change involved (i.e., high, medium, low), but merely on the existence of this discontinuity.

Remember, before the rise of professional workers, management was unchallenged. It could operate precipitously, and often did, without negative repercussions. It was unchallenged, because there was nobody of comparable authority or competence.

Over the years, however, with professional workers becoming increasingly the voice of authority through the exercise of *knowledge power*, qualitative change and discontinuity have been gaining momentum. To deny this qualitative change, or to suggest that it is of no consequence, does not reverse the pattern.

What's more, incipient organizational catastrophe does not depend on the specific conditions that regulate organizational behavior (e.g., policies and procedures, formal structures and infrastructures, and chains of command). What it depends on is *the number and complexity of these restricting indices*. It follows—the greater the number and the more vigorously they are enforced, the less effective they become. Eventually, the formal organization accedes to the demands of the informal organizational network.

Catastrophe, in this case, does not depend on the cause-and-effect relationship between existing conditions and resultant behaviors, but merely on the empirical fact that such relationships exist.

Given the situation described on these pages, the American organization is 'out of control' with power 'falling between the chairs.' Yet, the panic to preserve conventional control prevents this fact from being acknowledged. While management continues to attempt to dictate organizational behavior, professionals sensing that they are victims of the system—wait to be rescued from their predicament. They fail to see themselves as the rescuers. Management, on the other hand, valiantly attempts to play 'rescuer'... a role for which it is no longer suited. Consequently, organizational frustration reigns supreme. Physical and psychological safety are at risk, which impacts negatively on performance for all.

As experience tells us, "something's gotta give!" The time for circular logic is past. As much as management resists this fact, it is evident that the thinking which created the problem is not sufficient to resolve it. We have no choice but to view the American organization differently. This is no time for halfway measures. It is this obvious *discontinuity* that signals imminent catastrophe.

When the Great American Dream Explodes

The course of the American organization has, over time, been charted in terms of challenges and responses. An external threat has consistently enhanced us, while an internal threat (which we have difficulty acknowledging) has consistently diminished us. Palpable threats have always been more real than our dreams, yet it is our dreams that bury us. This has never been truer than in America since mid-20th century.

The early growth of the American organization was accelerated by World War II. It was in that conflict that America first experienced the intoxicating sense of invincibility. We could do whatever we wanted, and without challenge. Whereas World War I found most American 'doughboys' arriving just in time to join the Armistice Parade, World War II was different. The years 1942-1945 demonstrated to the skeptical world that Americans could accomplish whatever they set their minds to do.

This brought the United States to political and economic preeminence throughout the world, but principally in Europe and the Far East. Meanwhile, at home, it radically changed the fabric of society, threatening America's moral and psychological foundation.

The war years pried many women from their homes into the defense industries, and many soldiers loose from their family farms. Women went hesitantly into the factories, while their men went reluctantly off to war. When the war ended in 1945, many women stayed in the factories, while few men returned to the farm. American society began the process of building itself around the complex organization.

Corpocracy, or society as bureaucratic organization, replaced the simple life and pastoral domesticity of the nuclear family. And with that change, institutional society, as it was known, hit a historical snag. Corporate farms replaced ancestral farms, with machines replacing farm hands.

Suddenly, the identity of the farmer with the land became a memory. On another front, automation and mass production separated factory hands from the products they once produced with pride. *Alienation* and *anomie* became familiar words in the social vocabulary of disillusioned American workers.

Protests were faint, however, because American workers were taking home more money than they had ever dreamed of making. Their *standard of living* zoomed, exceeding their wildest dreams. Parents who had not gone beyond grammar school saw their sons and daughters graduating from college. A new middle class emerged with but one desire: to see their children better off than they had been.

Economically, many of their wishes were fulfilled, but not as envisioned. Their children, surprisingly, found little happiness and joy, and, therefore, projected little goodwill. They did not experience pride in work or trust in relationships. Nor did they discover a sense of achievement in life. Somehow, they had 'everything and nothing at all.' They were full of themselves, but empty of fulfillment. Greed became their creed. As they became materially satiated, they became spiritually bankrupt. As the song goes, "they were laughing on the outside and crying on the inside."

Nevertheless, for a remarkable 20 years (1945-1965), American commerce could do little wrong, and so the dream as nightmare was conveniently denied. Whatever we had to sell, there was a captive world market waiting to 'buy American.' While the frontiers of American power and prestige continued to expand, the integrity of the American dream commenced to contract.

The game of *making things,* never America's long suit, finally caught up with us. It became a 'zero-sum' game, with *quantity* the winner at the expense *of quality.*

Ironically, the world's most gifted teachers in the art of management and quality control—W. Edwards Deming, J. M. Juran, and Peter Drucker—were Americans, but not appreciated for what they had to offer at home. They had to go abroad to apply their trades. Deming created a 'science of quality' around statistical process control; Juran developed foolproof quality management systems to detect and resolve chronic problems; and Drucker invented the corporation as we know it. They recognized the error of our ways, and cautioned the 'authorities,' but nobody was listening. They couldn't hear for the ringing of the cash register. [2]

Blinded by success, and translating that success into self-righteous exceptionalism, the United States assumed yet another role—the definitive model of enterprise and the policeman of the world. This implicitly and explicitly projected the cultural biases of the American society, thus magnifying its *ethnocentrism.* The belief persisted that everyone wanted to be an American and, therefore, to value what Americans valued.

We had no clear purpose in mind, save that of 'making the world safe for democracy,' which found Americans in Korea in the 1950s and Vietnam in the 1960s and 1970s, then after the Twin Towers terrorist attack in September 2001, in Iraq and Afghanistan. The cost of these incursions, both in terms of blood and treasure, has led to a skyrocketing national debt that future generations of American taxpayers will have to pay.

The stalemate of the Korean War came on the heels of the 'ecstasy of victory' in World War II. America, and Americans, have never been quite the same. Dreams die hard, however, even in the face of the nightmares they sometimes create.

This has been personified in a series of presidencies in which blunders and misfortunes seem to have haunted the Office of the President. They extend from Kennedy, Johnson and Nixon in Vietnam, resurfacing again in the two Bush administrations with wars in Iraq, then culminating in the Obama Administration. The pathos resembles Shakespearean tragedy. Kennedy is cut down by assassination, Johnson by a "guns & butter" policy, Nixon by Watergate, the two Bush presidencies by inconclusive wars in Iraq, then Obama pulling out of Iraq and Afghanistan, while mainly unable to intervene in the civil war in Syria, to persuade Iran to abandon its nuclear program, or for Russia's Vladimir Putin to honor the national integrity of the Ukraine.

Yet, even with a lack of effective leadership with always a penchant for the absurd, the United States has managed to recover miraculously from one crisis after another to go on for another day.

It wasn't until the 'me' generation—the children born after WWII—came of age that this *continuity* brought about a new discontinuity. Disgusted with established precedence, no longer accepting of conspicuous materialism, members of this generation distanced itself from parents in blatantly obtrusive ways. Young men burned their draft cards or fled the country to Canada to avoid the Vietnam War draft. Young people flunked or dropped out of school. They quit, or were fired, from their jobs. They rejected the idea of family and formed communes with open relationships. They got in trouble with the law. They accepted the tag of 'flower children,' 'hippies,' and 'yuppies'... 'Not trusting anyone over thirty.' They saw war for what it was, ugly and inhumane, becoming the first disenfranchised generation in American history to stop a war without the vote. They chose not to be a part of something that their values could not support.

They were witness to the United States' *Fall From Grace*. Sons and daughters of putative American patriots, they turned inward against authority and the values of a confused, schizophrenic society. [3]

The *Fall from Grace* precipitated the emergence of a new 'self-directed' mentality. This mentality differed dramatically from the 'other-directed' orientation of their parents. They had a high need to *Please Themselves*, whereas their parents had a high need to *Please Others*. They could no longer comply with an American society that, to their minds, was veering dangerously off course.

Hardly anarchists, as some would see them, they were actually patriots in a new sense of American tradition. Indeed, they deemed the *continuity* of letting 'the powers that be' do their thinking and determine their destiny as pure madness. Survival as rational human beings demanded the discontinuity of thinking for themselves.

Against this background, the momentum of international economic and political influence, which the United States had enjoyed since WWII, was now thwarted by the industrial resurgence of Europe and Asia.

Denial of this resurgence was ignored, while the decline in industrial dominance was denied, as corporate America refused to renovate plants and equipment, to focus on quality, to upgrade the skills of the work force, to develop the competitive intelligence required to meet changing market needs, or to commit to long-range strategies. Instead, corporate America continued to operate with only cosmetic changes in the workplace, and to address the global marketplace as if it were still an American captive.

Small wonder American refrigerators never sold in Japan, when they were nearly as large as most Japanese kitchens. The same was true of American automobiles in Europe and Asia. Forget the gasoline consumption problem, these American cars looked like boats trying to negotiate narrow channels in these more congested surroundings.

In any case, this encroaching discontinuity was ignored not only by industrialists, but also by American universities, where scholarship is supposed to register some objective detachment from passing events. Ironically, in terms of 'competitive edge' and 'competitive advantage,' virtually all of the *grand strategies* now emanating from our pristine universities are actually reactions to this resurgence, rather than in anticipation of it. Catch-up modalities are not strategies at all, but declarations of panic... behavior suggestive of impending catastrophe.

The absence of American product quality and the consumption hysteria of the American people better describes the disposition of *The Great American Dream*. It has become a nightmare. Conspicuous consumption has become 'therapy for an anxious age.'

Chances are that, today, 'consumption' is of a product made somewhere other than the United States. These purchases have made foreign manufacturers rich. With their foreign exchange, some have bought large blocks of American metropolitan real estate, while others have purchased American companies. This willingness to invest in America has created the illusion that the United States is healthy, productive, and in charge of its destiny. But is it?

A close scrutiny of the various prescriptions designed to get America back on track have one thing in common: *none would radically restructure the organization.*

Quite the contrary. The continued maintenance of managerial dominance continues to be seen as the legitimate means of organizational renewal. Since the 1980s. countless endorsements for organizational change, and of work and the workplace, have strangely, required little or no change in management.

Equally preposterous, and symptomatic of our dilemma, are attempts by our elected representatives to blame our economic woes on Japan and European nationals. This tends to confuse them, because they see America's foreign trade policy as fuzzy, inconsistent, and frequently ill-informed. The shifting of responsibility, and the failure to think through our problems, have become the legacy of America's self-indulgence. We would have the world change toward us, but, of course, we don't want to change ourselves. We want nothing to disturb our illusion of stability.

Thus, we find nary a book written about 'atavistic management,' nor about the anachronism of the bureaucratic organization. While being the soul of reasonableness, the formulators of 'ameliorative prescriptions' fail to emphasize the importance of structure on organizational behavior:

Individual behavior follows organizational structure.

We are failing as a society because we are no longer organized to succeed. What worked in 1950, when the demographics of our society were quite different, is sure to fail today.

Meanwhile, there is the dream that technology will save us from ourselves—that we need only to perfect our grasp of this, and the future is ours. But technology has already changed us. It has made the organization anachronistic, and management irrelevant. Simultaneously, technology has changed the nature of work and created the professional worker. Yet, scant attention is given to how powerful, important, and significant this worker has become.

Some would even go so far as to blame this development on the Internet and Information Technology, and how mobile devices have changed work and our social life. This has not been the cause, but simply the quickening from a tectonic shift to warp speed.

Precedence or Prophecy?

Looking backwards sometimes helps us to see things more clearly. When World War I was followed by the 'Roaring 20s,' the common man was not invited to the party. He was either taken advantage of or for granted. In a word, he was exploited. Conditions were so bad in most industrial facilities that workers had little recourse, but to organize into labor unions. Today, we think of the *American Labor Union Movement* as if it has always been with us. But that is not true. It is essentially a phenomenon of the early 20th Century.

The labor union movement won early support (1933) from President Franklin Delano Roosevelt. At the height of the *Great Depression*, FDR declared war on the instability of the American economic system. With the cooperation of the unions, he constructed a governmental protective umbrella over the common man. What Roosevelt saw was *physical and economic deprivation* of the American worker (i.e., poor working conditions, unsafe equipment, inhuman treatment, dangers to health and safety, and enslaving wages). Labor rode on the back of Roosevelt's somewhat naive compassion, as he became the 'Patron Saint of the Downtrodden.'

Not until this president's commitment to labor did management pay attention to the worker. But was it the right medicine for America?

Unwittingly, the patrician Roosevelt moved the common man away from experiencing and dealing with his own pain. Without the pain of growing through adversity, the American character started its emotional decline. The worker went from self-righteous interdependence *The Culture of Contribution*, to management dependence *Culture of Comfort*, declining into counter dependence on the company for the worker's total well being *The Culture of Complacency*. This is where we see most workers today whether blue-collar or professionals.

Unfortunately, unions contributed to this decline by sacrificing workers' control of their work... for more money. With each contract settlement, workers improved their economic status, but at the expense of planning, organizing, and controlling what they did. This growing dependence on management, and subsequently on the organization, found many American workers trapped in extended adolescence, finding it easier to be taken care of than to take hold; easier to adapt to the system than to challenge it.

While these American workers were experiencing the post-WWII economic bonanza, Europe and Asia (especially Japan) were struggling for survival in the aftermath of a crushing defeat. They had no choice but to confront the reality of their failure and to deal with it accordingly. That the *Marshall Plan* and the *Truman Doctrine* were important contributors to European recovery cannot be denied. But Europeans did it. It was not done for them.

On the other hand, the miracle of Japan is due, in no small measure, to Japan's acceptance of defeat and embracing the natural resistance to this truth. Devastated by war, the Japanese could rationalize their plight. Instead, they admitted that the only enemy they had to overcome was the enemy of self-contempt. They had a choice: see themselves as victims or find their way back to victory. And victory they are realizing. They are winning the economic war we are now fighting—which is, in reality, World War III.

Meanwhile, Truman's *Fair Deal*, Kennedy's *New Frontier*, and Johnson's *Great Society* all rose out of the common soil of Roosevelt's *New Deal*. Each of these domestic policies reminds me of the old football adage, "When in trouble, punt!" FDR taught the government, "When in trouble, spend!" Throwing money at a problem thus has become the quintessential panacea, and his greatest legacy. Yet, each iteration of this policy of spending has driven the United States further from its reality and deeper into the illusion of economic progress.

Today, American professional workers find themselves in a similar, if not exactly the same situation as those earlier American blue-collar workers. What professionals today are faced with is not socioeconomic deprivation, however, but *psychological dep-*

rivation. Economically, they have fared quite well, benefiting appreciably from the success of blue-collar unions.

Psychological deprivation is more subtle, and less definable. That does not make it less mortifying. On the contrary, professionals are better equipped to deal with physical than psychological abuse. *Psychological deprivation* is frequently expressed in the:

- Constant threat of redundancy exercises, as companies continuously downsize;
- Freeze on promotions and wages;
- Reduction in benefits and entitlements;
- Need to complete inane projects;
- Failure to be given challenging work;
- Combining of jobs without assigning adequate support resources;
- Monotonous staccato of reorganization;
- Competition between husband and wife for determining who has the most economic clout in the family;
- Failure of children in school because parents are enslaved to demanding jobs, and have no time for them;
- Climate of panic that permeates the working environment so pervasively that panic is treated as routine;
- Requirement to attend endless meetings that accomplish little, other than preventing deadlines from being met;
- Failure to give recognition, appreciation and honest feedback on performance;
- Sense of purposelessness and powerlessness in the face of it all.

Management is not paying much attention to these psychological contingencies as they are too abstract and beyond management's compass. Consequently, in the eyes of many managers, they do not exist. Yet, it is the psychological climate that suffers, as it is not a matter of conscious design, but no longer knowing who has the actual power, and what constitutes *real work*.

While blue-collar workers are quite vocal about their complaints, feeling they have nothing to lose, professionals are of a different stripe. Because they wear the same uniform, they feel a kinship with management. Some identify with 'the management tree' as the most obvious avenue for their career development. Yet others feel somewhat tenuous about their real contribution to the organization's success.

Clearly, they see blue-collar workers, because they do and make real things, at an advantage, whereas their primary contribution is less obvious. What professionals have to sell are ideas and knowledge, which may eventually become 'things,' but the distance between concept and product is a long and complicated one. It is easy to have 'your idea' lost in the shuffle.

Therefore, professionals often become cynical about performance, seeing *packaging perceptions* as a fulltime activity. 'Making an impression' takes precedence over making a difference. They see careers as delicate designs that, unfortunately, must incorporate a belief that personality has much greater impact on career enhancement than performance. Indeed, they have adopted the same 'short-term/short-range' perspective as the organizations they serve.

On balance, professionals feel they have everything to lose if they are too open about their dissatisfaction. They conceal their contempt for management in surreptitious ways—ways that are difficult to discern. These are the *silent killers*, or the *'Six Mad Monarchs of the Madhouse'* that will be profiled later.

It is this *psychological deprivation* that is killing the organization. There is no way of knowing how long American professionals will continue to accept management's euphemistic words as substitutes for real action, or how long restive passivity will preoccupy them, perpetuating what the German's call 'the American Disease' (See Foreword).

Chances are professionals will continue to feed the dream with their illusions until the dream explodes into reality. That will be the moment of catastrophe.

The Fall of Rome... or, The More Things Change...

The fall of Rome illuminates today's dilemma. It came about when loyal Roman subjects turned inward against their rulers. What precipitated the fall was the eroded integrity of the Roman leadership and the growing disenchantment of Roman citizens, combined with escalating challenges from outside.

From a technological perspective, there was a change in military technique. The development of armored cavalry was overwhelming the Roman infantry legions, and their light cavalry. This was due to a *denial* of this technological change on the one hand, and, on the other, the *failure* of Rome to anticipate urban growth and its consequences.

The Romans neglected their agriculture—seeing themselves as warriors, not farmers. This neglect meant they could not support the cavalry with the necessary fodder, while properly feeding the swollen urban population. Moreover, years of warring had pried many peasant soldiers loose from their ancestral land.

Meanwhile, the idle urban proletariat, which was drifting into Rome in ever-increasing numbers, was contributing to the urban sprawl. This disenchanted citizenry would ultimately harness their political discontent into open rebellion.

In this political and psychological climate, the Huns shook the empire, and the Visigoths and Germanic invaders shattered it. These Northern tribes were products of the heavy, well watered soils beyond the Mediterranean fringe, where abundant fodder could be had. This allowed them to hold the technological advantage of an armored cavalry. Meanwhile, Rome was demoralized by psychological turmoil and political chaos, which enhanced this edge.

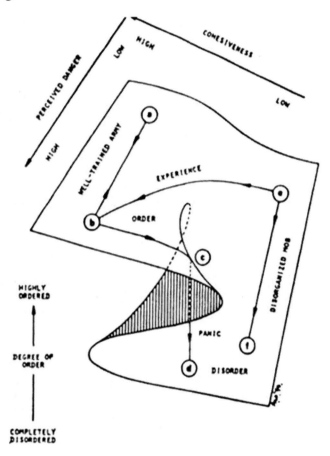

Figure 2-2: Social Order vs. Disorder in Times of Danger. [4]

Thom uses his catastrophe theory to describe a society in turmoil (See Figure 2-2). It could be the Rome described above, or it could be the United States today. What we have is *social order* and *disorder* in a time of danger. Whether the danger is perceived or not, it exists.

Thom considers the control factors of this topology to be cohesiveness and perceived danger. Cohesiveness is the tendency for individuals to identify with their group and its mission.

Danger, on the other hand, is based on the perceived level of danger, not on the actual danger confronting the group. This is because rumor can be just as detrimental as solid facts in determining behavior.

[Since September 11, 2001, when two hijacked aircraft crashed into the World Trade Center in New York City, while a third smashed into the Pentagon in Arlington, Virginia, and a fourth into a field near Shanksville, Pennsylvania in a seies of coordinated Al-Qaeda attacks with 2,996 killed, the United States of America has been in a state of heighten paranoia, and irrational engagement. This commenced with the preemptive invasion of Iraq in 2003 and remains a country in the advanced stages of hysteria as these words are written. A threat that has come out of the shadows by a rag tag group has been embolden into a worldwide terror organization, largely build on this fear and elevated anxiety. No nation, not even Nazi German, Imperial Japan or the Soviet Union has had such an impact on this nation.]

Path a-b in Figure 2-2 indicates that soldiers are conditioned to regard the integrity of their unit as of paramount importance. Most managers are, in that same sense, good soldiers. They will do nearly anything to sustain this integrity.

This cohesiveness actually increases as danger is perceived to be increasing… as when the threat of competition becomes greater. In a societal sense, the danger could be the threat of physical survival, as in the case of Pearl Harbor being bombed in 1941. Or, in a psychological sense, the danger could be the perceived damage to our pride, as in the case of Russia assuming the edge in space with Sputnik in 1957.

[The financial crisis of 2007-2008, which nearly led to another Great Depression, was a global financial crisis. It resulted in the collapse of major financial institutions across the globe with national governments forced to bailout these banks. It became known as "the Great Recession," and it is still with us as this is being written. It marked the collapse of the real estate market, and many major industrial enterprises, such as the automotive industry, which required major bailouts by national governments. The evaporation of financial liquidity can be traced back to August 9, 2007, when suspect business practices completely unraveled.]

But cohesiveness decreases, for example, when soldiers see comrades flee. The breakdown of the army maybe sudden (b-c-d) because *panic* has set in. This represents catastrophe.

This is what happened with the stock market collapse in October, 1987, and again in October, 1989. The army of stakeholders in American enterprise took to the hills.

This sometimes happens in a business when key people sense impending disaster and flee so as not to be brought down with the collapse.

With mob behavior, this gets a little tricky. True, mob behavior becomes less orderly as danger increases (e-f). But even this can be misleading. For example, if the mob's sense of cohesiveness increases steadily over time, while the danger is also rising, an ill-organized group can become orderly—as did the Chinese Communist forces in the 'Long March' of 1935. It was this march—a remarkable achievement—that ultimately overwhelmed the Nationalists in 1949.

China had never, in modern times, been organized under one political system. In the so-called *skunk works* [5] of industry, the same kind of growing cohesiveness and achievement can find order growing out of chaos.

The unpredictable behavior of large groups at critical moments of stress has shaped much of history. Take the *French Revolution* and the crowd that stormed the Bastille in 1789. It was coherent and purposeful at a critical moment of stress and danger, while the military contingent guarding the Bastille broke their cohesive ranks, losing their sense of solidarity under supreme stress.

What happens at such moments is evidence of a 'crowd mind' of immense unconscious energy. Obviously, the quantitative levels of tension were different, respectively, for each individual revolutionary and soldier, but the *Qualitative behavior*, the storming of the Bastille and the capitulation of the military, were group phenomena.

[French social psychologist Gustave Le Bon sees the crowd as a study of the popular mind. [see Le Bon's"The Crowd," 1896] He writes, "At certain moments a half dozen men might constitute a psychological crowd, which may not happen in the case of hundreds of men gathered together by accident. On the other hand, an entire nation, though there be no visible agglomeration, may become a crowd under the action of certain influences." We need look no further than the rise of Osam bin Laden for confirmation of this premise.]

On a more familiar level, Thom's model makes it easy to see how rumors can be demoralizing, or how failure to address real issues vital to the group's interests can foreshadow catastrophe. Learning that the official version of events is false can trigger a heightened awareness of danger, while diminishing group cohesiveness. It may spawn a signal that the leadership doesn't trust its followers with the truth.

These examples are presented because a small insignificant *faux pas* will eventually cause 'the jump' to a new stable state; to the dominance of the professional worker in the organization.

Next, we will explore the implications of this in terms of *"The Echoing Footsteps."*

Endnotes

(1) Woodcock, Alexander, and Monte Davis, *Catastrophe Theory: A Revolutionary New Way of Understanding How Things Change* (Middlesex, England: Penguin Books, 1978), pp. 20-22.

(2) These three great Americans, as octogenarians, were still active in the patient pursuit of bringing America back. The Japanese recovery after WWII is largely their doing. They created the Japanese miracle only after their appeals fell on deaf ears in the United States.

(3) *Schizophrenia* is a functional psychosis which is characterized by the progressive inability to make adequate and appropriate emotional responses, a loss of contact with the world of reality, and often the presence of hallucinations and the development of a highly individualized logic, with inappropriate intellectual reactions.

(4) Woodcock and Davis, op. cit. p. 122.

(5) Many companies are proud of their 'skunk works,' bands of eight or ten zealots off in the corner, often out producing product development groups that number in the hundreds. Tom Peters and Robert Waterman made these activities famous in their book. *In Search of Excellence* (New York: Harper & Row, 1982).

CHAPTER THREE

ECHOING FOOTSTEPS

"In modern-day business versions of Greek tragedy, executives are leading the charge on their own companies. They carry out Wall Street's orders to restructure, often before learning that their company is a target.

"The increase in self-restructuring is an important ripple effect of... hostile takeovers. Most restructurings occur not because the firm lost a takeover battle... They occur because top executives pull the trigger on their own companies. A defensive strategy of Downsize, Dismantle and Debt, of 'raid yourself first and be safe,' has taken hold... When top executives put their own restructuring into motion to 'save' the company... they usually bring on the same terror they hoped to prevent... Although the recent wave of corporate streamlining has greatly improved profit margins, it has so decimated executive ranks

that America may never recover... By the end of 1990 a million managers will have lost their jobs."

—Paul Hirsch,
Professor of Business, Northwestern University

"Whatever folly their kings commit, it is the Greeks themselves that suffer. Let Kings go mad and blunder as they may, the people in the end are sure to pay."

—Horace (65 B.C.-8 B.C.), Roman poet

THE CORPORATE BOARDROOM is under siege. Panic is in the air. The organization is going through a transforming, exchanging, and discarding phase as it focuses on 'cipher management' and other panic strategies. Although unrecognized, this is the precise *discontinuity* that is moving the organization from a *management power center* to a *worker power center.* The imminent catastrophe will come without warning, taking a 'quantum leap' from the stable state of management to a worker power base.

Because nobody is paying attention, an enormous amount of energy and destructive capacity is being expended in this transition. Although the current discontinuity forewarns of this happening, it continues to be denied. Meanwhile, it appears the organization could, literally, go quite mad before a sense of sanity and stability is reestablished.

Conventional tools for tracking and predicting these developments have proven inadequate. Because they fail to capture the social morphology of organization, demographic and psychometric/cultural (attitude) surveys cannot identify this type of discontinuity, nor can sophisticated statistical trend analyses. Quite the contrary! These 'exercises,' instead, conceal the situation, misleading the organization into either a more optimistic or pessimistic perspective—seldom a realistic one. Consequently, this finds some executives believing cosmetic changes will suffice, while others see precipitous action as the only recourse. Everything—even market standing, technology, and basic wealth-producing capacity—may be sacrificed in order to offset the immediate crisis, or to 'keep the stock price up.'

At any other time in our history, to behave in this manner would have been perceived as certifiable lunacy. Today, it is accepted as *SOP* (Standard Operating Procedure).

[WWMs argues that "six silent killers" (see Chapter Four that follows) are destroying the organization from within, silently, unobtrusively and passively with behaviors difficult to detect.

Indicative of the rise of professionals is sometimes displayed overtly in egregious behaviors that can, and often does have shattering consequences. This has been due to the failure of institutional leadership.

Nicholas Leeson, a young derivative broker for Barings Bank of Great Britain, an investment bank founded in 1762, conducted fraudulent, unauthorized and speculative trading from Barings's Singapore operation. This led to the bank's total collapse and insolvency in 1995 with losses that exceeded 208 million British pounds sterling. Barings then vanished.

Edward Snowden, a low level analyst in the National Security Agency (NSA) leaked sensitive highly classified secret documents to the public relating to NSA's spy program. These documents revealed how extensive the United States was spying on its allies as well as its enemies.

Bradley Manning, an enlisted man in the U.S. Army, a person working in U.S. Army Intelligence, released 720,000 highly secretive documents from the State and Defense Departments of the United States to Julian Assange, who promptly published them on WikiLeaks to the world on the Internet.

At this writing, Snowden is in Russia, which has no extradition treaty with the United States. Manning is in prison for violating the U.S. Espionage Act, serving a thirty-five year prison term. Assange is on the run, and in hiding, wanted in Sweden on a rape charge, and in several other countries for unethical and/or criminal practices.

These three men of no demonstrable distinction other than the brazen character of of their acts, are representative of the overt side of personhood, whereas the "six silent killers" are representative of the covert side of this cultural mindset.

Leeson, Snowden, Manning and Assange indicate in their behavior no countervailing common good restrain. They are the face of the world of tomorrow where individuals with special knowledge and skills will have the power to impact, disrupt, embarrass, or destroy ancient institutions with alacrity should they so desire. That is, if the responsible side of personhood does not prevail. And it will not prevail if it is not acknowledged to in fact exist.

These miscreants were not so much motivated by material gain, as for other reasons. Leeson was simply caught up in a game that became an addiction. He didn't profit from the game, or attempt to do so, as that was never his intent.

Snowden and Mnning were righteous whistle blowers, while Assange had an obvious issue with the power of institutions to command and dictate, as well as an issue with the money and celebrity classes. In various ways, these young men were driven by a misplaced morality code perceived in the context of personhood in what they came to see as an age of greed and duplicity.

They are the face of the world tomorrow when individuals of special knowledge can impact, disrupt, embarrass or destroy ancient institutions., that is, if the responsible side of personhood fails to be prevalent.]

To an organization under siege, just a slight stimulus can produce a shattering response. Forget the continuity the organization is struggling to maintain. *Discontinuity,* when it flexes its psychic energy (which is surely gaining momentum), will not be denied. Given this situation, an organization under siege can be suddenly demoralized or toppled by a single rumor, or in a single moment—by mass hysteria generated by corporate paranoia. Thus, the goodwill built over a hundred years can be destroyed with an irresponsible act. Many American corporations fit this description too well, yet they would be the first to deny it.

Organizational stability is controlled by *awareness* and *acceptance*. Awareness (i.e., conscious competence) compels the organization to be fully conscious of what it is (and is not), where it is, and how it got there, where it wants to go, and what it must do to get there. It sounds simple. Under siege, however, where the organization wants to go gets short shrift, overwhelmed by the flood of impulses to act compulsively. This is unfortunate, but almost inevitable. The *mind of the organization*, which is not quiet, cannot think clearly. It is caught up in the madness that it would attempt to avoid.

The problem is a simple one. These corporations are trying to solve *the problem* with the same kind of thinking that got them into it in the first place. All solutions are dominated by left-brain linear logic and labeling. *The left brain is the seat of logic, analysis, and rational problem solving. It is also the seat of language.* And, my, how language is used against itself to explain away the essence of the dilemma. In order to soften crushing reality, euphemisms become the order of the day; *fads* and *'quick and dirty'* solutions become life buoys in an economic maelstrom.

LEFT HEMISPHERE	RIGHT HEMISPHERE
Verbal	Nonverbal, visuo-spatial
Sequential, temporal, digital	Simultaneous, spatial, analogic
Logical, analytical	Gestalt, synthetic
Rational	Intuitive
WESTERN THOUGHT	EASTERN THOUGHT

Figure 3-1: Two Brains: Two Cognitive Styles.

Meanwhile, a corps of 80,000 new *MBAs,* epitomizing the quintessence of the verbal, analytical, and rational mode of 'left-brain thinking,' annually march out of American universities to exacerbate the problem rather than resolve it. [1] Remarkably, because we have turned to MBAs for salvation, we have fallen further into our own inferno.

MBAs appear to have developed no real, discernible skills to help them understand the problem, much less deal with it. The basic problem, you see, is not primarily economic—although there *are* economic implications. The basic problem is the utilization of American manpower, which is psychosocial in origin. The key issue is the American people, and how they deal with the reality they refuse to face.

This takes 'right-brain thinking,' integrated into the rationale of 'left-brain analysis.' In other words a holistic perspective. It is a combination of visual, perceptual, and intuitive thought, centered in the right hemisphere of the brain, acting in consort with the rational mode of the left hemisphere. Because it sees a problem in its smallest parts and as a whole, the right brain serves this thinking. Conversely, when the left brain takes exclusive charge of a problem, it moves hastily over *defining the problem,* placing most of its energies in the nightmarish labyrinth of *problem solving.*

Having said that, American corporations are throwing *Hail Mary passes* everywhere, hoping against hope that someone 'on our side' will catch them. Yet, at a time when the industrial world's economic forecasts for the 1990s are bright, the long business expansion generated in the United States during the 1980s appears to have ended. A deep economic slump looms on the horizon. Many American corporations that acquired large amounts of debt from leveraged buyouts and junk bonds are struggling. A period of slow growth could result in a wave of panic, followed by a large wave of bankruptcies that might very well thwart the American spirit to survive as a first rate international competitor.

In the face of these portentous possibilities, Americans continue to demonstrate irrefutable contempt for this reality. Take education, for example. Against Germany and Japan, its prime competitors, America is falling behind educationally. During the last decade of this century, one million American youth will drop out of school annually. The estimated cost of this dropout is $240 billion in lost earnings and unearned taxes over their lifetime.

In America, learning is primarily viewed as a necessity—like taking medicine when you are sick. Ironically, this medicine is most frequently confined to the classroom, not considered a lifelong experience. Many, once they are out of school, put learning on the back burner. The joy of learning and the privilege of a public school education are taken for granted—or not taken at all. Meanwhile, the quest for success, and the drive to attain it through education, finds German students going to school six days each week, and the Japanese more than a month longer than American students.

Likewise, Americans have a contempt for saving. We are the poorest savers in the industrial West! This thinking contaminates *both* the American government *and* the American corporate world. As U.S. trade deficits spiral, the Germans and Japanese are creating huge surpluses. Put more graphically, the average Japanese worker earned half the income of the average American in 1973. Today, he earns 20 percent more. German workers, who in 1973 were making two-thirds of our average income, are now a third ahead. If this trend continues, Americans will awaken one day to the lowest standard of living in the free world.

Before you consider this an exaggeration—if U.S. trade deficits continue at their present level, major borrowing from abroad will be required. This, in turn, will result in more buildup of foreign debt. The United States already has foreign obligations of over *$500 billion*. By the early 1990s, that figure could reach *$1 trillion*, requiring debt service of some $8 billion to $10 billion per month. [2] This is money that would otherwise be available to invest in such areas critical to American life as schools, police forces, anti-drug campaigns, medical research, environmental cleanup, and repairing of the infrastructure of American society.

But an even more debilitating barrier—after taking into account quality, marketing savvy, and exchange rates—involves the social and cultural implications of plummeting personal performance on the job. The decline of the work ethic and productivity is especially apparent among American professionals. This predicament is discounted by optimists who point out the $210 billion spent annually by employers on *training*. And, they remind us of our habitual technological leadership and economic clout (saying, for example, "The Gross National Product is double that of Japan, and four times that of Germany").

For one thing, we don't need to intensify our efforts in training. The whole rationale of training is wrong for these times and this work force. Training is what blue-collar workers have always been given, which remains essentially an indoctrination into the 'how,' but not 'why' of things. The 'how of things' is simply not enough to keep professionals interested, much less involved. This mechanistic formula is a legacy of the turn-of-the-century *cultural bias* towards workers, epitomized by Frederick Winslow Taylor, the father of 'scientific management,' who declared:

"… One of the very first requirements for man who is fit to handle pig iron as a regular occupation is that he shall be so stupid and so phlegmatic that he more nearly resembles an ox than any other type." [3]

This powerful bias towards workers is still extant today reflected in the fact that most training is confined primarily to instruction, not enlightenment; to the 'nitty-gritty' operant conditioning advocated by such lights as B. F. Skinner, et al. The focus of such training is on behavior modification, or of 'doing something' differently, not thinking differently; on behavior, not commonly held values, beliefs and expectations.

But we don't need more instruction. We need greater enlightenment; clearer insight into the futility of our present efforts. Obviously, we are working hard, but on the wrong things. *Training*, as pointed out elsewhere, fails to deal with the *cultural biases* of the organization, which are directly responsible for poor performance. Before we can change behavior, we must first attempt to change these biases. The capacity to change depends heavily on previous learning and the biases stored in the brain of each individual worker. Giving individuals uniform instruction without regard to the biases they bring to the learning effort virtually guarantees failure. Education, on the other hand, meets such biases head on.

When the *One Minute Manager* (1982) created such excitement, Catherine Tritsch observed, "Shamu the Whale may be better trained than most U.S. workers." [4] True, this book developed a precise formula for training. Apparently killer whales at Sea World's aquatic show respond positively to this mechanistic formula. Actually, this is not too surprising, for animals can be trained, but people must be educated. This has never been truer than today since the biases of the organization's culture have had such a powerful influence on performance. Consequently, conventional training, even with all the impressive devices of modern technology, has little capacity to change behavior or staying effect as performance everywhere indicates.

More importantly, however, training has little impact on *cultural biases*. Therefore, for all intent and purposes, these billions of dollars are being poured into a bottomless pit. This is because training is not designed to deal with cultural change. Only education can deal with the organization's cultural resistance to change because it uses previous learning as a basis for building a bridge to new learning experiences.

Education does this by assisting the individual worker in exploring their cultural basis of operation and how it meets, or fails to meet their performance needs. Such engagement, over time, generally finds them discarding the old and making way for the new. It is a slow and patient process that is generated by the momentum established by the will of the worker. Once this momentum takes hold, however, there is breakthrough to incredible achievement.

Meanwhile, training is too frequently a panic response to an ill-defined problem. Regrettably, when this occurs, training comes to be known as an activity for its own sake and little more.

As for technical leadership and economic clout, these are evanescent when it comes to individual will and creative spirit. *Will and spirit* are intangibles that personify the thrust of a national psyche. Here reside the sense and will to survive, founded in common values and beliefs. These abstractions are energized by the pain of history and the challenge of reality. But when the twin cultural narcotics—*comfort and complacency*—invade the American psyche (as they surely have), then there is little sense of the danger ahead, for few can hear 'the echoing footsteps.'

Ironically, it is the gift of technology that has deadened the senses. There is only one reason man has survived on this planet: the *human brain*. The brain is a necessary apparatus for human survival, with the human mind the software recording of that struggle. What is imprinted upon the mind dictates the way human beings behave. Paradoxically, as technology has pushed back the veil of ignorance, it has lost the coordinates of wisdom and humor.

Whether science or religion, whenever either becomes dogma or ritualistic consensus, civilization takes a step back into the *Dark Ages. Awareness and acceptance* have become buried in these times, yet the situation *mandates* that the American people disavow their resistance to reality and embrace what reality demands. Our inclination, however, is denial. Today, defensiveness, excuses, justifications, and denials combine with *comfort and complacency* to depict the *landscape of catastrophe.*

Unfortunately, these are words. Only words. If they are not felt, not valued, not believed, not understood, the echoing footsteps of catastrophe will not be heard. What is so disconcerting is that this seems to be the case.

Organizations... because they refuse to deal with workers differently than in the past... appear helpless in the face of mounting challenges. Despite expending enormous amounts of energy, time, and money, it seems impossible for them to see the situation clearly.

American organizations are currently throwing prodigious amounts of resources at their *cant nemesis*—poor quality. Quality has become the New Messiah, with 'salvation through quality' the new litany. "It will save us from ourselves, and win our redemption." This is a panic response to the strategic issue of "how do we get back on track?"

Global issues require global strategies. But we are not comfortable thinking in such terms. Global strategies require a conceptual framework and theoretical speculation. But thinking conceptually gives us a headache, and we have little time for theories (or, for that matter, for theoreticians). Such a framework entails qualitative analysis, or subjective thinking. But we are extremely skeptical of this type of analysis, finding it too abstract and fuzzy-headed.

We prefer quantitative analysis, with concrete references. This we see as objective and 'value free.' No matter how often this disappoints or fails us, we invariably return to the 'quick and dirty' solution, the newest fad, or the 'miraculous.' We live in the *Prison of Panic Called 'Now,'* and have little desire to escape its punishing comfort. This, then, explains the popularity of Harris Polls, questionnaires, statistical analysis, and astrology. It is reduced to quantitative mathematics, neat and tidy summaries—not messy, inconclusive speculation.

We want something that deludes us into thinking, "If we do this (reduce cost) and this (improve quality), the problem will automatically solve itself."

This implies that our problems are more quantitative than qualitative; more operational than psychological. Therefore, cost-cutting and continuous quality improvement necessarily will improve the health and stability of the organization.

None of this is true, of course. On the contrary, it is a cultural issue. If you design a bad system, and the people believe in it, it will work. If you design a 'perfect' system, and the people do not believe in it, it will invariably fail. It is true that Western Europe and Japan (now China, and sometimes Brazil) are setting the economic pace in the world market. But to focus on their quality and productivity as an exclusive algorithm would be unwise!

Western Europe, in particular—because the culture is so richly nurtured and maintained—has been responsive to almost any economic system. Max Weber's *authoritarian bureaucracy* is firmly in place. The Germans, especially, are a resourceful people and respectful of their authoritarian tradition. This resourceful-ness is not to be confused with being industrious, which they are not. Certainly, they are not nearly as industrious as Americans.

Germans can be accused, however, of working smarter than Americans. They are more apt to concentrate on the "right things" that make 80 percent of the difference than doing everything right. That said industrious effort, alone, is not a reliable gauge of productivity.

So, when they work, they work. They find little solace in 'working for work's sake.' Moreover, with an average annual vacation of five weeks, and an additional nine to 14 paid holidays, they make the average American's two-week vacation look anemic.

Ironically, Europeans seldom carry vacation over to the next year, whereas this is common with American workers. There is a saying, "When Europeans are working, they are thinking about their holiday. When Americans are on holiday, they are thinking about their work."

New Period of Genesis... or, The Japanese Talent for Survival

What about the Japanese? They are different than we think. Robert Christopher—neither an academic nor a sensationalist—offers insight in his book, *The Japanese Mind: The Goliath Explained* (1983). Here are a few enlightening gems from Christopher's book:

The men who manage the Japanese economy know that they must de-emphasize traditional industries and reorient the Japanese economy around highly sophisticated technologies in which Third World nations cannot hope to make themselves competitive. [5]

Japan is the most homogeneous of the world's major nations, explaining why it has been able to westernize its society and yet preserve a sense of its own identity. [6]

Japanese are not inherently a mystical people. Confucianism dominates the value system of Japan, which is more an ethical system than a religious faith. Its emphasis is on loyalty, personal relationships and etiquette, with a high value on education and hard work. [7]

Survival is not a phantom but very real to the Japanese. Consequently, in their heart of hearts, they have only one absolutely immutable goal—the survival and maximum well being of the Japanese tribe. Because of Japan's almost total dependence on imported energy and the fact that it possesses few natural resources required by modern industry, the Japanese never forget that any prolonged interruption of their imports would signal their doom. This makes for tribal pride and, paradoxically, helps to account for their drive and efficiency. [8]

The Japanese understand limits and accept them with stoic fanaticism. Japan is about the size of the state of Montana, but nearly three quarters of its land is mountainous. Because of a history of typhoons and earthquakes, the Japanese prefer living on the flatter parts of the country. Therefore, roughly 120 million of them are jammed into an area significantly smaller than the state of Connecticut. [9]

Japanese fanaticism is personified in a national addiction to electronic gadgetry. Robotics greet the visitor everywhere, and taxi cab doors are opened and shut with automatic control devices. Anything electronic holds them in awe. [10]

Young people are into *now*. A 1980 government poll found youngsters between 15 and 19 simply doing what they wanted to do (50 percent), as opposed to working toward future goals (28 percent). There is a hint of a cultural break with Japanese tradition in that these young people are attaching more importance than their elders to self-gratification and a privately centered value system. [11]

It is inconceivable to the great majority of Japanese of achieving true stature and success other than being identified as part of the group. [12]

The Japanese people are essentially law-abiding and disciplined because they choose to be. It is a case of automatic controls regulating behavior. In all of Japan in 1979, crimes involving handguns totaled only 179; the same impressive statistics are true of other crimes. Over the past two decades, crime has been on the decline in Japan. On the other hand, 99 percent of those people brought to trial for crimes are found guilty... but only four percent go to jail. The prime objective of Japanese justice is not to send an offender to jail, but to secure his confession, repentance and reform. [13]

Japan is not a litigious society. Civil lawsuits filed annually represent only about five percent of those filed in the United States. Consider this against the fact that the Japanese population is approximately one half the size of the U.S.A. What actually discourages litigation is the deeply held conviction that taking someone to court constitutes a breach of community harmony, to which they attach a great value. [14]

Their distaste for confrontation benefits them in their society, but frustrates them in dealing with foreigners. Generally speaking, if you accommodate them in matters of style, they will likely accommodate you in matters of substance. [15]

Japanese youngsters appear literally smarter than American youngsters on the basis of *I.Q. scores*. In 1982 British psychologist Richard Lynn conducted a study of children between ages of 6 and 16. The average I.Q. score of the Japanese youngsters was 111 compared to 100 for their American peers. *Only two percent of all Americans had I.Q.'s of 130 or more, but more than ten percent of all Japanese did.* While this does not necessarily mean they are intrinsically smarter than Americans, they do learn better because schools in Japan are an extension of the home, and teachers are accorded the same respect as family members. [16]

Thoughtful Japanese believe the information process will prove as much a turning point in human history as the Industrial Revolution. That is why it has become an *Information Society*. [17]

Both the United States and Japan are democracies, and both are concerned about individual rights. But the words *democracy* and *individualism* mean different things to them. Japanese democracy is more structured and hierarchical, while individual Japanese tend to seek self-fulfillment through identification with a group. [18]

World War II destroyed the feudal system which dominated Japanese society. People in prewar days stuck to the community to which they were born. When Japan was reindustrialized, the company became the new community as people flocked to the central industrial complexes, as the old sense of geographic community largely disappeared. Now, the new feudal lords of the manor are the executives of industry. [19]

Japanese workers have not been brainwashed into docility by their bosses. Japanese executives manifest precisely the same attitudes, values, beliefs and expectations as their assembly-line workers. These executives have worked on the line. What they would have their people do, they have done, and will do again.

Humility and identity with the worker are indigenous to their function and success. Therefore, dedication and hard work are more prized than brilliance. [20]

Individual survival, corporate survival and national survival are all woven from the same cloth. Cooperation between unions and management lie in the recognition of this fact. [21]

Japanese executives find their American counterparts too aristocratic. They see everything in the American organization as organized to separate executives from the workers. For Japanese executives to be effective they find they must be a valued member of the working community; integral to and not separated from it. Their primary role is *to serve* that community by serving the workers. [22] (See Figure 3-2)

The Great Separators

Executive Perks	Employee Eligibility
40 percent **Chauffeur Service**	One-tenth of 1 percent
63 percent **Company Plane**	Three-tenths of 1 percent
30 percent **Executive Dining Room**	Top executives only
55 percent **Country Club Membership**	One-half of 1 percent
62 percent **First Class Air Travel**	Seven-tenths of 1 percent
19 percent **Health Club Membership**	Top executives only

Miscellaneous Perks
In addition to salaries, bonuses and stock options

• **Car Telephone**	Free to top executives
• **Company Car**	Free to top executives
• **Legal Advice**	Free to top executives
• **Financial Planning**	Free to top executives
• **Interest Free Loans**	Free to top executives

Figure 3-2: American corporate executives take care of their own. [23]

The *Japanese System,* with its heavy emphasis on the survival of the institution, forces managers to think constantly about the long term. Conversely, American managers are judged by their stockholders on the basis of the quarterly profit, which forces them to focus on the short term. [24]

The basic difference between Japan and the United States is not economic, but one of differing social systems in the organization. Americans are individualistic and pride themselves in being independent-minded, whereas the Japanese are conditioned from birth to be group-oriented. Group orientation, of course, sponsors long-term planning, which the Japanese concede is the primary reason for their business success to date. And it is always conducted on the basis of a consensus model. [25]

But even planning differs philosophically between the two countries. In Japan it is a flexible rather than rigid process, eclectic, intuitive and somewhat chaotic, driven by a strong tribal consciousness to consensus. Therefore, it is more qualitative than quantitative; more abstract than concrete; more understood as a *doctrine* than a document. [26]

Japanese corporations are far more ready to mortgage the present in order to secure the future than are American firms. [27]

As of 1982, the productivity of American workers as a whole was still more than one-and-one-half times that of Japanese workers. This is largely because of the 'dual economy' of Japan. More than 70 percent of all Japanese industrial workers are employed by companies of fewer than 300 people, and more than half of all Japanese manufacturing enterprises employ fewer than five people. Only about 30 percent of the Japanese work force enjoys 'lifetime employment' for one of the megacorporation's. [28]

The Japanese receptivity to robotics is attributed to the influence of Buddhism, which, unlike Christianity, does not place man at the center of the universe. Buddhism, in fact, makes no distinction between the animate and inanimate worlds. Therefore, Japanese do not instinctively feel threatened by machines with human attributes as Westerners tend to be. [29]

The per capita *Gross National Product*—the value of the goods and services produced by each citizen—which is one half of the

United States in 1990, is expected to be 20 percent higher than in the United States by the year 2000. [30]

The Japanese chief fear, based upon how the United States has managed its economy and conducted its foreign policy, is that America may have lost both the will and the ability to maintain the kind of international milieu which Japan needs in order to survive and prosper as a free society. [31]

Japan once looked upon the United States as teacher. Now it sees them both as students of economics, with the better marks going to the Japanese. Therefore, it would like this equality to be recognized, and then for Japan to be treated with at least the same respect that the United States accords to substantially less dynamic allies, such as France and Great Britain. [32]

Robert Christopher concludes that Americans have little idea how the Japanese 'think,' and he concedes that ignorance of our top economic competitor can be very dangerous. If the Japanese have one advantage over the United States, he believes, it is their ability to fuse a sense of individual responsibility and achievement with the discipline and consciousness of the group.

Ultimately, Christopher argues, every Japanese achievement is rooted in the dictates of a primitive tribe, and shaped by a *sense of impending catastrophe* and the overwhelming need to survive. These primordial urges, as well as a short age of land and natural resources, explain the sometimes violent Japanese reaction to the outside world, and their intense competition and desire for group consensus—at any price.

"Just Say Noh"

A document that surfaced in late 1989—*The Japan That Can Say 'No': The Case for a New U.S./Japan Relationship,* by Akio Morita and Shintaro Ishihara—gives credence to the warning that Americans must understand the Japanese Goliath' better. This document, passionately xenophobic, written exclusively for a Japanese audience, is tacitly nostalgic for the dominance of the

Emperor and a return to the feudalistic consistency of such a society: "… Our honest and sincere emperor is the tribal symbol within our national polity and our culture; indeed, he is like the father of our family…" [33]

Just as Europe is firmly established culturally as an ancient authoritarian, paternalistic society, the Japanese are dedicated to the same feudalistic premises of ancient Japan. It is a feudalistic bureaucracy, as Europe is an authoritarian bureaucracy. These social systems work surprisingly well today for their respective cultures. A primary reason is that, as gifted as the European and Japanese people are in science and industry, they continue to be dominated by a submissive, blue-collar mentality; not by the equivalent of the American professional. And blue-collar workers respond positively to delimiting constraints of bureaucratic processes. That should give us little comfort, however.

The United States, on the other hand, has always been a renegade society—from the opening moments of its history, when it deserted the authoritarian and feudalistic confines of Europe for America. It is a violent society in which 'the right to bear arms' is considered as much an inalienable right as is the right to free speech.

In more than 300 years of violence, turmoil, and abrasive individualism, America has not satisfied its anger against itself. Everything is treated as a 'war'—marriage, work, sport, leisure, education, health and business… even religion. Consequently, there is little room for spirituality in *anything*, let alone organized religion.

In his book, *The Pursuit of Loneliness* (1970), Philip Slater wrote of America at the cultural breaking point in the Vietnam era. He reminded us of three basic human desires that are uniquely frustrated by the American culture:

- The desire for *community*—the wish to live in *trust* and *cooperation* with one's colleagues in a visible collective entity.

- The desire for *engagement*—the wish to come to grips with social and interpersonal problems and to confront an environment that is not composed of ego-extensions.

- The desire for *dependence*—the wish to share responsibility and control of one's impulses and the direction of one's life.

So, the inter-psychic war that ensues in every dimension of American society is essentially between *community* and *competition; engagement* and *noninvolvement; dependence* and *independence.*

While Americans struggle against themselves in psychic *war games* on every front of American life, the economic war is being taken away from them by the European and Japanese cultures, which have not been permitted the luxury of surviving by subordinating these basic human desires to their opposites. Ironically, that subordination has been a principle pastime of Americans. And the result: competition, noninvolvement, and independence represent the main constructs of that vague entity called the *American Character.*

The American character, in truth, remains that of a child. And like a child, the focus of America's existence has always been on *becoming,* rather than *being;* on the *competitive drive,* rather than the *spirit of cooperation;* on the preferred role *of spectator* to the *participant;* on the *illusion of progress,* rather than *reality.*

In these times—when professional workers (as a group) are coming to recognize these character flaws within themselves—they sense that the construction of the American organization is leveraged against them. Increasingly, they see management as caretakers of an anachronistic cultural system that frustrates them in pursuit of basic human dignity. But before their minds can totally come to grips with these frustrations, their behavior displays covert *rebellion* in what are called here *Six Mad Monarchs of the Madhouse* (which we'll explore in Chapter Four).

Given this predicament—and perhaps inevitably—the United States (where consumption has replaced creative contribution) has come in for some good economic bashing; primarily by the Japanese, but also by Europeans. This is because Europe and Japan are counter dependent on the American market for their products and on American military might for their security. Yet, despite all this, there is nothing in the world to compare to the United States.

From Europe, the 'U.S. bashing' instructs us that "American business is not serious." While Akio Morita, chairman of Sony (coauthor of *The Japan That Can Say 'No'*), says, "Americans look ahead 10 minutes, while Japanese look ahead 10 years."

There is some truth in all of this, but what it means is that 'the gloves are off.' The bowing and polite smiles have turned into nervous grimaces. Europe and Japan are tired of playing 'second fiddle' to the United States. They demand leadership, and find they must take the game away from the United States because we either cannot, or will not, lead.

Writing about superconductivity as a key to the future of Japan, Shintaro Ishihara, Morita's coauthor and former Japanese Minister of Transport, says:

"This type of technology does not exist anywhere in the Soviet Union or the United States. It exists only in Japan and West Germany. If the giants in the economic field and the politicians can join together around this type of technology, it would open up new possibilities for our advancement. Whether or not this can be achieved depends upon our large and small choices in the future; in sum it is a question involving the sensibilities of our politicians." [34]

When you take this document and its implicit discord, and all the recent events in Eastern Europe—from the precipitous collapse of East Germany and the Berlin Wall to the climactic breakdown of the Ceausescu regime in Romania—you have manifestations of Thom's *catastrophe theory* in action.

The discontinuity begins with words, and—ultimately, but precipitously—continues with actions. None of the world's writers could have predicted that the Soviet bloc of nations would respond this quickly, and in this manner, to *glasnost* and *perestroika*.

It is clear that World War II is finally coming to an end. Men of reason everywhere are putting military warfare behind them. Now, they are struggling frantically to create the best advantage for their people in the great economic war (World War III), which has replaced it.

Beyond this, what Europeans and Japanese say about the United States can easily be refuted by the indispensable role America played in their miraculous recovery from World War II and their emergence into world prominence. As Mike Royko asks:

"I just wonder: Is that what the Japanese would have done for us if they had won World War II? Would the United States now be an open society, run by Americans? Would we be exporting cars to Japan? Would Japan be letting us sell almost anything to them, while we turn away their products? Would Japan have let us—indeed, helped us—become an independent, economic world power?" [35]

But even beyond this obvious self-conscious defensiveness, what Europeans and Japanese are saying can be reduced to this reality:

Europeans and Japanese want to buy fewer and fewer things made in the United States, while Americans want to buy more and more things made in Europe and Japan.

The trade imbalance between the United States and the combined European/Japanese market has widened, producing 'the thunder of echoing footsteps.' Clearly, time is running out. Longstanding assumptions about these allies are changing:

Europeans want Americans to 'go home,' while the Japanese are learning to say 'no.' This is a switch—from traditional European hospitality and Japanese equivocation, to candor.

The Japanese are 'calling America's bluff with their tough economic stand. They believe they will ensure their security, and benefit all of mankind, by increasing their technological lead.

Meanwhile, these principal confederates in the world economy know that they need the United States. And they worry that America can never again restore its effective productivity. This is not the worry of humanitarians… it is the concern of partners who feel that, if America continues to sink into lethargy, we all may go into bankruptcy together.

This is moving Europe to the *European Economic Community* of 1992 and is driving Japan away from the United States' protectionism, if not markets. An outspoken critic, Ishihara insists, "Japan needs Asia more than America." He goes so far as to advocate revoking the U.S. Security Treaty and establishing a much greater deterrent capacity of their own.

Although confidence in the United States is not yet lost, it has definitely become tentative. A growing concern is that—due to our economic self-indulgence, lack of discipline, and corporate executive greed—the United States is doomed as a super power. "The time will never again come when America will regain its strength in industry," says Morita. "We are going to have a totally new configuration in the balance of power in the world." Ishihara is even more pessimistic, arguing, "There is no hope for the United States." Economic warfare is the basis for existence in the free world and, according to Ishihara, America continues to fail in this warfare.

At another point in *The Japan That Can Say 'No'*, Ishihara foresees "the end of the modern era as developed by white Westerners." History, he insists, is entering a new period of genesis. Indeed, this document is a lecture on America's sloth, decadence, and racism. The revealing shock of this comes through foreign eyes, which strip away the illusion.

Is it polemic? Of course. The United States is the melting pot of nations, a multiracial, multinational, multicreed, pluralistic society. Only one percent of the Japanese population is not Japanese. And that tiny minority's involvement in that nation's munificence is hardly visible.

What is equally true is that, as communism collapses, the world is moving toward freedom and free enterprise. At a time when the world is emulating American society, the United States seems distracted from its course. America's failure to keep-up-the-pace is an argument that is seldom challenged by Americans or foreigners. Instead, they nod ruefully and think perhaps Arnold Toynbee was right; that Western society is doomed.

Yet, it could be equally argued that the United States 'is the world.' And that America may be moving towards its apogee, leading the way into the next millennium, motivated by the certain message of those 'echoing footsteps.'

The More Things Go Around They Come Around

The robust Japanese economy Post WWII resulted in Japan feeling superior to its teacher, the United States. "Just Say Noh!" came to be the battle cry to America's influence.

Japan saw itself as solvent, fiscally responsible, its people prudent savers, living within their means, banks and the government working together and alway on the same page, with the automotive and technology industries increasingly dominating the global marketplace. *The Land of the Rising Sun* assumed the swagger and hubris to rival that of its teacher, taking pride in its solidarity as "Japan, Inc."

This Post WWII economic miracle lasted until the early 1990s, or when WWMs was first published.

Subsequently, Japan suffered a series of political troubles, experienced economic volatility, and endured nightmarish natural disasters. This found Japan entering the 21st century with a sinking economy and political instability that never could have been anticipated.

Japan stumbled into the new century marred by a recession due to imprudent financial decisions from both households and the Japanese government that have affected the future stability of its economy. This lingering economic catastrophe was exacerbated in 2011 with the Tohoku-Fukushima earthquake and the tsunami disaster that resulted in the Fukushima Daini Nuclear Power Plant meltdown and the closure of scores of Japanese factories.

A series of elections failed to adequately address Japan's economic woes. This resulted in the 1990s coming to be called "Japan's Lost Decade."

Given these circumstances Japan was not prepared to deal with the worldwide recession of 2008. So, at this writing, it is still struggling economically and politically, as it has failed to regain its former world status as an economic power. It would appear no entity can escape these 'echoing footsteps.' [36]

Aspirin Management and Other Home Remedies

Revolution is clearly at hand in the American organization. All the 'polite' books notwithstanding, America will never come out of this deep swoon if we do not pay attention to the collapsing infrastructure of the American organization. America is not performing because it is not *organized* to perform. It is organized to perpetuate the 'American disease'—Corpocracy.

Aspirin management and other home remedies will not suffice. 'Aspirin management' is pontificated by consultants and authors who win large contracts by acting as architects of 'failsafe strategies' for management. They contrive the redundancy exercises, the cost-cutting programs, the leveraged buyouts, the fads, the 'leadership guides,' the 'copycat' formulas to greater productivity—all the maneuvers, the quick and dirty fixes, to chronic organizational problems.

Home remedies, on the other hand, are the entitlement programs, the compensation dances, the management creep games, the problem avoidance' processes (including Total Quality Management, Quality of Work, Quality of Work Life, etc.), and all the other exercises to educate responsibility *out* of the work force, crippling it forever with *learned helplessness.*

Treating workers as 'patients' with aspirin management has given the organization a headache, rather than relief. But this is nothing compared to what 'home remedies' have done. They have given the patient a migraine and the *organization* a terminal illness.

In short, the American organization has remained fixed in antiquity, while everything within it and around it has changed. It has become a veritable madhouse, as illustrated:

- By workers who are there, but not there;

- By frenzied activity that finds those involved further behind at the end of the day than when they started;

- By the appearance of order, control, stability, and purposefulness when, in fact, everything is 'out of control,' and chaos reigns supreme.

Why is this? It is because the organization is organized to frustrate the individual, forcing them to resort, as a coping mechanism, to one or more of the six silent organizational killers… the *Six Mad Monarchs of the Madhouse,* which we will now discuss.

Endnotes

(1)   For comparison, Western Europe, which represents a population of approximately 100 million more citizens than the United States, produces only 4,000 MBAs per year.

(2)   Garten, Jeffrey E., "Japan and Germany: American Concerns," *Foreign Affairs,* Winter, 1989/1990; p. 91.

(3) Taylor, Frederick Winslow, *The Principles of Scientific Management* (New York: W. W. Norton & Co., Inc., 1911), p. 59.

(4) Tritsch, Catherine, "How To Be A One-Minute Trainer," *Successful Meetings*, August, 1983.

(5) Christopher, Robert C., *The Japanese Mind: The Goliath Explained* (New York: Simon and Schuster, 1983), p. 28.

(6) Ibid. p. 44.

(7) Ibid. p. 46.

(8) Ibid. p. 55.

(9) Ibid. p. 119.

(10) Ibid. p. 127.

(11) Ibid. p. 136, 301.

(12) Ibid. p. 148.

(13) Ibid. pp. 163-164.

(14) Ibid. p. 156.

(15) Ibid. p. 174.

(16) Ibid. p. 193.

(17) Ibid. p. 207.

(18) Ibid. p. 215.

(19) Ibid. p. 243.

(20) Ibid. p. 245.

(21) Ibid. p. 248.

(22) Ibid. p. 249.

(23) Source: "Special Report of Executive Perks" for 325 Fortune 500 companies, *Wall Street Journal*, April 18, 1990.

(24) Christopher, op. cit. p. 250.

(25) Ibid. p. 253.

(26) Ibid. pp. 253, 255.

(27) Ibid. p. 253.

(28) Ibid. p. 262.

(29) Ibid. p. 292.

(30) Ibid. p. 298.

(31) Ibid. p. 299.

(32) Ibid. p. 313.

(33) Buruma, lan, "Just Say Noh," *New York Review*, December 7, 1989, p. 19.

(34) Lewis, Flora, "Japanese-U.S. Bashing Is Instructive," *The Tampa Tribune*, November 17, 1989.

(35) Royko, Mike, "Japanese... Why Are They Complaining?", *The Tampa Tribune*, November 17, 1989.

(36) Langfitt, Frank, Japan's Economic Woes Offer Lessons to US, December 21, 2012 (www.google.com); Mauldin, John, Japan Is On The Brink Of Disaster, May 26, 2013 (www.google.com).

CHAPTER FOUR

THE MAD MONARCHS OF THE MADHOUSE

"Whatever liberates our spirit without giving us mastery over ourselves is destructive."

—Johann Wolfgang von Goethe
(1749-1832) German poet, novelist and philosopher

"When people are free to do as they please, they usually imitate each other. Originality is deliberate and forced, and partakers of the nature of a protest. A society which gives unlimited freedom to the individual, more often than not attains a disconcerting sameness. On the other hand, where communal discipline is strict but not ruthless—an annoyance which irritates, but not a heavy yoke which crushes—originality is likely to thrive.

It is true that, when imitation runs its course in a wholly free society, it results in a uniformity which is not unlike a mild tyranny. Thus the fully standardized free society has perhaps enough compulsion to challenge originality."

—**Eric Hoffer** (1902-1983),
Longshoreman philosopher

THE CRIPPLED GENIUS of the American worker contains many paradoxes. Take the way Americans behave when they are *full of themselves,* contrasted with when they are not. In case of the former, they are obsessed with *self,* spending an inordinate amount of time preoccupied with *things.* American workers have an essential drive *to acquire,* but an equal need *to give.* Yes, the paradoxical nature of the American character takes on many forms.

A few years ago, after a winter thaw, the Mississippi River at Waterloo, Iowa, threatened to flood the city. Faced with this crisis, the city mobilized its resources, and people of all ages filled sand bags, mounted them on trucks, and distributed them throughout the city to form man-made dikes.

Hundreds of citizens worked 'round the clock'—beside neighbors and friends and, yes, beside strangers as well. The separate identities of age, race, religion, values, and profession dissolved into a faceless common challenge. For a brief moment, a *sense of community* possessed their consciousness.

After the crisis had passed, several participants were asked why they did it. The consensus was "because it had to be done; the city had to be saved!" Would they do it again? "Yes, of course," they replied in unison. They would submit themselves to the demands of *crisis management.* Waterloo, that moment, had no *insiders* or *outsiders*… it was a community with a *common mission.*

This is but one event in the kaleidoscopic spectrum of American *self-forgetfulness* in times of 'perceived crisis.' As previously mentioned, whenever *physical survival* is at stake (e.g., WWII), or *psychological survival* is an issue (e.g., launching of

Sputnik)—whenever the threat comes from *outside*, the sense of belonging to a communal tribe is apparent. But the key words are *perceived crisis.*

Throughout American history, tension invariably produces *music,* while relaxation typically generates *noise.* If we don't feel it, as with the current economic crisis, it doesn't exist. Yet, tension is as natural to the American spirit as joy is unnatural. We are tense and intense, and find difficulty in dealing with things that are going well. We are always waiting—even anxiously—for the other shoe to fall. For some reason, we have to work very hard at enjoyment. Leisure is, in fact, intimidating.

The odyssey of American workers and their quest for satisfaction has not been a particularly joyous one. When you see joy on their faces, it is likely a mask concealing the tension of struggle and fear within—struggle to become what they are not; fear of being found out for what they are.

Pretend and *pretension* – both derivatives of tension – are prominent features of the American character. Show me a youngster smiling easily in play. Instead, we have seven-year-olds playing football as if they were in the NFL. Their parents-as-coaches can be heard yelling at these prepubescent youngsters, whose bones have not yet matured to take such punishment. "Put your head down and take him out," they cry. "Hey! Hey! What's your problem, fellah, where's your toughness?" Would that such energy and enthusiasm were directed at their education and enlightenment. Their minds are quite nimble for such challenge, if their bodies are not.

On the distaff side, watch six-year-old baton twirlers, toothy grins barely covering actual grimaces, displaying little joy in the exercise. How many chose such activities? How many more are playing out someone else's fantasy?

There is a much greater pull in the American culture to *please others* than to *please self-*… justified by "it is good for you." More often than not, it is *parental authority* over adolescent powerlessness and its *need to please*. What this creates in a developing youngster is *self-doubt* and internal conflict.

Translated, this is *tension*. It is an American disease, orchestrated on the young by well-meaning parents. "Doing what is right" is inadvertently interpreted as "doing what is expected." Disquieting at best, the whole process turns to viciousness when the aspect of *competition* is added.

American workers assume that competition is as inherent to their nature as breathing. They wear it as a badge and swagger with a sense of what they think it means. Author W. W. Rostow sees it otherwise. He believes that before America can *compete*, it must first learn how to *cooperate*. It must first discover its tribal capacity for communal action. Rostow fears America may go the way of Great Britain which, between 1870 and 1971, went from 32 percent of the world's industrial production to generating only four percent. He suggests the only way out is to develop an organizational infrastructure of cooperation. [1]

Toward the Fully Developed Human Being

Competition imitates initiative in a deceptive manner, obfuscating understanding. The competitive person trains to 'outperform' the competition. Providing they are successful, we imagine they enjoy a sense of initiative. Not so. They are in a reactionary mode. They are becoming the other person... only better. The standard is not what they are capable of doing, but what the other person can do. This develops the veneer of skill and the appearance of competence. Taken to the extreme, it can actually reflect what is hated.

Roger Bannister, on the other hand, typifies the innovative person with initiative. A British medical doctor, Dr. Bannister was the first person to break the legendary barrier of the *four-minute mile*. He did this, not by being more competitive or imitative of the training of past great middle distance runners, but by studying his own physiology. He then trained against this standard, expunging from his mind the psychological limitations imposed by competitive zeal since the age of the Ancient Greek Olympiad, more than 2,000 years ago. Thanks to Dr. Bannister, today well over a hundred individual runners have broken the four-minute mile in little over a thirty-year span.

Compare this to the *organizational climber.* Competitive? Yes. Competent? Probably not. With success comes the almost certain requirement of initiating policy and dealing with situational ambiguities demanding original thinking. But this person is groomed to think imitatively—to adopt the 'party line' (otherwise known as getting promoted)—so functional imagination is out of the question. Resourcefulness has been trained-out of the individual, who only knows how to imitate existing patterns and thinking. Besides, the individual is 'safe!' Given a challenge, such a person is in 'uncharted territory,' with neither the freedom of mind nor the passion of heart to create new forms. When old forms fail, it is an invitation to become ruthless to survive... typical behavior under duress.

True organizational leadership requires the capacity to see and the ability to serve. The organizational climber is devoid of both. In fact, there is a lack of vision in most American corporations today, and little sense of service to the organization. Service is either self-aggrandizing or beholden to the traditional power structure. The organization is myopic; structured to encourage relentless campaigning for promotion (Figure 4-1). It has not always been so.

Henry Ford is credited with mass producing automobiles, and Thomas Edison with inventing the incandescent light bulb. Neither of these achievements compares with their visionary leadership, however:

In 1914, when most industrial workers were earning less than a dollar a day, Ford created the $5 work day. This created a guaranteed market for Ford automobiles. Beyond that, he created a $30 million profit-sharing plan and other incentives, which helped to establish the working middle class.

Edison, on the other hand, envisioned the city being eternally illuminated. To accomplish this he invented the Pearl Street Municipal Utility in New York City, the first central electric-light power plant in the world... in 1881.

Think of it. Ford never got beyond grammar school, and Edison was essentially self-taught, dropping out of school at an early age due to a hearing disability.

This is the rich stuff of our American heritage, but it has been replaced by 'hype' and 'pedigree.' Most of the men who built America couldn't get an interview today, much less a job in their own companies. They were *doers*, not takers; *performers*, not personalities.

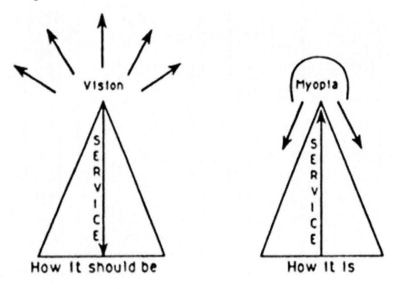

Figure 4-1: The leadership requirements of the organization are the *capacity to see* and the *ability to serve*.

Erich Fromm wrote, "Man himself, in each period of history, is formed in terms of the prevailing practice of life which in turn is determined by his mode of production."[2] Man's primary motivation is to contribute, not to consume. Capitalism makes the wish *to have and to use* the most dominant of human desires. A man so dominated, Karl Marx reasoned, is a 'crippled genius' with the ambition to *acquire* overpowering his desire to *accomplish*. Yet, neither private property nor profit is man's mission, but the free unfolding of his human powers. Fromm captures the essence of this:

"Not the man who has much, but the man who *is much* is the fully developed, truly human being." [3]

This is the crux of our problem today. Materialism is out of control in the American culture, and spiritualism has taken a holiday.

Since WWII, each succeeding generation has been more contemptuously materialistic, and the current *spoiled brat generation* (ages: 25-44) is especially deceptive. Young professionals don't talk about greed—they practice it. They don't flagrantly violate the Judaic Christian ethic—they ignore it. They simply strut their stuff. They retreat into the 'silent killers of organization,' wearing a mocking smile that says, "*Gotcha!*" They have become custodians of the *Mad Monarchs of the Madhouse*, otherwise known as the six silent killers:

- Passive aggression
- Passive responsive
- Passive defensive
- Malicious obedience
- Approach avoidance
- Obsessive compulsive behavior

These 'silent killers' eat away at the very sinews of an organization, and workers who display them are unscrupulous performers. They differ from their parents in that they are caught in the crunch between hypocrisy and hype, turning their frustrations unwittingly inward. They are looking for leadership in a leader-less society. They are looking for direction when nobody admits to being off course. They are looking for real work in the chaos of activity. Wherever they look, they find confusion:

- Nobody knows who has the *power.*

- Managers and workers alike—equally frustrated—spread these silent killers.

- Nobody is in charge. Management no longer has the power, and workers are reluctant to embrace it, but would relish the power without its concomitant responsibilities.

- And so power slips silently between them.

Management has given today's knowledgeable worker every-thing but meaningful challenges. Why management believed it could succeed at work when it was failing miserably at home is a persistent mystery. The sins of permissiveness, abdication, omis-sion, and commission—all committed at home—now play havoc with the organization. Clearly, little learning has taken place. The kids who weren't taught proper behavior or responsibility at home, are now refusing to behave responsibly at work.

Our problem, suggests Karl Zinsmeister of the American Enterprise Institute, is (at root) a moral disorder traced to the destroyed family. American children today are growing up in unstable homes, he notes, without regular and consistent support from one or both parents. This is leading to demonstrable intel-lectual and moral scars.

What makes this family disaster doubly dangerous, Zinsmeister insists, is that the trend pervades our society at a time when there is a significant decline in things material throughout the world. Clearly, there appears a counterbalancing upswing in the importance of the capacities of mind and soul everywhere else but in America. Zinsmeister puts it candidly:

- On a societal level: "National riches are now toted in human aptitudes and attitudes, not ounces of bullion."
- On a personal level: "Poverty is increasingly a function of character, or personal behavior." [4]

Put otherwise, the world is losing its patience with our anachronistic self-indulgence as it moves away from us spiritually as well as economically. Should the reader think these perceptions dated, a generation later after this book was first published, members of the Millennial Generation, those 18 to 33 years old in 2014, are less religious, less likely to see themselves as patriotic, less likely to be environmentalist, and more likely to support gay rights than Generation X (34-49), Boomers (50-68), or the Silent Majority (69-86). The drift away from the "common good" to personhood continues seemingly unabated.[5]

Why Johnny Won't Work

A better question than "Why won't Johnny work?" is "Why should he?" *New York Times* Journalist Daniel Rodgers writes, "We have exaggerated the death of the work ethic largely because its converts have so greatly exaggerated its existence." The work ethic has always been a minority phenomenon in American life. The idea that hard work is the greatest good in life never cut deeply into the South. It was violated in scores of 18th century frontier settlements, in rich men's ballrooms, and in most of the nation's workshops and factories. From the beginning, it belonged to a fraction of the population, primarily the Northern Protestant propertied classes (White Anglo-Saxon Protestants, or WASPs).

WASPs were an immensely influential minority, who did their best to nationalize their intense faith in hard work. They drummed it into school children, poor recipients of relief, freed slaves, immigrants, and industrial workers of all sorts. The lessons never fully took, however, so the story of the 'work ethic' is one of conflict and commitment.

Yet, the dreams of self-made success continued to win converts to the work ethic through the 19th, and well into the 20th century, as thousands of Europeans and Asians sought the 'American promise.' Once immigration was restricted, the ranks of the believers diminished dramatically. Hard times took up the slack, as did economic relocation, and with them a renewed respect for work arose temporarily. In the 1930s—the years of the *Great Depression*, when work was hard to find—respect for work grew appreciably.

But since the late 1940s, the workplace has become a veritable war zone. The struggle for the eight-hour day, resistance to job changes and increased production quotas, broke repeatedly into public view. Despite this, American factories a century ago were much more turbulent, with employee turnover double what it is today, and absenteeism better than ten percent.

The dramatic change was primarily caused by *leisure*, not work. There was little leisure for most Americans a century ago, so it wasn't threatening, as it is today. In fact, many Americans today refuse to take their accrued vacation, some being proud of their disdain for it. They would rather be paid for this benefit than face the break in their routine.

Indeed, the conflict between work and leisure is a real one. Seeing *work and leisure* as part of the same whole is seemingly incomprehensible to the majority. So, leisure is grudgingly compartmentalized. Like a giant cavity to be filled, leisure time is crammed with frivolous goods and entertainment, the opium of an impatient people.

This was illustrated dramatically by the 1960s 'furlough experiment' at Bethlehem Steel and Aluminum Company of America (Alcoa). In *Crisis in Bethlehem* (1986), John Strohmeyer explains how such steel industry excesses actually crippled 'the goose that laid the golden egg.' Steel workers in the 1960s, when the 13-week 'furlough' program was inaugurated, already had practically every benefit and financial concession imaginable. This program allowed the senior half of the work force to be given an additional 13 weeks of paid vacation every five years. This was also true of Alcoa, among others.

The furlough experiment was designed to manage manpower requirements more effectively, to give the work force the incentive to pursue self-enhancement interests (including educational pursuits), and to improve productivity. What it did, instead, was produce a nightmare. Most furloughed workers acquired second jobs. When the time came for them to go back to work, because they needed the additional income to maintain their 'new' standard of living, many continued their second jobs. Attempting to manage two jobs soon resulted in poor performance on both. So, for many, instead of a broadening experience, it was compressed into anger and resentment... directed at its benefactor, the company. Work was what they knew, and work was what filled the 13-week void. [6]

What's The Point of Working?

Despite this ambivalence, the price of freedom is still 'work.' When Adam and Eve exercised their freedom by disobeying God, they were driven from the womb of nature and into the real world of work. A prejudice against work has prevailed ever since. But late 20th century life played a trick on this cultural bias. Most work today is more playful, weightless, and more spiritual than leisure, no matter how much we try to see it otherwise. In the words of poet Kahlil Gibran, it is *"love made visible."* We have been driven back into the *Garden of Eden.*

With instant communications through electronics, with the Internet and metadata increasingly available far beyond the confines of narrow authority, what constitutes work, workers and the workplace are yet to be defined. Nothing is as it was, everything has changed or is changing. Small wonder that 21st century man doesn't know what side is up, much less what side is down. All institutions are antiquated, anachronistic, all positions of authority and accountability are atavistic. Yet, they all exist with those in leadership roles operating as if nothing has changed, exercising infallible authority and overseeing business as usual practices. It is not only managers and workers, but life itself that has been ill prepared for this new paradise. As a result, irrelevant conflicts and wars aggravate the times. This is what happens when no one is in charge.

Meanwhile, 'work' continues to be treated as punishment. Work is made into what it is not. Studs Terkel commits this error in his book *Working* (1974) with the opening: "This book, being about work, is, by its nature, about violence... to the spirit as well as the body." That was obviously true at one time. The historic horrors of child labor and Dickensian squalor now translate into robotic busy work on the production line, and the pretense of work in the office.

Digital software has advanced to where products can be manufactured without a single human hand being involved in the process. Increasingly, if we do not find other activities to involve people, the violence Terkel describes for work will be turned inward on us and each other. We are already seeing evidence of this with recreational murder and mayhem.

For many of us, struggle has gone out of work, pain has taken leave, and the motivation to work has become confused. Work has gone from the toil of moving the great stone of mortality... to moving the weightlessness of the human spirit. It is hard to measure 'work' when you are mainly spectator to it.

Guilt holds closest to Terkel's dictum. As is man's inclination, work is avoided whenever possible. Now, when it is not necessary to avoid it—when work is not threatening—Americans appear obsessed with it. Their priorities are out of control. Madness has taken center stage.

The modern American is ill-prepared for this development. Work for economic survival is fading. It is primarily sustained by spending money before it is earned, or being forever a loaner rather than an owner. Clearly, self-management is at issue.

Actually, when work as struggle abates, the *motive* to work changes. Traditionally, American parents worked to provide a better life for their children. But this, too, is fading. Disillusioned by the insolence of their spoiled brats, parents are retreating from this noble objective. Many, after surrendering their homes and possessions to their children's whims, are too tired or burned-out to complain.

The *spoiled brat generation* feeds on itself (the more it gets, the more it wants). It has no sense of purpose; no vision or reason for being. And, therefore, this generation marches to middle age suspended in extended adolescence.

Work has been distracted by leisure—doubly so because work and leisure have become interchangeable. Given this predicament, there is an insane effort to make the simple, difficult; and the banal, profound. It is the cultural bias of 'non-thinking thinking,' generating 'non-doing doing' of 'non-thing things.' Work, too, is feeding on itself. The principal product of work today is more work. With no discernible outcome, other than more work, it has become essentially counterfeit.

With the *Great Depression,* the *Dust Bowl,* and the *Bank Holiday* [7], now mainly forgotten, there is little sense of pain for these events of the 1930s. Even recession and inflation are hardly felt experiences.

[Readers might point to the global economic meltdown of 2007-2008, as the exception, when the fear of a second Great Depression threatened world economic stability. But here six years later (2014), it is apparent that nothing has been learned. The United States govern-

ment, with the rationale of "too big to fail," bailed out the automotive industry and Wall Street, while European and Asia countries did the same. Six years later, the same economic risks, the same disregard for economic prudence is demonstrated across the globe, as it is business as usual.]

Today, elaborate financial cushions, including unemployment insurance, pension funds, union benefits, welfare payments, and food stamps have taken much of the catastrophe out of unemployment or economic downturn. It would take total economic collapse to get most people's attention. We are prisoners of the organization—going from a sense of individualism and independence to a sense of organizational counter dependence. From the *Culture of Contribution*, through the *Culture of Comfort*, to where we are now—the *Culture of Complacency*. (See Figure 4-2).

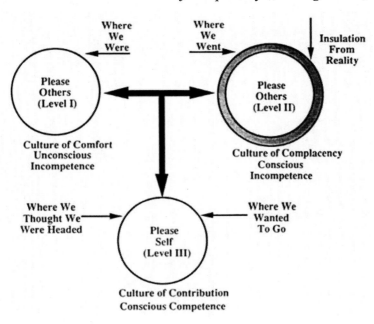

Figure 4-2: The Present Dilemma Illustrated.

Work today—being geared more toward impressions than outcomes—is respected for the identity it provides more than the satisfaction it gives. So, what is the point of working?

Think about it. What gives us the greatest satisfaction? It is being useful in the service of others. Now! It is no longer a vague ideal, but a real possibility. Work has gone from punishment to pleasure; from something we *have to do*, to something we *want to do*; from a vocation to an avocation; from *work* to *play*; from extrinsic interests *(outside demands)* to intrinsic interests *(inside commands)*. We have choices we've never had before.

Almost imperceptibly, the spiritual component of *giving* is competing with the conscious pursuit of *getting*. For the first time in man's history, masses of people across advanced societies no longer must focus on work as the central concern of their existence. They have the luxury of harboring ideals and giving them life. They may choose to work or ignore it in pursuit of other interests. Unfortunately, when it comes to such choices, most Americans are essentially primitives – with little appreciation of things other than work. To them work remains defined in terms of *struggle*.

Work, so defined, is the only thing they understand. And now that work is more ambiguous, they are confused. Americans have reached the age when rote learning and robotic behavior, which has hitherto dominated the requirements of most work, is not enough to keep body and soul together... something ignored without penalty by most Americans, until now. Suddenly, work has become manifestly spiritual and self-directed, which is beyond the comprehension and experience of the majority.

While America's ancestors struggled for economic survival in the New World, most Americans today have little sense of economic deprivation. Consequently, turning from the *concrete world of getting* to the *abstract world of serving* is baffling. *Service to others* is more subjective and qualitative, whereas the objective world of quantitative measurement, the cynical world of greed, is the world they know best.

Paradoxically, Americans are on the threshold of having enough leisure time to create a better world, but they continue to be trained and conditioned for a world that no longer exists and, therefore, what they are doing appears to be *out of control.* In a time of conference calling and Fax machines, microwave ovens and home computers, a study, entitled *Agenda for the 1990s,* finds time pressures and resulting stress levels getting worse (Figure 4-3). The result is that American professionals are finding it impossible to meet both their personal and professional demands. This study, examining lifestyles of 1000 businessmen and women in 14 industries, discovered that time savers and efficiency-enhancing technology, oddly enough, contributed to the dilemma.

Working More and Enjoying It Less

- 85 percent said they work more than 45 hours per week

- 48 percent feel stressed every day 65 percent work more than one weekend a month

- 89 percent take work home with them

- 53 percent spend less than two hours a week looking after their children

- 4 percent said child-care facilities were available at their workplace

---

Figure 4-3: Agenda for the 1990s survey of 650 men and 350 women professionals. [8]

These Americans are working for technology, rather than technology working for them. With so much information available, and so little time to deal with it, they have become *proactive* (a buzz word of these times) in producing even more technology. The increasing volume of information has become a demon—demanding more hours and causing more stress, creating a *decision-making dilemma*. More and more decisions must be made in a finite period of time. Thus, qualitative decision making is subjugated to the quantitative demands of 'non-doing doing' of 'nonthing things,' which, increasingly, is the basis of most work today.

[Evidence of working more and enjoying it less became quite apparent after the economic meltdown of 2007-2008, and continues as the subsequent recession that followed still lingers.

Companies and professions not only retrenched after undergoing downsizing, they made "superjobs" of what formerly were discrete well defined responsibilities. As one expert put it, "Job descriptions are now written in sand and the wind is blowing."

Emboldened by the unemployment crisis, businesses and professions of all sizes now ask employees to take on extra tasks that had little to do with their primary roles and expertise: engineers making sales calls, accountants working in customer service, financial officers running divisions on the side, medical practitioners (formerly nurses) acting as surrogate doctors diagnosing patients, signing prescriptions, and ostensibly acting as if physicians.

While mulitasking is strangely celebrated by those forced to so perform, recent research suggests that multitasking can reduce productivity, because it takes mental energy to switch from one task to the next. The sheer number of hours demanded by the superjob also can impair performance as the brain becomes fatigued.] [9]

Panic is in the air. When genuine leisure is a distinct possibility, the leisure society in America is a myth. In 1989, for example, the sales of the Filofax Company, whose elaborate notebooks help people navigate through the clutter of their lives, hit $4.2 million, double its sales in 1987. Meanwhile, more executives, professionals, self-employed people, journalists and bureaucrats confess to thriving on 60-70-hour work weeks and the fast pace of the electronic workplace. Yet, economists trained to study the impact of this frenetic activity fail to discern any appreciable benefit to the American economy. One explanation might be that many of these people are just 'spinning their wheels;' that working longer and harder is a subconscious way of avoiding the pain of working smarter… a repressed way of avoiding the discomfort of changing their behavior patterns. Consequently, the average professional is destined to spend at least three years of their life in desultory meetings and more than two years playing telephone tag.

Now we have added to this the sometimes mindless activity of tweeting, texting and surfacing the Internet, as the newest catharsis for the anxious age.

This preoccupation with vacuous *doing* deprives professionals of the time to embrace their transcendental heritage. In the early 19th century, Ralph Waldo Emerson expressed this uniquely American spiritualism with his celebration of experience. Emerson's famous essay, *Self-Reliance* (1844), emphasizes the wisdom of self-trust and perspective:

"To believe your own thought, to believe that what is true for you in your private heart is true for all men… that is genius."

Where is our genius today? Why do we embrace madness when our transcendent al past—the world of Emerson, Thoreau, Melville, Poe and Hawthorne—provides a more relevant education? [10]

Emerson had a different vision of the educated American than the *professional-technical elite* we have produced. He envisioned a person with a strong bent for experience, supported by a spiritual insight into being; a person with a sense of balance.

Emerson believed education should promote the ability of the common man as much through experience as from books. For him, the basis of a democratic education was the cultivation of ordinary experience to its spiritual essence. From this faith in the sovereignty of the individual sprang his vision of the unity of self, nature, and society. Emerson could see experience melting into the essence of the national character, producing a model of the possibilities of a democratic culture for the world. Repeatedly, he expressed the sanctity of *individualism,* combined with the responsibilities of *self-reliance.* America has drifted far from this transcendental course.

Consider the arrogance of individualism today and the conspicuous lack of self-reliance. Where is the sense of place and space; the sense of experience or self-determinism? American workers, by their own admission, find little joy in work, less joy at school, and still less joy in their private lives. They are being 'taken care of,' and they resent their *organizational counter dependence.* They lash out silently at phantom obstacles, failing to realize they are both the enemy and ally of the organization—the silent killers of lost momentum, as well as the secret weapon to newfound hope. They live the remorse of Eugene O'Neill:

"We talk about the American Dream, and want to tell the world about the American Dream, but what is that dream, in most cases, but the dream of material things? I sometimes think that the United States, for this reason, is the greatest failure the world has ever seen." [11]

But if this is so, who can change it if not American workers!

Enter... The Mad Monarchs of the Madhouse

Somehow this has been forgotten. Workers continue to spread their discontent throughout the organization, so that the damage control crew (otherwise known as management) has all but abdicated. Management, floating on a sea of self-pity, takes ownership of all that goes awry. It is the plague all over again—a disease with which everyone is contaminated, but no one can see the source of the disease because it is too obvious. Isolated under the microscope, however, this disease takes the form of six silent killers—*the Mad Monarchs of the Madhouse.*

Mad Monarch no. 1: Passive Aggression Behavior

Coming to work late; leaving early; doing as little as possible to get by, not as much as one is capable of doing.

This silent killer is invoked, somewhere in America, at least a hundred thousand times every hour of every working day, at a cost in productivity in the *billions* of dollars. Small wonder America can't make its mortgage payments.

Passive aggression has several interesting components:

Component: Perceiving Being Wronged

Passive aggression—a strategy (not always conscious) of punishing someone for a real or imagined slight—is actually an oxymoron. It's a play on the words 'passive' and 'aggression.' While in an apparently passive mood, the mind is racing with some kind of belligerent thought or punishing behavior to 'put a hurt' on someone or something. The perception of 'being wronged' may build to a defiance that is manifested in counterproductive behavior.

Component: The Need to Challenge the Rules

Authority becomes symbolized as 'the enemy.' Having a sense of powerlessness against authority, the next best thing is defiance of the rules. This is demonstrated by doing the opposite of what 'policy' calls for in the conduct of work—not enough to be flagrant, just enough to be an irritant. Workers typically demonstrate this by coming to work three minutes late and leaving four minutes early.

Component: Personal Fixation

Occasionally *passive aggression* takes a strange turn back on the person. They become so fixated with 'being wronged' that they take it out on themselves... by eating too much and becoming fat (because 'thin' is in), or disregarding normal hygiene (because 'appearance' is important), or using uncouth language (because 'maturity' is promoted). In the twisted logic against 'the self' the idea is to punish 'the system' that 'made the behavior necessary' in the first place.

Remember, the *passive aggressive* person is trying to get back at *something* or *someone* who has *wronged them*. What triggers this could be a failure at home, work or school; a failure to be recognized or appreciated; a failure to be included in a select group or event; a relationship gone awry; a loved one lost (yes, being mad at God can precipitate this behavior); a failure to get an expected promotion... even self-contempt for not being healthier, happier, more attractive, more intelligent can produce such reactive behavior. Being contemptuous of healthy, happy people can take the form of being insolently unhealthy and unhappy in their face.

Therefore, *passive aggression* is often a failure to communicate with oneself, which precipitates this ambivalent behavior. It rises out of a sense of powerlessness and low self-esteem. It is a way of 'getting even' without getting hurt or being discovered. *Passive aggression* is devastatingly disruptive, and yet the organization cultivates a climate for it.

Mad Monarch no. 2:
Passive Responsive Behavior

Never doing anything until one is told; never doing anything that one is not specifically told to do; leaving one's mind at home while bringing one's body to work.

One word describes how you are likely to feel about this person... *frustrated*. No matter what you do, nothing happens:

- You flatter them; nothing.

- You reprimand them; nothing.

- You boost their salary; nothing.

- You praise them before their colleagues; nothing.

- You reprimand them in public; nothing.

- You give them a letter of commendation for their file; nothing.

- You threaten to put a letter in their file; nothing.

- You give them a vacation day with pay; nothing.

- You give them time off without pay; nothing.

- You promise them a promotion; nothing.

- You threaten to fire them; nothing.

- Nothing; nothing; NOTHING.

Not a single thing you can imagine doing seems to get through to them. They appear inexplicably beyond your skills of comprehension and communication.

What frequently happens is that managers become obsessed with them. The *rescuers* are going to *save* them; while the *tough-minded* bounce them around the organization like a tennis ball, only to find they never land for too long in any given spot. Yet, they endure. It is management that does not.

Ultimately, in frustration, the manager *documents* their every action. The cost of this in terms of wasted time, energy, and expense is beyond calculation. The rationale that justifies it is this: *It's the principle of the thing.*

Take the case of the manager who documented a person who was tardy for the 167th time. This documentation, submitted to *The Marginal Employee Program* (a program for dealing with difficult employees) ran to seven typewritten pages, single spaced.

When asked what was so magical about 'the 167th time,' the manager scratched his head and said, "I really don't know."

Characteristically, such managers take ownership of the *passive responsive* person's problem, and—probably as far back as there have been managers—others have done the same. Over time, that person's sensitivity erodes to the point they become totally insensitive to everything and everybody. No matter what the stimuli, they become utterly nonresponsive.

Every time an opportunity *to fail* occurred, somebody broke their fall, buffering them from the incident, and *saving* them from an important learning experience. Such *protectionism* may rise out of love, guilt, a sick need to dominate, or every other shade of human conduct that prevents growth through self-knowledge. It is a diabolic deception of life to be cut off from the struggle and pain of experience—carried on the back of *a savior.*

How, then, do you turn such a person around? You don't! You cannot overcome 25 to 30 years of mismanaged development. You can only neutralize their impact, cutting them off from the mainstream, putting them in inconsequential jobs. Any flicker of behavioral change is rewarded, of course. If none occurs, it is *their problem*—not the organization's. The organization's mission is to establish a productive work climate, not save workers from themselves.

Parenthetically, *Time & Attendance* (T&A) is not a very meaningful performance gauge. Focusing on punctuality projects the implicit message that conformity and obedience count more than contribution. America is brimming over with workers who have never missed a day, or have seldom been late. Many of these same workers are unlikely to make a smidgen of difference. *Showing up* is their major contribution.

The *passive responsive* person is an emotional cripple who causes pain to everyone they touch. The irony is that they generate so much concern that people want to help them when only *they* have that capability.

There are basically three types of workers in the organization (Figure 4-4). There are *the winners* (leaders, victors or "hard chargers"). They represent about 15 percent of the organization. No matter what management or their peers do to them or for them, they go forward successfully. They are usually well ahead of the learning curve, understand (and accept) the naked reality of the organization, and deal with it accordingly. They *use the organization* to foster (and promote) their personal and professional interests (and requirements).

Then there are *the losers* (lagers, victims or "foot draggers"). They also represent about 15 percent of the organization. *The Mad Monarchs of the Madhouse* frequently fall into this category. Not only are *passive responsive* people losers; they are perhaps the biggest losers of all, because they not only visit this haven, but live there. Losers seldom understand the organization and refuse to deal with it as it is. They practically never see what the organization can do *for them*, choosing instead to see what it does *to them*.

The balance of the organization—70 percent—falls into the broad category of *the followers* (the soldiers, or 'obedient'). Followers move in the direction the organization is going. The organization is dynamic, so some of them occasionally move either into the winners or losers categories; but very few. Given the current structure and culture of the organization, chances are best for them to move into the losers' category. Incidentally, perhaps as much as 90 percent of management are 'good soldiers' and, therefore, fall into the 'followers' category.

The *winners*, ironically, are mainly winners despite, rather than because of the organization. American management demonstrates more uneasiness with winners than losers, clearly preferring followers. Meanwhile, followers increasingly confused by management's ambivalence, are displaying these *invisible behaviors*.

Passive responsive people, by the way, are likely to *think* several of the things actually *said* by *passive defensive* people (we'll discuss them next). While *passive responsive* people give the appearance that they could care less, in reality they are probably just hardened to life's vicissitudes. Robert Smith captured this in his book about children with the catchy title, *Where Did You Go? Out. What Did You Do? Nothing* (1974).

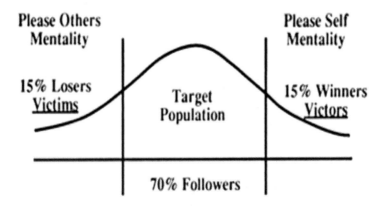

Figure 4-4: Normal distribution of working population.

- Winners will contribute regardless of management style.
- Followers will move in the direction of the dominant culture.
- Losers will seldom contribute no matter what the style or culture.

Passive responsiveness is a safe place youngsters learn to go early in life. It is an easy way to pretend "I don't care," or "You don't understand." Most of us visit this as a temporary haven. When it becomes a home, we are in trouble.

Mad Monarch no. 3
Passive Defensive Behavior

Always having an answer for why something isn't done ("It's not my job; nobody told me; how was I supposed to know; I never got that kind of training; I didn't get the memo; I can't read your handwriting; I wasn't there when you gave those orders; you must have told somebody else and forgot; I can't read your mind; I'm waiting for somebody to tell *us* what to do; this is where *they* told us to go; I'm new around here; *we* followed instructions—how were *we* to know *they* were wrong?"); or always having a CYA (Cover Your Ass) memo for every contingency ("The best offense is a good defense"); or being an expert finger pointer in SYA (Show Your Ass) games.

Passive defensive people represent an intriguing psychology. They seem aggressive, even confident, but manage to commit blunder after blunder, which is inconsistent with their image.

As the conflict between *what is valued* and *what is not* grows more acute and distorted, the organization is enjoying a bonanza in producing *passive defensive* behavior, which takes these forms:

CYA games. Practitioners have an amazing faculty—no matter what they do or fail to do—to make another person feel responsible.

SYA games. Practitioners go from self-love, to self-hate, to self-pity, to the attack. Having painted themselves into a corner, they come out swinging with a 'red pencil,' caustic remark, or looking for the exception. Their singular strategy is to throw others off stride; and once their adversaries are off balance, to take full advantage of them. Due to a massive sense of insecurity, they receive a secret delight in humiliating others.

Reckless Abandon Games. This is *passive defensive* behavior at the point of no return. Psychologists call this *Type 'T' Personality,* or high-risk-taking, thrill-seeking, rule-breaking, creative-abandon persona. Being primarily *left brain* dominated, their reasoning easily gravitates to the bizarre. Paranoia, which is busily fermenting under the surface, comes to dominate their minds. They are looking for trouble, and invariably find it; or for enemies, and find themselves surrounded by them. They are under siege, and feel they have no recourse but to do something precipitously, which they do repeatedly.

The first two forms of *passive defensive* behavior are familiar to most of us. There are times, I'm certain, when we all resort to *CYA* and *SYA* games. These brief lapses are part of our defense mechanism, which the organization is structured to encourage.

Because most of us don't reach the limits of our emotional resources, we seldom encounter *Reckless Abandon* games. It is a stage where the person leaves the herd and enters the wilderness out of which there is no escape. It is a dangerous place that an improbable number of talented people are, in these times, rushing to enter.

But *CYA/SYA games* and *Reckless Abandon games* are not confined to individual behavior. Of late, in fact, many organizations have been seduced by the intoxicants of *passive defensiveness,* which makes it worthy of special consideration here. The intoxicant may be money, power, status, glamour, immortality, fame, ambition, lust, or any other variation of the seven deadly sins.

Reckless Abandon Games— or When the Bizarre Becomes Absurd

What do Martin Siegel, Ivan Boesky, John DeLorean, Gary Hart, Dr. John Darsee, Jim Bakker, former President Richard Nixon, John Dean, the Manville Corporation, Continental Illinois Bank, E. F. Hutton, and Chrysler Corporation have in common? The answer is 'passive defensive behavior.' Let us now examine how.

The Siegel/Levine/Boesky/Milken Connection

While still in his thirties, Martin Siegel had everything—a Harvard education, a prestigious position with Kidder, Peabody

& Company, a $3.5 million home, a $4 million annual income. It wasn't enough. *Siegel had the whole world in his hands, and dropped it.* He agreed to share privileged information ('inside trading') with Ivan Boesky and Michael Milken.

During his 15 years at Kidder, Peabody & Co., he became known as the firm's "takeover specialist." This led in 1986, at the age of 38, to be made managing director of Drexel, Burnham, Lambert. The following February, 1987, he was indicted by the Security and Exchange Commission (SEC) for securities conspiracy. [12]

Why did young Siegel break the law; why did he turn his back on life's promise; why did he deceive himself, and in so doing, cheat many?

Only he knows. But the fact remains that he was enamored of power and flattered that Boesky would pay attention to him; would treat him as a confidant. He was heady with the importance of success and being accepted by heavy-hitter Boesky.

Dennis Levine's connection to Boesky is a little less central to this den of thieves. He was more quiet than Siegel in his work in mergers and acquisitions, preferring research with a voracious appetite for information. Boesky was into buying information. Levine's profile became more prominent as he played a key role in the hostile takeover of Crown Zellerback and Revlon with Boesky using this inside information.

Ivan Boesky was an arbitrageur in the mid-1980s, and the spider in the center of this intrigue, with his precognitions proving to to be fraudulent. Rather then keep a running tabulation of all the publicly traded firms trading, he took a shortcut and went directly to the source of mergers arms of major investment banks. Boesky paid Leving and Siegel for pre-takeover information that guided his prescient buys.

He would use this information to pick potential takeover targets and invest before an offer was made. When the fated offer came, the target firm's stock would shoot up and Boesky would sell his shares for a profit. He hit home runs on about every major deal in the 1980s. [13]

With the cosmic soaring of his income, Siegel more than Levine spent with a compulsive fever. He was hooked on the narcotic, money. "If I have money," his behavior implied, "people will love me, people won't be able to hurt me." This *passive defensiveness* translates into a deep disabling spiritual bankruptcy known as insecurity.

Levine's motivation is less apparent, as he, four years younger than Siegel, seems to have been more the manipulated than the manipulator. The SEC used Levine's ambivalence to roll him, and he gave up Boesky, with Siegel caught in the net during the Getty Oil fiasco. With those three in hand, the SEC went after Michael Milken, who was always the SEC's primary target.

Michael Milken seems the quintessential Wall Street crook as he seemed, on the surface, to be playing the securities game fairly when he was deviously playing it according to his own rules. He takes the gold for complexity. He became a billionaire financier and philanthropist and was noted as the "junk bond king." The monstrosity of his securities fraud and racketeering puts Mafiosa types to shame. Even his charitable contributions in the 1980s had the taint of fraud. [14]

[Martin A. Siegel pleaded guilty to securities conspiracy in February 1987, and was sentenced to two months imprisonment and five years probation, and fined $9 million in civil penalties. He was a witness for the prosecution and the reason for his light sentence. He has assumed a low profile since.

Dennis Levin pleaded guilty in 1986 to charges related to inside trading, securities fraud, tax invasion and perjury. He was sentenced to two years in federal prison, fined $11.5 million, and $2 million in back taxes. He wrote a book, "Inside Out—An Insider's Account of Wall Street" (1991) in which he claimed most Wall Streeters were honest. Over the last 25 years, Levine has reemerged as a financial *consultant and global strategist for innovative technology trends. He also lectures throughout the world at universities and think tanks, and host's conferences on contemporary issues relating to business ethics to emerging technology developments.*

Ivan Boesky was fined $100 million and sentenced to three years in prison. He served 22 months. Today, he is 77, comfortably retired, as his wife, Seema filed for divorce in 1991, and agreed to pay him $23 million, and $180,000 a year for life.

Michael Milken was fined $1 billion finally reduced to $600 million, and sentenced to 10 years in federal prison released after serving two years. Today, he is again a billionaire, and a philanthropist focusing his efforts on medical research. For this work, he has been given credit for changing the face of medicine.] [15]

Immanuel Kant wrote, "Out of timber as crooked as that from which man is made nothing entirely straight can be built." Indeed.

John DeLorean

If ever there was an *ideal type* to depict the *reckless abandon passive defensive* personality, John DeLorean tops the list. A swashbuckling executive at General Motors, his creative flair, dress, and style made his more conservative associates cringe. He was successful—a winner—in a business where 'anything goes if you can sell automobiles.'

When he left GM and formed DeLorean Motors in Northern Ireland, he commenced to cheat with *reckless abandon*. Before, he had played the capitalistic game of business with panache and humor; mainly within the rules. Once outside GM's protective umbrella, he took on Nietzschean dimensions, personifying himself as the self-made capitalist. Thus, the fantasy wish of a capitalistic *superman* exploded into reality.

DeLorean, more a self-promoting salesman than a businessman, convinced Northern Ireland to stake him with $100 million. It did so because industry and jobs were badly needed. He betrayed that trust by going out of business. Before the failure was finalized, however, he did a merry dance, including attempting to rescue the venture by being implicated in cocaine-trafficking charges. This, as business writer Craig Walters observes, demonstrated a profound naiveté about the nature of small business:

"He [DeLorean] had no appreciation of the role GM had played in his success during his 17 years there, no understanding of his limitations, and no comprehension of the finite nature of capital." [16]

DeLorean got caught up in the high risk, high-rolling game of self-deception and fell like a stone to the bottom of his dream.

[John Zackary DeLorean, born in 1925 of immigrant parents in Detroit, Michigan, rose from such common roots that his success was nothing short of spectacular. At General Motors, he was best known as the developer of the Pontiac GTO muscle car, Pontiac Grand Prix, and Chevrolet Vega, all best selling cars when GM's sales were declining because of Ralph Nader's devastating book on the Chevolet Corvair, "Unsafe At Any Speed" (1965).

From the beginning, he was an apt student and successful at every level from grammar school to high school to technical college to university, always receiving top academic honors in music and the arts as well as engineering. He was blessed with Hollywood good looks, and was GM's "golden boy" at only 42, heading the company's Pontiac Division.

Politics and his maverick style came to clash at GM leading to the creation of DeLorean Motors in Northern Ireland in 1981. The operation made only 9,000 DMC-12 stainless steel body cars with gullwing doors, and was bankrupt by the end of 1982 when the British government stopped the operation.

In an apparent attempt to save DeLorean Motors, he was charged with cocaine trafficking. He managed to escape the charges proving entrapment by federal agents.

In 1994, he filed a patent with the US Patent and Trade Office for a raised monorail, which was never built. To the end he kept redesigning his DMC-12, hoping to resurrect DeLorean Motors. The Internet was used to sell DeLorean Time, a stainless steel watch priced at $3,495 in the interest of generating funds to renew automotive production. He died in 2005 without a watch being built or sold in his lifetime.] [17]

Gary Hart: Inside Outsider

No political leader on the American scene was better prepared, harder working, or more focused on national issues than former United States senator and presidential candidate, Gary Hart. His devotion to new ideas about American life brought depth and vigor to an otherwise lackluster 1988 presidential campaign. Enter the *femme fatale*, in the person of Donna Rice, and you have the beginning of Hart's demise. Who shot down Gary Hart? Was it Donna Rice? The press? Or was it the *reckless abandon* of his *passive defensiveness*?

A half century ago, in the 1940 campaign for the presidency, Republican candidate *Wendell Willkie* openly campaigned with his mistress. He had a good relationship with the press and refused to hide the complexity of his marriage. *Reckless abandon*, to be sure, but things were different then (for one thing, the press at that time was not yet into journalistic voyeurism). Willkie was soundly defeated in the election, but the war was already underway in Europe, so his behavior had little to do with his defeat.

[Gary Warren Hartspence (actual name), born in 1936, served in the US Senate from 1975 to 1987, ran for the presidency in 1984, and again in 1988, where he was considered a front runner, was waylaid by an extramarital affair.

Since 1989, he has been a consultant to the national security, public speaker on a wide range of issues, including Homeland Security. In 2001, he earned a doctorate in politics from Oxford University,

Cambridge, England. He is currently a professor at Colorado Universiy, and is author or co-author of several books and articles, including four novels. His pen name is John Blackthorn.] [18]

No, Ms. Rice did not shoot down Gary Hart. His *reckless abandon* did the trick. An interesting study, it perhaps started with Hart changing his name, then progressing to coyness about his age, then moving on to finding difficulty in 'telling it straight' to friends. Finally, he was an inside outsider, alone; with the world that needed him so badly playing on another circuit. As one friend put it, "He was a time bomb waiting to explode." [19] And of course, it did.

Dr. John Darsee: The Ultimate Disappointment

Dr. Darsee had a spectacular career from 1974 through 1979. His research and hospital charts were written with bold, impeccable handwriting. One of his senior medical colleagues described it as "meticulous, beautiful, almost like calligraphy." An envious peer went even further to suggest "you could almost photograph his notes and publish them in a text book." The clarity of his mind and the scope of his vision was legendary, and he was barely thirty.

Dr. Darsee had it all: a quicksilver grasp of complex scientific concepts; high skill and compassion as a physician; the drive of a perfectionist; and the charisma of a born teacher. He was popular among his younger colleagues and much admired by his influential seniors.

Dr. Paul Walter, a prominent heart specialist whose name appeared as coauthor on 15 of Darsee's published scientific works, thought of him as "clearly one of the most remarkable young men in American medicine." Dr. Walter was right, but not for the reasons he thought.

It appears that most of Darsee's convincingly presented data were, in fact, cunningly crafted lies. Walter, like dozens of other researchers, was dazzled by Darsee's talent, productivity, generosity (e.g., sharing credit), and skillful use of flattery. Consequently, they were remiss in closely scrutinizing the data he was churning out.

Lengthy investigations at Harvard Medical School, where he graduated with honors, and at Emory, have uncovered a pattern of deception that is remarkable in the expanding annals of research fraud. Seventeen of his full length scientific papers have had to be retracted from the scientific literature, as have 47 abstracts (short summaries of research results). But it goes beyond this.

Many scientists have used Darsee's published works as reference to their own research, so more than 241 scientific reports have been compromised. Yet, the scientific community is asking, "How could it happen?" and that is the wrong question. *Why* it happened is more appropriate.

This demonstrates the laxity in the medical profession to be qualitatively driven. Because it is structured to be captivated by quantitative indices, this is a system vulnerable to deceptive manipulation. Making a clever impression with brightness and hard work, coupled with an imposing bibliography, is the passport to academic success. This gets closer to the 'why.'

The drive to succeed at any price, and in the shortest space of time, promotes cheating. While these good doctors are lamenting how they have been deceived, they might better deplore why the system encourages such behavior; *why the system is not the accused.*

[Dr. John Darsee, born in 1948, well after the scandal at Harvard and misconduct at Notre Dame was made public, wrote an apology in the New York Journal of Medicine, in which he said he "was sorry for allowing these inaccuracies and falsehoods to be published in the Journal, and apologized to the editorial board and readers."

Dr. Darsee was subsequently awarded a clinical fellowship in critical care medicine by Ellis Hospital in Schenectady, New York. He worked there until June 1983, when the New York State Board of Regents revoked his license to practice medicine in the State of New

York. It is believed that he is now practicing medicine as a physician in Indiana.] [20]

Be forewarned. For every Dr. Darsee discovered, there are literally thousands preparing to take his place. Darsee represents a reactionary frame of reference that is the kingdom of *passive defensive behavior.* [21]

Jim Bakker's Ladder Is Gone

William Butler Yeats once wrote, "Now that my ladder is gone, I must lie down where all ladders start, in the fowl rag-and-bone shop of the heart." [22]

Only in America could two otherwise ordinary people rise and fall as quickly as did Jim and Tammy Bakker. Their Praise The Lord (PTL) television club was a resounding success, largely due to their commonplace familiarity. They were 'like the couple next door.'

But somewhere between *their* house and the homes of millions of Americans, Tammy's mascara and war paint and Jim's cherubic grin became diabolical. Essentially nice people, they got caught in the war of ratings and the insatiable appetite of television for dollars. Long before Jim's sex scandal surfaced, the PTL club had become 'show biz,' departing from its religious and spiritual intent. It became entertainment with a capital 'E.' When that happened, the Bakker's commenced to behave like superstars, with other peoples' money. The mansions, the Mercedes, Tammy's shopping sprees—all became part of the scam that led to Jim's dalliance with Jessica Hahn. *Reckless abandon passive defensiveness* had come to dominate their lives and lifestyle. When that happened, they became 'a born-again disaster.'

[Jim Bakker was sentenced in 1989 to 45-years in prison for mail fraud and conspiracy; served eight years and was released; wrote a book in 1996 denouncing his prosperity theology in "I Was Wrong"; set

up a new televangelist program in Branson, Missouri called the "Jim Bakker Show" in 1998; created a development called "Morningside," which resembles the upscale Heritage USA of his PTL Club years: and with a new wife, the 74-year-old is in demand, although he owes the IRS $6 million.

Tammy Faye Bakker divorced Jim Bakker after 31 years of marriage in 1992, remarried, and died in 2007 at the age of 65.] [23]

President Richard M. Nixon

While a law student at Duke University, where his diligence gave him the nickname 'iron butt,' Nixon's drive betrayed him—as it would throughout his remarkable career. One night, not able to handle the suspense of waiting until grades were posted, he broke into the dean's office to see his grades; only to be caught. It is beside the point that he had top grades, or that he finished third in his class. His anxiety at not knowing became master of his destiny.

Years later, this behavior would be repeated. Far ahead in the polls, he would resort to the Watergate break-in. Countless Nixon biographers make much of this in terms of his legendary paranoia. By their assessment, one of the great American presidents in terms of foreign affairs, Nixon demonstrated a disconcerting capacity for senseless behavior. Obviously, there are many contradictions in his character: from a Quaker upbringing, to a tough minded hawkishness; from an extreme discomfort around people, to a public boldness bordering on bravado. It is within this chiaroscuro that his *passive defensiveness* resided.

[After December 1974, former President Nixon planned a comeback. He had resigned from the presidency, the first American president to do so under the threat of impeachment, and was subsequently given a pardon by President Gerald Ford. At the time, he wrote in his diary, "So be it."

He was practically broke with only $500 in the bank, never being that interested in money, he set about being an elder statesman. He wrote ten books starting with his "RN: The Memoir of Richard Nixon" (1978). The book revealed the quality of his mind, and implicitly, his disappointments, paranoia, and anxieties. It might be said he was neither comfortable with success nor disengaged by failure as he was inclined to soldier on as much by the one as the other.

Not surprisingly, his books and life beyond the presidency received mixed reviews subjectively following political persuasions. Richard Reeves "President Nixon: Alone in the White House" (2001) suffers for this as did many others. Journalists are not historians but they often write as if they think they are.

He continued to write, lecture, meet leaders across the world, especially in Third World countries. In 1990, the Richard Nixon Library was established in Yorba Linda, his birthplace, and a year later, the Nixon Center, a think tank. He died in 1993 at the age of 81.] [24]

John Dean & Blind Ambition

When values and beliefs are tabled, and one enters the no-man's land of experience, one encounters *reckless abandon.* John Dean in his biography, *Blind Ambition* (1977), candidly admits that 'making it' took precedence over everything. Cheating became not only the rule of convenience, but necessity. Cutting corners became an art form of Machiavellian perfection, with the ends justifying any means. Dean operated quite successfully in this cynical world, where cunning, duplicity, and bad faith were part of the arsenal of deception. But when he was made to take the fall for the entire Nixon Administration, he reneged.

Since then, he hasn't gotten 'religion' as have several other Watergate conspirators. Instead, he has chosen a quiet withdrawal from ambition; blind or otherwise.

[John Dean was born about 50 years too early as his temperament, "blind ambition," as he puts it, and his loose morality and loyalty would fit in nicely with the personhood of the times.

During the Watergate scandal of the Nixon Administration, the FBI considered Dean the "master manipulator of the Watergate cover up," which he quickly retreated from once indicted, becoming a witness for the prosecution against President Nixon.

Today, Dean is an author, columnist, commentator on contemporary politics, critic of conservatism, and the Republican party, and was a supporter of efforts to impeach President George W. Bush when he was in office.] [25]

Corporate Malfeasance

It would be inappropriate to end this discussion on *passive defensiveness* without giving evidence of its corporate appeal. The American corporate landscape is rife with it. The examples cited here are representative of this disturbing trend.

Manville Corporation

Once this giant was known as Johns Manville Corporation. Now, it is in the process of disintegrating as one of its principle products, asbestos, brings it down.

For many years, it appears, the Johns Manville medical department doctored data regarding the dangers associated with asbestos inhalation; duplicity that goes back at least to the end of WWII. Consequently, there is no way of estimating how many former employees suffering from debilitating lung diseases can trace their ills to working for Johns Manville. The cover-up, in any case, falls into *CYA passive defensiveness.*

What is particularly disturbing is the motivation behind it. A lawyer recalls how, 45 years ago, he confronted Manville's corporate council about the company's policy of concealing chest X-ray results from employees. He asked, "Do you mean to tell me you would let them work until they dropped dead?" The corporate attorney replied, "Yes, we save a lot of money that way." [26]

Such *CYA* behavior represents the least troublesome way to solve a dilemma. Yet, a company is deemed of a higher moral order than the individual. The pure absurdity of thinking 'anything is justified,' as long as it 'saves the company,' apparently never occurred to anyone. *Human rights* were not considered—only organizational survival. Concealing information, then, whatever its nature, is sometimes considered a way of protecting 'the product,' and therefore 'the company.'

[In 1982, Johns-Manville faced unprecedented liability for asbestos injury claims. It voluntarily filed for bankruptcy protection under Chapter 11 of the US Bankruptcy Code. It was, at the time, the largest United States company to have done so. In 1988, the bankruptcy was resolved by the Manville Trust to asbestos claimants and emerged from Chapter 11 as Manville Corporation. To date, the Manville Trust, which is still active, has paid out $4.3 billion to claimants. In 1997, the company changed its name back to Johns Manville without the hyphen. In 2001, Berkshire Hathaway bought the corporation. In 2012, Mary Rinehart was appointed the new CEO. She had been the CFO for Johns Manville, and has been with the company over 33 years.] [27]

Continental Illinois Bank

From the ninth largest bank in the United States to oblivion is the history of Continental Illinois. Similar to the gigantic fiasco of the thrifts and the multibillion-dollar 'bail out' of 1989, this bank now belongs to the Federal Deposit Insurance Corporation (FDIC) to the tune of more than 80 percent of its assets.

It was a different matter in 1976. Continental had a dream that, through leveraged lending, it could become perhaps the seventh largest bank in America. Corporate officers became aggressive pursuers of borrowers everywhere, bent on realizing that dream.

Their diligence paid off. They found a rich captive market in poorly capitalized Oklahoma oil producers. With this discovery, they began to bet enormous sums on their dream. Eventually, a cool $1 billion worth of dreams found its way into Continental's portfolio, and another cool $1 billion of depositor's money flowed out to pay for it. The trouble started when the price of oil collapsed.

Continental had become so spellbound by lending, it didn't look deeply into how growth had been achieved. When the borrowers had dry holes and idle drilling equipment, the fat interest rates dried up, too. Under the *reckless abandon* of growth, the sharp shrinkage of assets caught the attention of internal auditors. The dream died almost immediately. The auditors, without even trying, stumbled on the bottomless pit of deceit upon which the dream was built.

For example, one loan officer had purchased $800 million in gas loans from Penn Square Bank in Oklahoma City, where he had also borrowed $565,000 personally. He was issued a minor reprimand for this behavior. It wasn't until Federal prosecutors entered the picture that such incidents of charity were called what they were—kickbacks.

As with Johns Manville, internal control mechanisms flashed danger signals, but they were either ignored or treated as routine. The bank was 'on a roll,' and nothing was going to stop it. Once the word got out, however, the bank's instability nearly put it under; saved only by FDIC. Of course, the big losers were the bank's thousands of shareholders, and more than 2000 employees who lost their jobs. Continental is now a small bank made modest by a big appetite for cover-up.

[In 1984, Continental Illinois became the largest bank failure in United States history. The bank held that distinction until the fail-

ure of Washington Mutual in 2008 during the financial crisis of that year, which ended by being seven times larger than the failure of Continental Illinois. To avert the total failure of Continental Illinois, the Federal Deposit Insurance Corporation (FDIC) infused $4.5 billion to rescue the bank. In 1984, Congressman Steward McKinney during Congressional Hearings on the bank coined the phrase "too big to fail." The bank was renamed Continental Bank with the federal government owning 80 percent of the company shares. In 1994, Continental Bank was acquired by Bank of America, which owns several banks in the Chicago area.] [28]

E. F. Hutton

No 'fall from grace' was more shocking to the national television audience than that of E. F. Hutton & Company. The television commercial, "When E. F. Hutton speaks, everyone stops to listen," epitomized Hutton as *the* financial institution to be trusted.

E. F. Hutton—the nation's second largest independent broker finally pleaded guilty to about 2000 counts of mail and wire fraud. This brokerage firm systematically bilked 400 of its own banks by drawing against uncollected funds or, in some cases, against nonexistent funds. It would cover these funds after enjoying interest-free use of the money.

It was a scam. Perfect. Who knew of this scam, or how many, nobody will ever know. Yet, it rivals Watergate in the sheer complexity of the cover-up.

Hutton paid a modest fine of $2 million plus government investigative costs of $750,000. Additionally, $8 million has been placed in reserve for restitution to the banks. A pittance. True, several officers lost their jobs. Many others still are under indictment. Yet, at best, it represents a slap on the wrist.

The investor's confidence level in Hutton is quite another matter. We don't forget something as spiritual as trust nor as emotional as money. The irony is that most television viewers are not investors. They were offended regardless—not because they lost money, but because their trust in an image was violated, and that's even worse. In that respect, not only E. F. Hutton was tarnished by this act, but an industry.

[As a result of several mergers, the remains of old E. F. Hutton are now Smith Barney, a subsidiary of Citigroup. In 2009, Citigroup sold 51 percent of Smith Barney to Morgan Stanley, creating Morgan Stanley Smith Barney, which was formerly a division of Citi Global Wealth Management. E. F. Hutton was revived in April 2012 with its original name.] [29]

Chrysler Corporation

Thanks largely to Lee Iacocca, Chrysler had again become a household name, with automobile sales setting new records. Then, a story of odometer tampering and damaged vehicles being sold as new shook this image.

In one case, a 1987 Turismo driven by a Chrysler executive hit a pocket of water on a highway, flipped on its side, and slid into a ditch, rolling over. After repairs, it was shipped as a new vehicle. In at least 40 instances, Chrysler cars were shipped as new after being involved in collisions or accidents severe enough that frames were bent or doors damaged.

During an 18-month period (July, 1985, through December, 1986), Chrysler sold more than (60,000 vehicles as new cars that had been driven by company managers with their odometers disconnected. The hidden odometer mileage often exceeded 400 miles, as managers drove these automobiles to and from work, and even on personal trips. When caught in this deception, the Chrysler chorus sang, "Everyone takes a free ride." [30]

When there is a tendency to explain away clearly unacceptable behavior—be it intentional or accidental, corporate or individual—*The Mad Monarchs of the Madhouse* are at work.

[In 1998, Chrysler merged with Daimler-Benz AG to form Daimler Chrysler. It proved contentious with Chrysler being sold to Cerberus Capital Management and renamed Chrysler LCC in 2007. Chrysler was hit hard by the automotive crisis of 2008-2010, and filed Chapter 11 bankruptcy reorganization in 2009. Two months later, it emerged from the bankruptcy proceedings with the United Auto Workers Pension Fund, Fiat, and the United States and Canadian governments as principal owners. By 2011, Chrysler LCC had repaid what it borrowed from the US Government five years early. On January 1, 2014, it announced a deal to purchase the rest of Chrysler from the UAW Retiree Health Trust. The deal was completed on June 21, 2014, making Chrysler Group a wholly owned subsidiary of Fiat.] [31]

Mad Monarch no. 4:
Approach Avoidance Behavior

Accepting assignments that are never completed; volunteering to support initiatives, but never coming through or even showing up; indicating a desire to be challenged, but avoiding sacrifices and inconveniences (e.g., taking risks, working late, or learning new things); appearing to be doing something, but actually refusing to do it. An engineer might describe such a person as having high RPMs and low torque.

Approach avoidance represents a flirtation with expected or required behavior, but no intention of performing. Children forced to eat 'what is good for them' and showing mommy a clean plate while the dog under the table licks its chops are perfecting this behavior.

The behavior involves *approaching* (or agreeing to act in a certain manner); then *avoiding* the consequences demanded of the act or situation. Telethon campaigners know the behavior well:

A person calls in to make a generous pledge, and then ignores the frequent mailed reminders of this commitment.

But that is not the classic form of *approach avoidance* in the organization. More typically, people 'drop the ball' on a project by failing to contribute their part. Such failures might be a report not completed on time, an important reference not checked out, the right people not invited to a crucial meeting any number of important 'little specifics' that make for the proper completion of projects, and thereby spell 'organizational success.'

We're all guilty of such faux pas occasionally. But the seasoned *approach avoider* consciously strives to find ways of producing disassembly. Some make a career of it.

What may trigger this behavior is the conflict between the *Need to Please Others* and the *Need to Please Self.* The antagonism here is demonstrated by keeping the organization—and the people in it (especially those in authority)—off stride and at bay. Irritation is practiced as an art form.

Of all *The Mad Monarchs,* this is the most ambiguous. A morality play is going on inside the individual. On the one hand, these people are driven by 'what they should be,' (their *Ideal Self*); and on the other, by 'what they are' (their *Real Self*).

The conflict between these *self-demands* causes people to misconstrue *situations,* preferring to see things as they would like them to be, not as they are. This finds them accepting assignments—only to be stopped short by such *self-demands* as, "How could they ask *me* to do that? Don't they know who I am?"

Self-demands take precedence over *role demands*—or the assignment that needs to be done. If this sounds confusing, imagine individuals who are experiencing the ambivalence. If they *can* misinterpret the demands made on them, they *will.* When captive to such wrong-headedness, they are seldom apt to do what is expected; especially not *when expected.*

It's the old game of 'fight or flight,' with one part wanting to fight (approach), and the other part wanting to take flight (avoidance). Put otherwise, it is the problem of 'engagement' and 'noninvolvement,' which is, as pointed out earlier, endemic to the American character.

Approach avoidance embraces stress and anxiety. When they are in the throes of *approach avoidance* conflict, the practitioners' pulse quickens, and their temples throb. They feel the need to avoid whatever is causing it, and this is when confusion sets in (Figure 4-5).

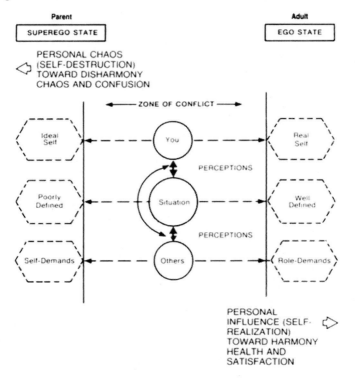

Figure 4-5 Fisher Model of Conflict and Stress

"Anxiety is how the individual relates to stress, accepts it, interprets it," says Rollo May. "Stress is a halfway station on the way to anxiety. Anxiety is how we handle stress. [32] The problem with people subject to *approach avoidance behavior* is that their emotional circuits are flooded, and they are crippled by distress.

This ambivalence of character finds them being given less meaningful assignments, because they cannot be trusted to complete them, which reinforces the behavior. Ultimately, at the extreme, they are labeled—and treated as nonpersons.

Mad Monarch no. 5: Obsessive Compulsive Behavior

Being obsessed with what one does not have and is not, at the expense of what one does have and is; always seeing the grass greener on the other side of the fence. This is an idiosyncratic American disease elevated to an art form.

Obsessive compulsive behavior is characterized by the presence of *obsessive* ideas and *compulsive* actions. It can be diagnosed as a *psychotic disease,* but is much more prevalent in the organization as a neurosis. There are at least four ways to examine *obsessive compulsive* behavior as it affects organizational health:

- Cultural
- Psychological
- Political
- Economic

No society in recent history has been as successful as the United States at exploiting this sickness coincidental to its economic benefit as well as anguish.

Cultural 'Obsessive Compulsive' Behavior

Culture, as defined here, is the working climate of the organization in terms of shared values, beliefs, and expectations of workers. Culture is a recent managerial obsession, triggered by emphasis given it by Human Resources. Over the past several years, these professionals have attempted unsuccessfully to untangle the sins of the organization with cultural manipulations.

Now, senior managers mouth such words as 'culture' and 'climate' without the vaguest notion of what they mean or imply. Put more directly, senior management fails to understand that *cultural bias* dictates the behavior of the organization more than any other single factor. Therefore, focusing on behavior rather than on this *cultural bias* is an important contributor to the ineffectiveness of the organization today.

Established *rites and rituals* dominate the *will* of the organization, with the *informal organization* controlling the ebb and flow of information and activity. Inherent in this informal construction are *cultural biases*. These biases dictate what is tolerated, expected, believed, valued, and experienced. Put succinctly,

Cultural bias is the mechanism of the organization that governs all organizational behavior.

There can be no discernible change without first understanding and dealing with this reality. This is because the organization tends to resist change, preferring to sustain its value and belief system, or that which is known. To ignore this fact spells inevitable doom for organizational change.

The formal organization has come to exert *little* real influence on *behavior*. Management has either disavowed this phenomenon or chosen to embrace panic. Panic is reflected in the frenetic pace of faddist activities... from 'T' groups, to Quality Circles; from team building, to sensing sessions; from Muzak, to ergonomic work centers; from worker wellness programs, to company-sponsored beer blasts on Friday night; from 'Management By Objectives (MBOs),' to 'Total Quality Management (TQM);' from 40-hour work weeks, to flex time; from Day-Care Centers, to Employee Assistance Programs (EAPs); from shared management, to symbolic management... *and on it goes!*

There is no strategy—only the panic of buying time by embracing new fads. *Real work*, by implication, has gotten a bad name; or has been lost in the shuffle. Meanwhile, *value change*, which is essential to exercise behavioral change, is served poorly by these cosmetic changes.

This notwithstanding, the 'fad merchants' know their client—management. Management wants quick fixes; not carefully calibrated assessments of why the organization behaves as it does. They are impatient for solutions; so solutions they are given. Around it, meanwhile, ever-increasing numbers of workers are refusing to work.

Management is so obsessed with the *idea* of culture that it has become compulsive in its *actions* toward its own organization's culture. Management thought that whatever it was inclined to do would get it to where it wanted to go. But that has proven false (See Figure 4-2). For all this preoccupation with fads, the organization has actually gone from the *Culture of Comfort* to the *Culture of Complacency*, and at the expense of the *Culture of Contribution*.

Psychological 'Obsessive Compulsive' Behavior

The *'Psychological'* may be defined in terms of relationships within the organization. Americans are far more adept at managing technology than managing, motivating, and leading people. So, we deal with what we know, which finds workers treated more as things than as people.

Relationships suggest conflict. And as Georg Simmel has observed, conflict is the glue which bonds people together, yet it is avoided. *Managed conflict* keeps the organization 'on course,' and so is essential to its health. Yet, conflict is frequently perceived as bad; and disagreement as disruptive. Consequently, the disgruntled are either ignored, denied, or put on short tethers. Meanwhile, elitism is sponsored (i.e., favoring one group over another), while authority hides behind its position power.

The implicit message here is that 'loyalty to authority' takes precedence over 'loyalty to self.' Human nature has trouble with this. The effect of this perversity of relationships is a psychologically sick organization.

Paradoxically, the more the organization resists the plurality of human nature, forcing a standard by which all must abide, the more intense the levels of organizational stress and strain. This impairs its ability to perform against ever accelerating and changing demands. Ultimately, the organization becomes traumatized, polarized, and unable to function effectively. Management may 'say the right words' in an attempt to avoid this predicament, but its actions tell a different story.

Contribution is based on the authenticity of relationships. This means all behavior must first pass through the successive filters of *politeness, suspicion, fight,* and *cooperation.* Only through this distinctly human process are communication and cooperation achieved. Conversely, attempts to go from politeness to cooperation—by avoiding suspicion and fight—achieve compliance instead. Compliance, which is always coercive or involuntary, propagates *The Six Mad Monarchs.* Cooperation, because it is freely and voluntarily given, generates contribution (Figure 4-6).

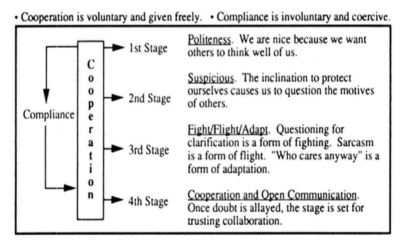

Figure 4-6: Sequential Chronology of Interpersonal Relationships.

The 'Obsessive Compulsive' Personified

Going from 'politeness' to the *cooperation* stage requires work. It is not neat, clean, and predictable. On the contrary, relationships are often messy, volatile, inconclusive, and troubling. Consider this against obsessive compulsive individuals, who want everything to fit. Their primary drive is to avoid confrontation, work, the unpleasant, and the uncomfortable. With them, there is a fatiguing preoccupation with the negative (Figure 4-7).

They use *life style,* for instance, as a distraction: spend as much as you make, live for Saturday night, and find your opiate in 'whatever.' They have a mania for fun, not joy—and a preoccupation with self as opposed to serving others.

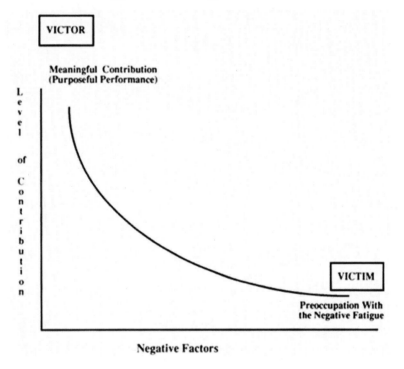

Figure 4-7: Fatiguing Preoccupation With The Negative.

This may take the form of being obsessed with losing weight, getting into shape, becoming more cosmetically attractive. So, diet books are bought, but not read; exercise equipment is purchased, but not used; medical advice is sought, but not followed. The obsessed keep psychotherapists, psychologists, phenomenologists, astrologers, and Tarot Card readers in business. And big business it is! America is in love with its sickness and consumed with seeing it prosper.

The late Jackie Gleason once bragged that his six pack-a-day cigarette addiction and voracious appetite for booze and food was justified because, "You only live once!" Such obsessions are not living; rather, compulsive forms of suicide. Other celebrities equally compulsively addicted were John Wayne, Humphrey Bogart, Yul Brynner, Nat 'King' Cole, Steve McQueen, Edward R. Murrow, Richard Burton, Desi Arnaz, Sammy Davis, Jr., and Chet Huntley. All died before their time.

Work continues to suffer due to *obsessive compulsive* preoccupations. Take AIDS… the current obsession with AIDS has actually spawned a *new* disease—'pseudo AIDS.' This disease is described as the anxiety that occurs when people experience recurrent fatigue, diarrhea, night sweats, and prolonged fevers, which are also early symptoms of AIDS. Given the sickness in society, this could one day blossom into hysteria.

Meanwhile, drug and alcohol abuse in the workplace is compulsively out of control. As many as one American worker in four uses dangerous drugs on the job at some time. Nearly seven young people out of ten coming into the American work force have used illegal drugs. Nationally, in 1988 alone, alcohol and substance abuse cost the U.S. economy more than $100 billion in lost productivity. Even worse, 95 percent of business owners surveyed said they'd had some direct experience with drug abuse among their workers. [33]

Corporate 'Obsessive Compulsive' Behavior

Corporations are replete with instances of *obsessive compulsive* behavior. Take the controversy over the Procter and Gamble trademark, which demonstrates how absurd it can get.

For more than 140 years, P&G's trademark showed a man in the moon, with 13 stars representing the original American colonies. Suddenly, this logo was condemned by certain accusers as a symbol of Satanism and Devil worship. These condemners urged a Christian boycott of all P&G products, including such popular brands as Pampers, Duncan Hines, and Folgers's coffee. This grew into a litigious fixation that caused P&G great cost and inconvenience.

Figure 4-8: Procter & Gamble Trademark.

Accusers went so far as to point out that, when a mirror is held up to the logo, the curlicues in the man's beard become *666*—the sign of the anti-Christ (Figure 4-8).

To refute these claims, P&G eventually filed a three-inch-thick brief that included a map of the United States showing the sweep of the rumors geographically; tallies of the rumors, state by state; compilation of the queries to consumer services departments; computer printouts, day-by-day, of the nature of the complaints; and literally tens of thousands of follow-up tallies.

P&G's obsession with its critics resulted in expensive and compulsive denials, and paranoid counterattacks. These actions by a relatively sophisticated organization were advanced as a result of a psychological threat of no substance, but of *telling* behavioral consequences. In defeat, P&G finally modified its logo—although, to this day, it is not actually known who the accusers were. One lingering epitaph goes: "In the beginning God made the tree. Where does Satan get Charmin?" [34]

There is no organization that cannot be reduced to rubble, indicating how fragile the collective psyche of even an exceptional corporation.

[In the 1800s when Procter & Gamble started, image not brand was dominate. So, from the beginning, P&G's logo has been important if not obsessively so.

From the beginning, the moon and stars in the company's logo was meant to touch people with its soap products in all phases of their lives.

This went well until the 1980s, when rumors spread that the "man in the moon" of the P&G image was a representation of a horned devil with hidden "666" combinations. Sales plummeted as the company was said to be Satanic.

Procter & Gamble's history clearly shows it has been preoccupied with its moon logo.

In the 1930s, the curls that made up the face of the man in the moon were so intricate that the image ended up hurting company sales. The next rendition in the 1940s had an image of the man with hidden horns and believed to be the "666" symbols in his hair and beard. During the satanic accusation of the 1980s, P&G decided in 1991 to straighten the man in the moon's hair. But in 1995, rumors resurfaced again of Satanism. This led P&G to go in a completely different direction with simply "P & G." In 2003, it cut down the ampersand's distance between "P&G." Then, later in 2003, the company decided to revisit history and return to the moon logo without a face and instead show a sliver of the moon with "P&G" in the center.

Procter & Gamble has been a very successful company throughout its history, but the Satanic rumors persist. The company was awarded $19.25 million in a civil lawsuit against former competitor Amway after that company reinvigorated the Satanism rumor in 1995.] [35]

Political 'Obsessive Compulsive' Behavior

Anyone who has read *Iacocca* (1984) knows executives can be as obsessed about themselves as characters on TV's *As The World Turns.* They constantly talk about themselves in obsessional terms. For example, in the denouement of *Iacocca,* the following could have been lifted from a 'soap':

"I never expected a showdown, but if it came to that, I was ready. I knew how valuable I was to the company... I was far more important than Henry [Ford], In my naiveté, I held out the hope that because we were a publicly held company, the better man would win.

"I was also greedy. I enjoyed being president. I liked having the president's perks, the special parking place, the private bathroom, and the white-coated waiters. I was getting soft, seduced by the good life.

"And I found it almost impossible to walk away from an annual income of $970,000... I wanted that million dollars a year so much that I wouldn't face reality." [36]

Perhaps it was this self-mocking candor that caused this book to be a resounding best seller. Behind the candor, however, was an *obsessive compulsive person.* Iacocca didn't invent the disease—he is just one of our more celebrated practitioners.

A less compulsive word than politics is *influence.* As much as Iacocca made of his perks, his more powerful obsession was power... the more blatant form of influence.

Dr. Lawrence Peter was one of the first to identify the cruel 'pecking order' game (see *The Peter Principle,* 1969). Promotion,

Peter found, was one of the most cynical ways of neutralizing an adversary, making it a common practice to promote people to their 'level of incompetence.' There they could do less damage and were easier to control.

Peter was looking at the organization in terms of competence, not influence. An educator, competence was important to Peter. Professors have little power, and even less influence, so are typically preoccupied with competency. The professional knowledge worker, incidentally, falls prey to the same trap. *The Mad Monarchs* were first given life in educational institutions. Professors, forced to conform to the whims of their 'less enlightened leaders,' rebelled covertly by embracing the six silent killers, resulting in an obsessional and—ironically—incompetent educational system. [37]

Competency is not a burning organizational issue, especially at the top. Power is all that matters, and competency gets only polite attention.

America's obsession with influence is reflected in John Kenneth Galbraith's *The Anatomy of Power* (1983). Ninety percent of his narrative is devoted to the 'origins of power,' with little attention to why it is amassed, or how it is used. Users of power, of course, don't have time to write books. Because he sees it as an outsider, Galbraith, like Peter, is fascinated with the power game. This is interesting considering he was a power broker as United States Ambassador to India, and as former dean of American economic liberalism. In any case, Peter and Galbraith agree that American corporate heads are power-hungry—if not power *mad*.

If madness there be, however, it doesn't stop at the top. Nor is the organization's obsession confined to results. The focus is far more entangled in the maddening web of gamesmanship in the transfer of power, where *The Divine Rights of Friendship* prevail.

When Lee Iacocca asked Henry Ford III why he was being fired, after leading Ford Motor Company to the two best years in its history, Ford shrugged his shoulders and said, "Well, sometimes you just don't like somebody." Indeed, the rights of friend-ship are very powerful—certainly equal to the transfer of power via royal bloodline. But as with royal blood, there are no guaran-tees that friendship will produce real leaders. Like a toss of the dice, it is risky business; hardly an appropriate means of handing off power. Yet, it remains the only game in town across corpo-rate America.

Economic 'Obsessive Compulsive' Behavior

The Japanese seem obsessed with people and realize profits. Americans seem obsessed with profits, but realize problems… with people. The irony is the Japanese understand and play the 'business game' far better than Americans, who invented it.

Alfred Sloan, the legendary leader of General Motors, once boasted that GM, although forced to lay off tens of thousands of workers, continued to pay stockholder dividends right through the Great Depression. A Japanese industrialist, even if circum-stances dictated such action, would never think of saying—much less boasting—of such a deed. Openly valuing profits above peo-ple would destroy his relationship with his workers. Well, guess what? It has the same effect in America… because it plays in America just as it plays in Japan:

- Focus on people, and they will focus on the needs of the company.

- Form a partnership with people, and they will work to sustain that partnership.

- Practice what you preach, and people will preach what you practice.

American management prefers managing *things,* and leaving the management of people to chance. The Japanese, on the other hand, find that working with, and through people is essential to organizational success. It is not so much that they do it especially well. It is the fact that they do it at all.

Moreover, the perception persists that American managers think first of themselves, then of the company image, and finally of the customer. Workers, for the most part, are believed to be taken for granted. Japanese managers, in contrast, are perceived to think first of their country, then their company and people, and, lastly, of themselves. And, as the record shows, these perceptions, managed or otherwise, pay handsome dividends.

When the American organization is in trouble, as it is now, how often does management seek the advice and support of workers for ways to increase performance? Infrequently, if at all. Why? Because management has little confidence in its ability to improve performance through people. It has more confidence in considering cost avoidance and cost reducing improvements— the 'world of things.'

Being *obsessively* analytical, management is *compulsively* driven to redundancy exercises, downsizing, organizational restructuring, resetting objectives, etc... *ad infinitum, ad nauseam.* This obviously impacts the lives of workers, for cipher management, which this is, is a way of dealing with workers without being involved with them 'head on.'

Unfortunately, Human Resources, as the 'agent' of such exercises, contributes to the folly by making constant assessments of 'worker satisfaction,' which, as we will see in the next chapter, only results in cosmetic changes and greater dysfunction.

There's no question that great energy is being put into making workers more productive. But that's the point. So much is being done *for* workers and *to* workers that workers are hardly involved in the process at all. They are on the outside of the problem— looking in—and then scornfully so.

Thinking of workers in terms of 'things,' management assumes, "If we throw enough money at the problem, it will eventually solve itself." So, training and development have become a multibillion-dollar business. But this is too frequently a *solution* looking for a *problem,* as the success record of such training clearly shows.

Management's overriding flaw is its Presbyterian sense of being morally and spiritually right, no matter what the cost; coupled with its sense, as *captains of industry* for half a century, of being right, on an earthly level, no matter what the cost. Clearly, management is more interested in being right than in being effective. Crazy, mindless energy, action for action's sake, and the American mania for being *right,* spell barbarism and stupidity in the workplace.

If workers are to *make a difference*, making a difference must be important to the organization. At this writing, it is not. There exists, in fact, a *cultural bias* against making a difference. This is illustrated each time workers are trained with new tools. Take Total Quality Management, which is currently in vogue. Workers are being trained in Juran Methodology, Deming's '14 points,' Taguchi's Design of Experiments, Nominal Group Technique, Statistical Process Control, Process Flow Analysis, teamwork, listening skills, coaching/counseling, and on and on. All of these are splendid tools extremely useful in establishing quality... if the culture and climate are appropriate for doing so. Consider these factors. TQM:

- Represents a *holistic* approach, while the organization stubbornly insists on being operationally focused on *anatomized* 'objectives' (MBOs).

- Is a *process* of incremental, continuous improvement. The organization, however, is *programmed* to schedule, output, and quotas.

- Is *qualitatively* driven. The organization has a *quantitative* bias.

- Is a *subjective* process. The organization has confidence only in *objective* measurements.

- Is an *attitude*, a mindset, a *philosophy* of doing business differently. It is a *doctrine* for doing business, not dogma for enforcing rules.

- Has a cultural bias for *quality* and a *long-term* perspective. The organization has a bias for *action* and a short-term perspective.

So, when workers trained in new skills return to the organization, they confront the dominant *cultural bias*, and that bias prevents them from using these new tools as they were designed to be used. For example, when it is an issue between doing a quality job and shipping the product on time, the *cultural bias* of 'meeting schedule' is likely to rear its ugly head, showing the true colors of the organization, with 'on time' winning out.

The failure of training *to make a difference* is largely due to an ignorance of *cultural biases*. It is the *culture* that prevents workers from behaving differently. This is the rule, not the exception. This must be understood and dealt with accordingly. Otherwise, workers, no matter how sincere these activities, are being trained more for 'training's sake' than to satisfy the needs of the organization. The net result: *everybody loses*. [38]

When Power Falls between the Chairs

Management's obsession with workers is actually a recent affair, because modern management, itself, is barely 50 years old. Yet, in that time, it has vacillated between taking advantage of workers and taking them for granted. Labor unions have contributed to this situation by surrendering to management the planning and control function of work in exchange for wage and benefit concessions. Obviously, with labor unions disintegrating at an alarming rate, and workers no longer content to go along with 'whim-of-the-week management,' this formula no longer works. The day of the 'organization man' has passed.

More than three decades ago, William H. Whyte, Jr. (*The Organization Man*, 1956), profiled this vanishing breed—the sycophantic worker—dedicated to the goals of 'his leader'—who, incidentally, controlled and dominated the organization. The 'organization man' was a loyal, obedient, conforming, and sacrificing individual who put the concerns of the organization above *everything* else, including himself and his family. But, over time, a peculiar thing happened. These working stiffs gradually came to feel that the organization belonged to them, with them having more of a stake in 'things' than anyone else.

As these 'organization men' moved up the ladder, they perpetuated the myth by behaving as if they *owned the company.* Today, atavistic leaders (e.g., Iacocca, et al.) are custodians of this deception. As 'organization men,' they appear to be running things—but they are actually running them to ground.

Remarkable changes are happening but, in the American tradition, we stubbornly resist their implications. *Power* has shifted from the 'barons of capitalism' to institutions that manipulate the *symbolic economy.* [39] We are seeing the collapse of real power and the introduction of synthetic power. Reality has taken a holiday, while the irrational fills the void.

Who would have thought multibillion-dollar corporations would ever be on the trading block, bankrupt, or driven to criminal activities for survival? Who would have thought the *Age of Capitalism* would die as it has, just as the *Iron Curtain* is falling?

Profits are imagined power. The organization is either more or less profitable, so leaders are either enhancing or losing their 'imagined' power base. The hysterical search for profits finds many organizations surviving on the basis of playing the money market. Galbraith predicted this catastrophe many years ago, envisioning capitalism giving way to a mandarin-like technocracy... where moving money around would take precedence over making things. [40]

In simpler less competitive times, this was workable. But, today, a tangible trade imbalance is real. And the intangible advantage of the mystique of America has all but disappeared. Now, rumor can throw an entire economy off its feet without having a basis in substance. The *compulsive currents* dominate this waning century, especially as they relate to America.

Peter Drucker, while more philosophical than John Kenneth Galbraith, sees the world economy in a state of flux, with classical economic theories no longer applying. The new *symbolic economy* of financial flow, he says, outweighs—by a ratio of more than 35 to 1—the *real economy* of traded goods and services. [41]

What is causing the demise of the real world economy is the *uncoupling* of the primary products economy from the industrial economy, and of the industrial economy from employment. The result is that capital movement, rather than trade, is driving the economy. And information technology and services are taking precedence over traditional labor.

Nothing is as it was. In light of these dramatic shifts, panic is in the air. We see a steady shedding of blue-collar jobs in America, with more than five million such jobs disappearing since 1975. America is experiencing an accelerated substitution of knowledge and capital for manual labor. Without such a substitution, Drucker argues, no modern nation can remain competitive. Yet, the *obsessive* attempt to preserve blue-collar jobs is actually a prescription for unemployment and further decline.

The problem is that the professional/technical elite have made most blue-collar jobs obsolete (few will argue with this assertion). Likewise, they have made *traditional* management irrelevant. It could disappear tomorrow and not be missed. In fact, should that happen, America could make such a turnaround that the mobilization miracle of WWII might look like child's play. This is, of course, contingent upon an atmosphere being created wherein the leadership and all employees of the organization collaborate to develop and reach common goals.

While professionals have most of the power and management little, you couldn't tell this by the way these workers behave. That is because they have been conditioned to a *cultural bias* which continues to insist management has the power. So, these professionals idle away their time perfecting *The Mad Monarchs*. Meanwhile, management attempts to exercise power, control, and influence, and can't because it doesn't have it. So, power falls between the chairs!

The Color-Blind Approach to Managing White-Collar Workers

Management's obsession includes seeing white-collar workers in blue-collar terms. Quality Control Circles (QCCs) are a case in point. QCCs, which have been a 'mixed blessing' among blue-collar ranks, have been a *disaster* with professional workers.

Blue-collar workers expect to be managed. Professionals expect to manage themselves. The point is that white-collar workers cannot be managed, except by themselves... and therein lies the critical difference between them.

Many blue-collar workers respond to the formalized type of problem solving provided by QCCs (Figure 4-9). And this makes sense, because they have definite production standards that clearly gauge their performance in quantitative terms. It is the nature of their work to do 'things.' And, they are treated like the things that they do.

But work is now an *integration* of thinking and doing. Thinking becomes a problem when the approach to work is not consistent with the demands of reason. You cannot tell workers in one breath that 'quality is everything' and in the next make quality simply a game of charades.

QCCs represent an attempt to get more productivity out of blue-collar workers, as if *they* were the problem. QCCs were designed as a voluntary system of worker participation, giving workers the opportunity to contribute to the decision making process of their own work center. As J. M. Juran has observed, however, such efforts are directed at solving the 'trivial many' problems of the organization, rather than the 'vital few'.

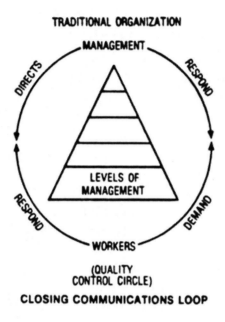

Figure 4-9: Communication Linkage of Quality Control Circles.

Juran states that only a 15-percent improvement in organizational effectiveness is realized if blue-collar workers solve 100 percent of the problems over which they have some control. Compare this to the 'vital few' problems, which Juran insists only management and the professional/technical staff have control, and the impact jumps to 85 percent.

Juran and W. Edwards Deming introduced the 'team concept' to the Japanese in the early 1960s. More remarkable is the fact that Joseph Scanlon originally introduced the concept in the early 1930s to the Empire Steel and Tin Plate Company, Mansfield, Ohio. And, by increasing union/management cooperation, it was instrumental in saving the company from bankruptcy. Scanlon's approach was a formula for sharing the firm's profits with all employees. At the same time, cooperation was aimed at reducing costs and improving quality. The wholehearted cooperation that ensued was instrumental in Empire Steel turning the financial corner. *The Scanlon Plan* hoped to establish a free enterprise system in which every worker would become a capitalist. [42]

The *cultural bias* of the organization doomed this innovative idea to failure. It is still happening today.

The General Motors assembly plant in the Van Nuys area of Los Angeles instituted the Japanese approach to the team concept in 1987. Three years later (in 1990), an incident indicated how badly it was failing. Barry Stavro of the *Los Angeles Times* tells the story:

"It was only one of the 3000 or so parts that go into a new Chevrolet Camaro or Pontiac Firebird. But for Larry Barker, a welder... one part summed up all that is wrong with the way GM builds ears.

"One night last fall Barker, along with the rest of the shift was sent home early after GM ran out of a reinforcement panel that is welded next to the wheel wells near the motor compartment... The panels come in pairs—one for the right side, one for the left—and when the plant ran out of panels for one side, the assembly line stopped.

"A night shift supervisor came down and actually took one of the panels from the other (wrong) side and literally tried beating it into place with a hammer and then welding it.

"The Rube Goldberg-fix-it took so long, Barker said, that GM decided 'it wasn't worth it, so then they sent us home.' But if the wrong part could have been forced into place faster, he believes, 'they probably would have run' the assembly line." [43]

The idea of teams was to give workers more say in how cars were built. Working in small teams, workers were supposed to have the right to stop the assembly line and fix the problem. It was all part of GM's continuous quality improvement plan to make better cars.

But the team concept didn't prepare the workers for trying to force a wrong part into a car. "There's a difference between having a part a little wrong, and beating one into place with a hammer," Barker confided. "They want quality, and they want you to be proud of what you're building. But how can you, when you see stuff like that?"

Based on such trauma and confusion, *The Mad Monarchs* are at work at Van Nuys. On a typical day, *17 percent* of the workers are 'no shows.' They see the 'team concept' as a joke. Morale is bad. Workers want to believe in what they do, but they don't have enough say in their jobs. They are discouraged from stopping the assembly line to fix defects, and they have not been cross-trained to do each other's jobs. "Management is too busy keeping the line moving," Larry Barker concludes. [44]

Professional workers are even more cynical of such processes as QCCs. They find this a one-dimensional world of linear logic that no longer fits their multidimensional work climate. [45] Increasingly, they deal in the symbolic world of work, in which conceptual design and the abstract nuances of information sharing take precedence over the *concrete* world of the making of things.

One of America's greatest economic challenges in the next several decades will be to find the formula for integrating people with these diverse talents and complex personalities into effective teams.

Attacking the 'trivial many' with blistering energy at the expense of the 'vital few' has been a reflection of America's *obsessive compulsiveness*. Look at any organization, and you'll find that nearly all of the glitches are within the purview of management and professionals.

American production workers, a vanishing breed, are not the problem. They have seen their jobs disappear and their lives ruined, believing in a system that no longer exists; a system that, at best, regarded them as interchangeable parts in a complex machine. They were never considered shareholders in enterprise, as Scanlon dreamed. This lesson has not been lost on professionals.

Power will continue to fall between the chairs if these professionals do not assume the responsibilities of self-management. To continue the organizational status quo is obsessional to the nth degree. The consequence of this ambivalence is the next silent killer—*malicious obedience.*

Mad Monarch no. 6: Malicious Obedient Behavior

Withholding information critical to the successful conduct of business for an individual/group/operation; hiding information required by colleagues to perform their jobs; giving false information; doing what you're told, even though you know it is wrong; circulating disinformation or misinformation that frustrates the organization from its purpose (including showing hostility by talking behind other peoples' backs); inventing rumors about the organization or an individual for the purpose of casting doubt; misusing property while having the appearance of doing nothing wrong.

Because it aims to punish as well as thwart the efforts of others, *malicious obedience* is the most insidious of the silent killers.

Take the case of Laurie Bernstein, age 30. [46] Laurie started at a small Southern law firm, getting distinctly icy treatment from the only other woman lawyer on the staff. When Bernstein was given one of her female colleague's cases to handle, resentment turned to spite. She discovered, to her frustration, she was not given the court documents and other important papers needed to handle the case. Late one evening, she accidentally uncovered them hidden in the other woman's mailbox. Ms. Sabotage was severely reprimanded.

"I felt terrible," recalls Bernstein. "I expected a camaraderie to emerge between us as the only two female lawyers at the firm. But quite the opposite occurred."

Malicious obedience is not exclusively a feminine complaint. On the contrary, it is becoming far more pervasive in our culture as the competitive struggle for jobs intensifies. With promotions stalling and management disappearing, professionals are turning their considerable skills on placing land mines in the way of their colleagues. Ironically, there is far more professional opportunity and satisfaction in cooperation. Regardless, more and more professionals are *falling on their own swords* exercising this silent killer.

Many of us are unaware *of malicious obedience,* yet most of us are prone to practice it on occasion. What is important to understand is that the word 'malicious' describes the intent, while 'obedient' describes how the behavior appears.

Malicious obedience is a paralyzing emotional trap in which we become victims of our own experience. With such a mindset, it is difficult to see or define our 'situation' clearly. Our frame of reference may be clouded by our competitive zeal, envy, or jealousy.

The buffers are self-reliance and emotional maturity, and they come when we accept what we are—*our essential essence* and exalt that uniqueness as our peculiar greatness. Unfortunately, we are not comfortable celebrating ourselves as great. We think that adjective applies only to others. Walt Whitman understood our conflict and gave it expression in his immortal *Leaves of Grass* (1871):

> "I celebrate myself, and sing myself, and what I assume you shall assume, for every atom belonging to me as good belongs to you. I loafe and invite my soul, I lean and loafe at my ease observing a spear of summer grass."

The irony is that the more we celebrate ourselves, the less we exalt ourselves; the more aware and accepting we are of our individualism, the less it gets in our way. *Personality*, on the other hand, is a mask we wear. It is not the *Real Self*, but the *Ideal Self*. It is driven by the *Need to Please Others*; to live up to their expectations for us, not our own.

Malicious obedience materializes out of this preoccupation as jealousy, envy, love, loyalty, ethics, competition, or any number of what are otherwise values and virtues.

What repeatedly happens is that the *maliciously obedient* person lies in wait for the right moment for subversive attack. One becomes worse than one's own enemy. What frequently goads them is the game of *success and failure*. But success to one is failure to another. So, it is a game of futility.

The tragedy is that *malicious obedient* people are neither particularly malicious nor obedient, and have little understanding of the severe consequences of their behavior. They have been wronged, and they want to hurt back, and this urge is more frequently fueled by impulse than by a conscious desire to destroy. "I don't get angry," they seem to say, "I get *even*." Vengeance is a corrosive disease, but so is indifference. To wit:

Secretaries were using VAX computers as word processors rather than personal computers. The cost of VAX computer time is *ten times* that of PCs.

- If they were doing this in ignorance, it was excusable. But if they knew the relative cost of computer time, it was *malicious obedience*.

- If an engineer observed them doing this and permitted the behavior to continue uncorrected, this, too, would be *malicious obedience*.

- If the section supervisor was aware, but chose to do nothing (not wanting to call attention to the budget), it would be *malicious obedience*.

- If the director was complacent because he planned to charge the customer in any case, it would be *malicious obedience.*

This situation may seem hypothetical, but it is not. It wasn't until the situation reached the attention of the vice president of operations that something was done. What happened to all the offending parties? Nothing.

Malicious obedience grows out of a contempt for the civilized needs of others and a scornful disregard for the irrefutable interdependent nature of those needs.

Many readers are too young to remember Ralph Nader's frontal attack on General Motors for what he believed was a cavalier disregard for automotive safety. This young lawyer wrote a book about the dangers of driving a Corvair, *Unsafe At Any Speed* (1956), which caused GM, compulsively, to seek to compromise Nader by invading his private life.

When no scandalous activity was uncovered, GM became obsessed with this young man. The result was that Nader grew into national prominence and General Motors descended to the ridiculous.

When a manager who is on a tight budget—and scrambling for breathing room to make *his numbers*—plays 'creative mathematics,' it is *malicious obedience.* The Chrysler executives who rolled back the odometers on 60,000 automobiles were *maliciously obedient.* They were guilty of knowingly doing something that hurt the customer. By the same token, anyone who was aware of their behavior and did nothing was also guilty.

The Watergate cover-up was a classic example of *malicious obedience,* with every level of the Executive Branch... all the way to the presidency... arrogantly disregarding ethics and/or common sense.

Similarly, the Iran/Contra scandal was incomprehensible to most Americans, who could not conceive of their government selling arms to terrorists—to a nation that had held Americans hostage for more than three agonizing years. As with the Great Depression, this rekindled the psychological fixation of helplessness in the face of adversity. And it gave the terrorists a paralyzing grip on the American psyche. Then, to hear America was partners with these criminals was more than we could fathom. This represents insolence as *malicious obedience*, or, "We know better than you what is good for you to know, because we are the wiser."

Surprisingly, *malicious obedience* often starts with innocence and builds to a crescendo of deception, climaxing in consequences clearly out of control. Such was the case of Lt. Col. Oliver North. With his steel-hammer commitment to following orders, he saw 'any means' as *justifying the ends*. Patriotic zeal was shielded behind the American flag.

North grew to epic proportions as the American people failing to see his behavior for what it was, *malicious obedience*—were captivated by his ramrod confidence. Elevated to epic hero, North was forgiven on a wave of patriotic emotion.

The Tragedy of Othello

Malicious obedience has intrigued man for centuries. William Shakespeare illustrated this deceptive behavior in *The Tragedy of Othello, The Moor of Venice* (1622). Othello deals with the struggle of evil and good in the human soul.

Iago, the villain—perhaps the most sadistically evil character in all literature—is maliciously obedient. An ensign serving under Othello, he had been passed over for promotion when Cassio was chosen instead as Othello's chief of staff. What followed was an intricate pattern of skullduggery, with Iago using Desdemona, Othello's wife, as bait.

Cassio, who loved Desdemona, was told by Iago that she loved him, Cassio, and not Othello. Iago then arranged a meeting between Cassio and Desdemona. While they were talking, Iago brought Othello into view of the pair and spoke vague innuendoes into his ear.

Afterwards, Iago would, from time to time, ask questions of Othello in a manner that caused him to wonder if Desdemona had been intimate with Cassio. Thus, the seeds of jealousy were sown, and Othello began to doubt his wife's fidelity.

When Othello complained to Desdemona of a headache, she offered to bind his head with her handkerchief, Othello's first gift to her. Later, she inadvertently dropped it, only to have Emilia, Iago's wife, pick it up. Iago, seeing an opportunity in this to further his scheme, took the handkerchief from his wife, and hid it in Cassio's room.

When Othello asked Iago for proof of Desdemona's unfaithfulness, threatening to kill him if he had no evidence, Iago said only that day he had slept in Cassio's room and had heard Cassio speak sweet words in his sleep to Desdemona. He reminded Othello of the handkerchief and said that he had seen Cassio wipe his beard with it.

Overcome by passion, Othello vowed revenge. He ordered Iago to kill Cassio, appointing the ensign his new chief. Meanwhile, overcome with madness, Othello smothered Desdemona to death, learning too late of Iago's treachery. Then, mad with grief, he plunged a dagger into his own heart.

Profile of the Maliciously Obedient

Shakespeare's kind of *malicious obedience* is a whispered presence in the wash rooms, company cafeterias, local eateries, social hangouts, workplaces, boardrooms, and dinner tables across America.

Demographically, because this seems a function of cynicism, and cynicism takes experience to acquire, the *maliciously obedient* are likely over 30, rather than under 25. These maturing 'baby boomers' are gloomy about their financial and emotional future. They worry about being squeezed between personal obligations and decreasing economic opportunity.

Psychologically, they are likely bitter because they have not made satisfactory progress in life, love, work, or self-realization.

They tend to take themselves too seriously and life not seriously enough, worrying pathetically about matters outside their control. Meanwhile, they view those who are successful as crooks; those more fortunate than themselves as having shady connections.

Economically, they are surprisingly successful, despite their idiosyncratic ways and their penchant for being difficult. They are more likely in the professional ranks than blue-collar workers. Indeed, the ranks of the *maliciously obedient* have grown as the white-collar working class has exploded into prominence.

Politically, they cover the total political spectrum, but are more likely narrow-minded than broad-minded; more likely extroverts than introverts; more inclined to be politically disinterested, if not naive, than sophisticated.

Put this profile together, and *malicious obedience* can be seen to be a crippling disease for an otherwise resourceful population. That is why it is so damaging to the organization.

Summary of Johnny and the Mad Monarchs of the Madhouse

This completes our long journey through the difficult terrain of *Why Johnny Won't Work.* We have traveled the contours of the six silent killers that have become prominently on display since the advent of the professional. They epitomize the irrational hold sick behavior has on the organization, making it a veritable madhouse, while proffering the face of sanity and sobriety.

Beneath the imposing facade of calm and control, there is chaos, the entropic deterioration of a *managed society* as it goes to seed. [47] Management, as we know it, is finished. Ninety percent of its function can be refocused on self-management work groups. On the other hand, leadership, as it was envisioned in the 19th century, must be revisited, because the management function is victim of incest (nepotism/friendship/collusion), lust (power), greed (takeover mania), suicide (complacent management), and history.

Meanwhile, as the process of deterioration continues, and the organization becomes increasingly impotent, the remedy prescribed is confined to treating symptoms. Take the position of educators. They teach as if the core of our American society were the factory, yet they fail to sustain the three R's—readin', 'ritin', and 'rithmetic. Instead, the academic climate implicitly demands obedience, punctuality, and discipline, with a curriculum and a grading system to match these anachronisms. Paradoxically, the more educators attempt to impose these values the less impact they have. Consequently, the classroom, in many cases, has been reduced to a war zone with more energy consumed in attempting to keep order than in educating.

On balance, the educational system in the United States is in a perilous condition with an under skilled, undereducated work force. Lester Thurow, M.I.T.'s Dean of the Sloan School of Management, has been diligently campaigning to increase our awareness of this fact. He cites the case of the IBM computer-chip factory in Burlington, Vermont. Here nearly 2,500 of its 7,500 workers have had to be taught eighth grade mathematics necessary to make the chips. If IBM has to teach basic algebra to its workers, Thurow reflects, "then the price of IBM semiconductor chips has to include the cost of teaching algebra." [48] Of course, if competition from abroad makes the same chips and doesn't have to teach elementary mathematics, because their workers have already learned these skills in school, Thurow reasons, "then the chips are cheaper than IBM chips and IBM goes out of business." [49]

Obviously, the *cultural bias* of American society remains tied to the factory machine. Against all evidence to the contrary, America remains preoccupied with maintaining a *managed society*.

Since Sputnik (1957), hysteria has invaded the classroom. To match Russia's professional/technical elite, the 'open classroom' and 'new math' were invented. Now, we have an organizational infrastructure to support a technocracy of layers upon layers of technical management; with our neglected production workers, essentially unschooled, unskilled, and poorly trained, responsible for making 'quality products.' And so, like Russia, we can mesmerize the world with our space program, but we can't sell our products at home or abroad.

Conversely, Germany and Japan have placed their emphasis on craftsmanship and workmanship, with far less accent on technocracy. Their commitment to efficiency and quality has proven a clear advantage. Little energy seems wasted in aborted activities from their consensus goal of excellence.

Compare this with the American approach. By the time the American technocracy gets past the design and product development phase and struggles through the lethargy of corpocracy, there appears little energy left for a commitment to excellence in the production of things other than with *words*.

So, Johnny won't work because he's not sure any more what real work is, and he hasn't been schooled to understand the challenges before him. The decline of the factory, the school, the family, and all the other supportive mechanisms of society's infrastructure represent a failure of America to pay attention.

The indicators are everywhere. The moral breakdown of the family is reflected:

- At home, with children dictating family life;
- In school, where the students set the norms, and teachers cower in compliance;
- In school advancement, where students are promoted socially;
- At work, where *non-doing doing* of *non-thing things* has become the norm;
- In the organization, where personality takes precedence over performance;

- In leadership, where making an impression wins over making a difference.

With college students not knowing what language is spoken in the Latin American countries, and 29 million Americans not able to read the cancer warning on cigarettes, our expectations have gone suddenly from optimistic to pessimistic, to 'forget it.' Suddenly, the American system has gone totally cosmetic. Struggle has gone out of enterprise, and measurement has become a joke.

The American spirit of risk and adventure has given way to passivity. Materialism, with a capital 'G,' has gone 'Hollywood.' Our worst sins are now projected as entertainment, with Mr. Gekko in the film *Wall Street* (1988) declaring, "Greed is good!" It has become a national anthem. *Making it* isn't the most important thing... *it's the only thing!* And this is happening at a time when America needs the very best of its people or it won't survive as America.

Endnotes

(1) Rostow, W. W., "To Compete, Americans Must First Cooperate," *International Herald Tribune*, March 16, 1987.

(2) Fromm, Erich, *Beyond the Chains of Illusions* (New York: Simon and Schuster, 1962) p. 41.

(3) Ibid. p. 41.

(4) Zinsmeister, op. cit.

(5) "An Age That's Less Religious, Patriotic," Pew Research Survey, February 14-23, 2014 (Tampa Bay Times, March 8, 2014).

(6) John Strohmeyer, Crisis in Bethlehem, Adler & Adler, Bethesda, MD, 1986.

(7) John Steinbeck captured the essence of this painful event in his book, *The Grapes of Wrath* (New York: The Viking Press, 1939). When the banks foreclosed on their land, Oklahoma sharecroppers left the "dust bowl" caused by

the terrible drought for the Promised Land, California. Steinbeck's book is a bittersweet portrayal of an uprooted family which had been devastated by the Depression. Many Americans, at the time, could identify with this family. Shortly after being inaugurated in 1933, President Franklin D. Roosevelt declared a 'Hank Holiday' by closing all banks to reorganize them. When they reopened, 100 days later, many Americans found they were 'wiped out' financially.

(8)   Cherry, Karen, "Study by Priority Management Systems, Inc.," *St. Petersburg Times*, January 20, 1990.

(9)   Ann Kadet, 'Superjobs'; Why You Work More, Enjoy It Less, Management (Internet)

(10)   Morrow, Lance, "What is the point of working?" *Time*, May 11, 1981

(11)   From "Give Me Liberty and...," an unpublished play by Eugene O'Neill as reported in Time [Source: Valentine, Alan, *Age of Conformity* (Chicago: Henry Regnery Company, 1954), p. 95].

(12)   Martin A. Siegel, Wikipedia; Wall Street History: The Boesky and Siegel Deal, Investopedia.

(13)   Dennis Levine, Wikipedia.

(14)   Michael Milken, Wikipedia; Michael Milken Explained, Investopedia.

(15)   Andrew Beattie, Top 4 Most Scandalous Insider Trading Debacles, September 7 2013, Internet.

(16)   Walters, Craig R., "DeLorean," *Inc. Magazine*, April, 1983.

(17)   "Rise and Fall of John DeLorean, *People magazine*, April 16, 1984.

(18)   Gary Hart, Wikipedia

(19)   Rosenthal, A. M., "Gary Hart Ought To Know Who Shot Down Gary Hart," *International Herald Tribune*, May 12, 1987.

(20)   Dr. John Darsee, Wikipedia

William J. Broad, "Notorious Darsee Case Shakes Assumptions About Science," June 14, 1983, New York Times.

(21) Knox. Richard A., "Medical Fraud: Rise and Fall of a Medical Legend," *The Boston Globe*, May 23, 1983.

(22) Yeats, William Butler, *Collected Poems* (New York: Macmillan Co., 1950).

(23) Jim Bakker, Wikipedia.

(24) Richard Nixon, Wikipedia. Richard M. Nixon, *RN: Memoir of Richard Nixon,* Grosset & Dunlap, New York, 1978. Richard Reeves, *President Nixon: Alone in the White House,* Simon & Schuster, 2001, New York.

(25) John Dean, Wikipedia.

(26) Gellerman, Saul W., "Why Good Managers Make Bad Ethical Choices," *Leaders of Humanity* (New York: Center for International Leadership, Bell South Management Institute, 1986).

(27) Johns-Manville, Wikipedia.

(28) Continental Bank of Illinois, Wikipedia.

(29) E. F. Hutton, Wikipedia.

(30) Kurtz, Howie, and Warren Brown, "Chrysler Named in Indictment on Odometer Fraud," *International Herald Tribune,* June 25, 1987 Associated Press, "Chrysler Defends Practice," *International Herald Tribune,* June 26, 1987.

(31) Chrysler Corporation, Wikipedia.

(32) May, Rollo, *The Meaning of Anxiety* (New York: W. W. Norton & Co., Inc. 1977) p. 113.

(33) Source: Greater Tampa Chamber of Commerce, National Institute on Drug Abuse, Research Triangle Institute Survey, *The Tampa Tribune,* January 15, 1989.

(34) Salmans, Sandra (*New York Times*), "Procter & Gamble Exorcising Devilish Rumors," *The Tampa Tribune,* August 1, 1982.

(35) Procter & Gamble and Satanic Charges, Wikipedia. Laura Stampler, "P&G Put A Moon Back into Its Logo," May 21, 2013, www.google.com.

(36) Iacocca, Lee, *Iacocca: An Autobiography* (New York: Bantam Books, 1984), pp. 120-121.

(37) See Smith, Page, *Killing The Spirit* (New York: The Viking Press, 1990).

(38) The complexity of the leadership in the automotive industry is revealed in biography and autobiography. Alfred P. Sloan, Jr., *My Years With General Motors, Doubleday*, New York, 1963. Robert Lacey, *Ford, The Men and the Machine*, Little Brown & Co., Boston, 1986; Peter Collier and David Horowitz, *The Fords: An American Epic*, Summit Books, New York, 1987.

(39) Reference to the *symbolic economy* is meant that money, credit, and capital are no longer tightly bound to the *real economy* of produced goods and services and trade. In place of this we have a new breed of bogus leaders managing Teflon organizations (i.e., corporate raiders who agitate stockholders into compliance with their take over schemes).

(40) Sony Corporation Chairman Akio Morita, addressing the 1990 graduating class of the Wharton School of Business of the University of Pennsylvania (May 14, 1990), warned that America will never get back on course if its best continue to 'chase the buck' instead of producing quality goods. Yet, only about 50 out of an MBA graduating class of 840 planned to get into manufacturing, keeping Galbraith's prophecy extant.

(41) Drucker, Peter F., "The Changed World Economy," *Foreign Affairs*, Spring, 1986, pp. 769-791.

(42) *The Scanlon Plan: A Frontier in Labor Management Cooperation*, ed. Frederick G. Lesieur (Boston: M.I.T. Press, 1964).

(43) Stavro, Barry, *Los Angeles Times* as reported in the *St. Petersburg Times*, January 28, 1990.

(44) Ibid. *St. Petersburg Times* (Section I).

(45) There are astute observers who recognize this difference and have done something about it. The 'resurrection of Ford' is a classic example. See Paul A. Banas, "Employee Involvement: A Sustained Labor 'Management Initiative at the Ford Motor Company," *Productivity in Organizations*, ed. John P. Campbell, Richard J. Campbell and Associates. (San Francisco: Jossey-Bass Publishers, 1988), pp. 388-415.

(46) Brand, David, "When Women Vie with Women," *Time*, February 1, 1988. See also Eichenbaum, Luise, and Susie Orbach, *Between Women: Love, Envy and Competition in Women's Friendship* (New York: The Viking Press, 1988).

(47) *Entropic* refers to the steady disorganization of a system to an ultimate state of inert uniformity. As used here, the management function is seen going from the presumed position of order to chaos…to the rebirth of the organization in which power is refocused on the professional knowledge workers while traditional management is relegated to history.

(48) Charles C. Mann, "The Man With All The Answers," *The Atlantic Monthly*, January, 1990, p. 60.

(49) Ibid. p. 60.

CHAPTER FIVE

THE THREE DOMINANT CULTURES OF THE ORGANIZATION

WHY WE CAN'T GET FROM HERE TO THERE

"The brain uses the principle of 'the match' by which incoming information matches, more or less exactly, the patterns stored in the brain, or else it is not recognized... Biasing involves all that is stored in the brain, relevant to a program decision, from experience, from plans, aims, fears, and from the current situ-

*ational input. To effect change of behavior, or 'open a new door'
to learning, we must try to change biases, not behavior directly
… Present learning depends heavily on previous learning and
biases stored in the brain of each individual. Giving individuals uniform instruction without regard to what they bring to
the learning effort virtually guarantees a high incidence of
failure."*

—**Leslie A. Hart**, Educational psychologist

Sisyphus Alone

IMAGINE A SMALL high tech operation in which 400 employees conscientiously come to work. This operation—once a highly competitive leader in its specialized field—suddenly finds itself in a desperate survival mode with executives working seven days a week (some ten to 12 hours a day), vainly struggling to keep the operation afloat.

In this situation, *work* means executives cordoning themselves off from other employees, frantically running from meeting to meeting—from marketing to sales; from engineering to produc-tion; from crisis to crisis. The operation is under siege, and no one has time to think, much less smile, as morbid activity fills a humorless void.

Meetings provide the *worry beads* for this anxious group with preparation for meetings leaving little time for calm reflection. *Work*, albeit undeniably laborious, finds no one with either the inclination or courage to call 'time out' for a sanity check.

Yet, at this most critical moment, the focus is shifted suddenly from 'the problem' and refocused on the demands of the corporate fathers for a *management review*. All energy is now rededicated to an elaborate presentation of the 'State of the Business,' com-bining *CYA* and *SYA* 'show and tell' documentation. A veritable *magnum opus* of 1300 pages is generated, with copies, of course, for all corporate fathers. The text is then featured in a four-hour, 400-viewgraph presentation *in living color.*

Someone from another planet watching this spectacle might conclude "there is no intelligent life on the planet earth."

The corporate fathers, numbed to the bone at the conclusion of this exercise, reciprocate by directing the staff to return to the drawing board and "simplify, codify and verify your findings."

After weeks of Herculean effort, you would think the profound shock of this would break staff members' composure—if not their decorum (Figure 5-1). Instead, you see faces filled with weary resignation (except the secretarial pool—their marriages are on hold, and to them, it is "enough already!"). As one secretary put it, "It's as if all my energies were poured down a black hole, without the slightest hint of light."

Figure 5-1: Sisyphus in Hades–condemned to roll a stone up a hill, only to have it roll down again as it nears the top for eternity.

This epitomizes *corpocracy* at its most debilitating stage. *'Non-thinking thinking'* to do *'non-doing doing'* of *'non-thing things'* becomes a matter of routine—or "if you can't dazzle 'em with brilliance, baffle 'em with bull shit." This was the effort of 80 men and women against an organization of 400.

Stated otherwise, 80 *self-appointed saviors* operated without the support, input, or involvement of the other 320. Yes—80 people were observed pushing the great stone of Sisyphus up the slope, while four times that number stood by and watched (laughing through their teeth).

"It's not our problem," the multitude sings in chorus. "Management got its tit in the ringer! Let management get it out!" These workers are 'having none of it.' So glib. So righteous. So comfortable in their ignorance. They are not irresponsible; merely nonresponsible.

Not one person interviewed stopped to think it was their job, not management's, that was on the line. Management takes care of its own. Shake the tree and it lands on different branches; or at the very least is given a *golden parachute* to break its fall. Not so for the workers. Poverty faces them. *Outplacement counseling,* two-weeks severance pay, and encouraging words don't feed a family.

When Getting Fired Looks Pretty Good

The *golden parachute,* at least in theory, was originally 'divined' to keep management honest with its focus primarily on the interest of business rather than self-aggrandizement. But that has not materialized in practice. In fact, with these golden parachutes, getting fired looks pretty good. For example, should Sidney Jay Sheinberg, the CEO of MCA, Inc., lose his job within a year of the company going through a 'change in control,' he would take home $16.8 million in cash, or roughly 23 times his normal annual salary. But it doesn't stop with him, for the severance package for MCA's top five executives would cost a minimum of $33.45 million. Add to this another 364 MCA employees guaranteed lump sum parachutes of three times their normal annual salaries, plus benefit packages and stock options. These additional parachutes approximate another $82 million.

Not to single out MCA, CEO John W. Amerman of Mattel (the toy manufacturer), faced with a similar firing, would get $5.5 million; Irvine-based FLUOR Corporation guarantees its top executives two to three times their annual pay plus cash payment to compensate for lost benefits; Los Angeles-based

National Medical Enterprises would give its top three people a total of more than $11 million plus stock and incentive items; Apple Computer would give its chief financial officer, Joseph A. Graziano, $2.4 million if he were fired, and senior vice president Delbert W. Yocam $1.6 million; and Carlsbad-based Decom Systems, Inc. guarantees its top officer four times his base salary if he is fired, twice his salary if he is unable to return to work because of a disability and a year's salary if he just decides to quit.

But possibly the most lucrative severance package is that of 92-year-old Armand Hammer of Occidental Petroleum. The value of his package exceeds $16 million. And if the IRS deems this excessive payment and imposes a 20-percent excise tax on it, Occidental agrees to pay that tax bill. Hammer is guaranteed his salary, bonus (adjusted for cost of living increases), perquisites, and employee benefits until the end of his employment agreement, which runs until 1998 when he will be 100 years old. [1]

[Dial up a quarter century later (2014), and what seemed extreme then has not only become a matter of routine, but has taken on the characteristics of the bizarre. To cite only one instance, CEO Marissa Mayer of Yahoo, hired Henrique de Castro as Yahoo's COO in 2012. It was her choice, and she made Yahoo pay for it. Castro was fired less than two years later in because she could never get along with him. Yahoo paid for the clash in personalities with Castro being given a $60 million golden parachute. Over his short tenure at Yahoo, he was given a total of $109 million. One might hope this was the exception, but clearly it is not. Executive compensation can be cavalier to the extreme, and golden parachutes are palpable evidence.] [2]

An Economic Holocaust

When a plant closes, it is an inconvenience to the management team, but a veritable disaster to the rank and file. Yet, this is typically the fate of American workers outside the decision-making process.

There are many horror stories which illustrate the devastating impact of 'plant closings,' but none more graphically than that of the grocery chain, Safeway Stores, Inc. The Leverage Buy Out (LBO) of Safeway Stores epitomizes a new level of employer insensitivity. Working in a food chain used to give one a sense of security, "Everyone has to eat, right?" In fact, the longtime motto of Safeway was:

"Safeway Offers Security."

After the LBO, it was changed to the *cipher management* lingo of:

"Targeted Returns On Current Investment."

Suddenly, employees went from being persons to being things.

More than 63,000 managers and workers were cut loose from Safeway through store closings, sales or layoffs. Many, when they finally found work in the grocery industry, went from an average of $12 to $4 per hour; many lost their homes; many went through divorce, serious illness or bankruptcy; a few even attempted or succeeded in committing suicide. The majority, however, took it on the chin without complaint as they watched the three investment banks that worked on the LBO receive a total of $65 million with law and accounting firms sharing in another $25 million. CEO Peter Magowan of Safeway and other directors and top executives received another $28 million for their shares in the company, with $5.7 million alone going to Magowan. He and 60 other top Safeway executives also got options to buy a total of ten percent of the new Safeway stock at $2 (in 1986) per share. Today those options, four years later, are worth more than $100 million or $12.125 per share. [As of March 13, 2014, a share of Safeway, Inc. was trading at $38.54, or that 1986 portfolio was now worth more than $300 million.]

Meanwhile corporate raiders, Herbert and Robert Haft, who orchestrated the unsuccessful hostile takeover, still managed to make $100 million by selling their Safeway shares they had accumulated to Kohlberg Kravis Roberts & Co. (KKR), the

LBO specialists who managed the reorganization. Incidentally, KKR charged Safeway $60 million in fees just to put the deal together. In a word, everybody made money (and continues to make money as the buyout group aggressively sells assets and consolidates profits)... at the expense of long-term, loyal and dedicated employees. Safeway was an economic pogrom for these employees no less psychologically damaging than the survivors of the *Holocaust.* [3]

Workers' perception of their role is to dutifully put in eight hours and 'the company be damned.' Let management worry about the health of the company. No one ever told them, and meant it, *'YOU* ARE THE *COMPANY!'* But they *are*!

Without workers, there is no company—only buildings. Management is not... nor has it ever been... 'the company.' In the past 50 years, however, management's function has gravitated increasingly to custodial powers without portfolio; which, even then, it treats shabbily.

Management's role, especially with the advent of the professional worker, is *to lead* and *to serve* its first customer, the organization's workers:

- *Lead* the organization, and it will realize its opportunities and adjust to its challenges.

- *Serve* the workers, and they will serve the organization... and, in turn, serve everyone.

But that's not what happens. There is a *cultural bias* that promotes *style* over *substance, conformity* over *contribution, loyalty* over *leadership.* This thwarts workers from doing real work, fostering instead the preposterous nightmare described above. Counterfeit work has become, as a result, an American institution.

The Law of Entropy

Something is terribly wrong with the American organization. The organization has become *The Prison of Panic Called NOW!* draining and depleting America's most critical resource—its people. Attempts to manage American enterprise out of this insane economic hell have driven it only deeper into the Divine Inferno of Sisyphus.

Workers and managers, rather than joining forces to attack the problem, too frequently have chosen instead to declare war on each other… with no one seeming to understand what is happening or why. Meanwhile, Europe and Japan 'run away with the store.'

What is wrong is that *entropy* has set in. Entropy, the Second Law of Thermodynamics, is what Einstein called "the premier law of science." *The Law of Entropy* states that energy can be changed in only one direction, from available to unavailable, from usable to unusable, from order to chaos. Entropy, then, is the *Law of Limits* (i.e., everything created eventually dies).

Paradoxically, out of chaos comes order, creativity, growth and development… a new level of consciousness. As Ernest Becker reminds us in *The Birth and Death of Meaning* (1971), when what we think no longer serves us, meaning must die to give birth to new meaning and a more valid culture.

Figure 5-2: You can liken the conscious/unconscious model to an iceberg.

To experience breakthrough or to surface some of these true motivators the worker must experience pain (discomfort). Also, management must decode what people say to what they mean. For example, "pay" is at issue when the person's self-esteem, sense of worth is on the line.

Despite this, man tends to create, out of freedom, *The Prison of Panic Called NOW!* The *Pathology of Normalcy* stubbornly maintains the status quo… when it is clearly destroying us. This is demonstrated each time management imposes its fiction on a problem, and thereby over-controls it.

Such behavior plunges us deeper into a 'hell' for which the 'only way out' is to deal with the pain and risk of *new experience*. Being aware and understanding of reality demands 'growing up'—demands reaching a higher level of consciousness. This once moved me to write:

"America is dead! Long live America!… On the eve of our 200th birthday, we have been shocked awake from our illusory dream. We have discovered belatedly that success is in the mind and not the body politic; that being Numero Uno is reaching after a child's fantasy; that

progress carries the seeds of its own destruction... America remains like a child. And like a child, the focus of America's existence has always been on becoming, rather than on being; on the competitive drive, rather than on cooperation; on the illusion of progress, rather than on reality... But alas! Thanks to a decade of corrupt and incompetent leadership, the wasting of our natural resources, the impatience of youth and discriminated minorities, the dream has died... And in doing so... we have embraced despair... despair is the only cure for illusion. Without despair... we will not grow up. Thus, on the eve of our 200th birthday, we are in a mourning period for our cherished illusions and protected fantasies... In the end, time runs out on a nation's adolescence. The youth must die to give birth to the man. That is why I proclaim, America is dead! Long live America!" [4]

The *American Century* is over, and the culture that made it so is dying. The sooner it is replaced, the better.

Cultures, be they societal or organizational, begin with the confidence of shared values and the infrastructures that support them. But once established, cultures irrevocably move in the direction of random chaos and waste. Waste can be defined as dissipated energy. Cultures inevitably die, but out of their ashes comes new life, as surely as the seed must 'die' to give birth to the flower's bloom. America is in the throes of this imprisoning dilemma:

- While most Americans appear economically well off, their standard of living is declining rapidly.

- There is little sense of this, however, because economic survival remains a phantom that is not felt.

- Therefore, the dying *status quo* is resolutely maintained.

Put tersely, America's prosperity is false, and the bills are coming due. The citadel of 'the illusion of normalcy' is the organization, which is decaying from the inside out.

Economist Robert Heilbronn finds America not only losing ground to Europe and Japan economically, but losing ground with respect to America's capacities as a society. What he sees as impoverishing America is "the inadequacy of our infrastructure, the public underpinnings without which a society cannot be healthy or an economy prosperous." [5]

Following WWII, spending on the infrastructure absorbed 6.9 percent of the nonmilitary federal budget. This share has declined ever since, plummeting to about one percent today. For this neglect, it will now cost (1985 dollars):

- $50 billion to repair the nation's 240,000 bridges
- $315 billion to repair our highways
- $25 billion to modernize air traffic control
- $20 billion for public housing

Inestimable billions for water supply and waste treatment facilities. These totals include only hard investments.

The 'soft' portion of our infrastructure—especially public education—is also badly neglected. Spending on elementary and secondary education reached 4.4 percent of G.N.P. in the 1970s and fell by ten percent during the past decade. This is important because the quality of our labor force is deteriorating rapidly, both at the bottom and at the top... and thus is a major reason we are falling behind.

This has happened, Heilbroner insists, because we have been unwilling to impose taxes on income, consumption, or even sin to pay for public improvements. Consider this against the fact that Sweden's 1985 tax structure was 51 percent of its Gross National Product (GNP), Germany's and Great Britain's were both 38 percent, while ours was only 29 percent. Among advanced industrial societies, only Japan's was lower at 28 percent. [6]

Additionally, *fear* of deficits—and the Russians—has immobilized us. While military spending more than doubled between 1980 and 1989 ($ 143 to $300 billion), and the deficit continued to climb, Heilbroner argues that the public has been misinformed. Without new taxes, we could pay for improvements to the infrastructure by doing what Corporate America does for plants and equipment—borrow. Corporations finance by writing checks against earnings. Precisely the same avenue of finance is open to the government because investing in the infrastructure now contributes to economic growth later.

Still, the fear that deficits will bankrupt us is a built-in *state-of-mind cultural bias*, which is unlikely to change soon. Applied to the improvement of our infrastructure, we can see a change in the quality of life, as the number of school dropout's declines, the air gets cleaner, the economy becomes more productive, and our society grows more decent. But none of this is likely if our *cultural bias* for maintaining the *Pathology of Normalcy* is not seen for what it is and dealt with accordingly.

Many organizations are obsessed with the need for *Tradition-Structure-Order-Control*. They fail to see that these obsessions keep them from responding to changing cultural and environmental demands. Likewise, they are intimidated by the ambiguous, the ambivalent, and the chaotic. They desire the madness of 'a place for everything, and everything in its place.'

The *Law of Entropy* implies that the best way to restore order is to accept the lack of it—even to embrace disorder and our resistance to it. Paradoxically, when an organization initiates a campaign to tighten control, it invariably loses it; creating, instead, islands of dissension, disorder, confusion, and mounting chaos. Such organizations are condemned to the fate of the legendary King of Corinth, Sisyphus, who rolled a heavy stone up a hill in Hades, only to have it roll back once it was near the top... for eternity.

An excellent illustration of this is the management of one organization of 4000 professional/technical employees where 'many things are changing, and nothing is changing at all':

The Total Quality Management (TQM) theme is promoted… but because the organization's cultural bias is being ignored—it's more a buzz word than a commitment to quality, and the operation is going pell mell into the *Madhouse of the Mad Monarchs*. This is not at all where it intended to go—which was into continuous quality improvement.

Were this 1945 rather than now, what management decreed might have been achieved… but not today. Work must be conducted on terms that are responsive to the needs and requirements of professionals, or it becomes counterfeit.

TQM fits the requirements of professionals when it is implemented appropriately.

- TQM requires a *process orientation,* which means shifting the focus from results to a concentration on processes. *Results orientation* reflects a commitment to linear objectives and standards through operational Goals and Objectives (G&Os). Close attention is given to the pecking order, with tight "top/down" controls. This is captured in neat, clean schematic flow charts that fail to acknowledge much less identify chronic systemic disturbances. Clearly, it is *management's game plan,* and so nothing happens as charted.

- *Process orientation* depends on subjective analysis of processes, which represents a consensus on what constitutes qualitative standards. The integrity of the operation is also an indication of mutual respect, trust, competence, and shared values and attitudes about work, or a common culture in a teaming environment. As self-management work teams, workers respond quickly to process change requirements because their focus is on the process, not on reports; on making timely decisions, not on waiting for approval.

- *Result orientation* demands a lot of checking and waiting; *process orientation* requires trust and some risk taking.

- *Result orientation* implies rigid standards, whereas a *process orientation* functions best with an *ad hoc* approach, which is more flexible and adaptable to situational demands.

- Order, control, conformity, and discipline are orchestrated to realize *results*; creative exchange and natural enthusiasm promote *processes*.

Given this disparity in orientation, tradition won out with TQM as if it were 'like any other program.' When it failed to take hold, management looked for a tool to discern its failure and set it sights on an old reliable, performance appraisal. So, a comprehensive *Performance Appraisal Attack* was inaugurated in which 350 managers and supervisors spent literally thousands of hours away from productive work.

As mentioned earlier, a typical work force finds 15 percent high and low performers, with the remaining 70 percent in the middle zone. Of the 4000 employees, then, roughly 600 (15 percent) should be having performance problems. But in this case, only six employees were declining in rating, and four were designated as 'needing improvement.'

This was clearly an exercise in futility, not a means to an end. Supervisors and workers participated in the charade because they had to, not because they were convinced it would improve performance. Getting workers and managers to talk to each other is worthwhile, but when that discourse becomes one-directional, it is a mocking personification of organizational ineptitude.

With nearly 80 percent of the work force currently 'professional,' and moving rapidly to 90 percent, the autocratic '*Parent/ Child*' management/worker relationship is no longer appropriate. The interdependent *Adult/Adult* relationship is obviously more suitable.

Workers are no longer expendable, interchangeable parts. Indeed, the critical shortage of knowledge workers is estimated to be as high as 16 million. These highly skilled professionals are indispensable to organizational success. The organization cannot survive without them. They have the power. They are in control. But, considering how they have been, and are now treated, the question is: *Do they have the will to take charge?*

Author Jeremy Rifkin insists that entropy must be felt as well as understood. This is especially true considering its apparent paradoxes:

- The more we attempt to improve order, the more chaos we create. Conversely, the more we accept chaos, and the creative verve flowing from it, the more quickly order is established.

- The more rigidly formal the structure of an organization, the less efficient; the more flexible the design, the more efficient it is. Informal processes, which dominate organizational culture, thrive in a flexible climate.

The most dangerous course is the safest course. A situation that does not permit risk and failure is a setup for contrived success. [7]

The *Law of Entropy* implies that the organization cannot survive if it continues to ignore the reality of its situation. Yet, as most organizations decline and slip into chaos, denial becomes a pressing factor. Many prefer to cling to the fiction of their situation than to deal with its reality. Ironically, this fiction can be promoted by resorting to *technological overkill...* that is, an inordinate dependence on robotics/computers, or creative finance, such as (but not limited to) capital manipulation, mergers, acquisitions, and leveraged buy-outs.

These 'solutions' accelerate an organization's mad dash to social disruption, discontinuity and, finally, maximum entropy, which is *organizational death*. This is when *incipient catastrophe* occurs.

The Changing Cultural Landscape of Work

For the past quarter century, the word, productivity, has been etched into the American psyche, reminding us of our decline. Since 1962, when the Japanese launched their full scale assault on American markets, three American citizens born in the first decade of the twentieth century managed to change the world: W. Edwards Deming, J. M. Juran, and Peter F. Drucker. Largely due to their synergistic efforts, war has changed from military to economic confrontation.

Dr. Juran came to America from Rumania as a small boy, and Drucker from Austria. Only Deming was American born. To put their contributions in perspective, Juran and Deming worked at Western Electric's Hawthorne Works in Chicago, when the famous *Hawthorne Study* was conducted. Moreover, they worked with Frederick Winslow Taylor, author of *Scientific Management* (1911), and inventor of the assembly line and mass production.

Meanwhile, Drucker—the youngster of the trio—became an early student of management and the organization. He is one of the premier social thinkers of our times.

America was late in 'hearing' the message of these distinguished Americans, who have had more impact on the rest of the world than on their own country. The Asian societies—particularly Japan, Singapore, and South Korea—offered these men a cultural climate conducive to their ideas. These societies create institutions to perform basic cultural tasks, ensuring that nearly all their children are well educated; keeping most families intact, systematically diverting money from consumption to investment, and attracting high talent into government service—which we have failed to do and which are critical to organizational success.

In *The End of the American Century* (1990), Steven Schlossstein finds that, compared to most East Asian societies, the United States has a disproportionate number of children who never learn the basic skills of modern life. Schlossstein considers these children as America's greatest competitive weakness.

On the other hand, academic standards in the best American colleges and universities are above those of South East Asia. The best evidence is that students from these countries flock to matriculate in the United States.

Most scholars of Asian education emphasize that their elementary and high schools succeed precisely because the worst graduates are so well educated. Applying that lesson to the ghetto schools in America doesn't work because, as professional-class consciousness has risen, the sense of the public good has declined. Once again the values of the *common good* have been superseded by *personhood*.

THE CULTURE OF COMFORT

"The lust for comfort, that stealthy thing that enters the house a guest, and then becomes a host, and then a master."

—Kahlil Gibran (1883-1931),
Lebanese-American poet

Gibran's transformation in values did not happen in a second. The *Culture of Comfort* (Figure 5-3) snuck up on America in the dead of a 1950s night. It was so quiet no one noticed. America, at the time, was the envy of the world in industry, commerce, and technology. It was slumbering in the twilight, seeing itself capriciously as 'the city on the hill,' with the world's eyes upon it. Indeed, America was tranquilized by the narcotic, 'what America touches, it makes holy.' It is an American illusion transposed to a 1950s conclusion.

For those who have forgotten the 1950s—or weren't around when America passed through them—that decade saw Rosie

Parks, a tired black working lady, refuse to move to the back of the bus in Montgomery, Alabama. America was unconscious of her fatigue; incompetent to deal with her simple demand. Thus, the *Civil Rights Movement* was ushered in, and it changed the American landscape.

The organization was paralyzed by *comfort* then, as it is now. Management ruled, but did not lead. It lacked corporate vision, will, and understanding. Moreover, management failed to perceive the shifting focus from middle class to professional class, as more Americans entered the work force after completing lengthy educations and attaining certain credentials. In the 1950s, these workers were less than a battalion, but today they are an army that is very suspicious of the *organization man.*

Meanwhile, Dwight David Eisenhower, the custodial president, was at the helm, ruling with a comfortable smile, fortuitous in being president when leadership might have gotten in the way. And, the generation that was to carry America into the next century was being born in comfortable ignorance.

Figure 5-3: Culture of Comfort (Motivation external to individual)

Against this backdrop, a managerial nightmare was taking shape. *Management creep*—an organizational cancer—was contracted in the post WWII euphoria of seemingly limitless opportunity. The disease metastasized at so comfortable a rate that no one paid attention. Typically, an organization of the 1950s employing 4000 people had:

- A general manager—who was not a vice president;
- A manager of operations—who was not a director (operations generally included Production, Engineering, Quality, and Shipping);
- A manager of administration—who also was not a director (administration usually included Business Administration, Personnel, Public Relations and Finance);
- Department foremen for the various operations, where the work was done...

And that was it. At most, the management staff totaled no more than 50. Today, that same organization has a management staff of between 250 and 400. Middle management 'takes the rap' as to where all the excess is located – but that's not true. There is a scandalous excess of first-line supervisors and top managers as well. As mentioned previously, if most sizable organizations cut top management by 15 percent, middle management by 25 percent, and first-line supervision by ten percent, there would be an immediate 100-percent improvement in operations.

The irony is that this malignant development has paralleled the rise of the professional working class. Better educated than their counterparts of the 1950s, they need much less supervision. Indeed, they resent being supervised.

What's worse, with all the organizational downsizing of the 1990s, management has essentially failed to downsize itself. Business publications cry out with ominous predictions of what drastic executive shrinkage could mean. Typical is the *Business Month* (November, 1988) headline caption:

"THE MANAGEMENT PURGES"

"Although the recent wave of corporate streamlining has greatly improved profit margins, it has so decimated executive ranks that America may never recover." [8]

Not to worry! Management continues to take care of management, if not business.

In one multinational corporation of 100,000 employees, worldwide downsizing was launched in 1986—with a vengeance. Human Resources was charged with managing the process. By 1988, the work force was reduced to 74,000 employees, but the management staff across multinational operations was reduced by less than three percent. Actually, Human Resources profited by the exercise—going from four to nine vice presidents.

From the top down, management is obviously preoccupied with its own survival—too frequently at the expense of the organization. It has used a not-too-subtle device to sustain itself—*crisis management:*

- First, management creates a climate that sponsors crisis situations.

- Then, it rewards itself for handling these situations successfully.

The American organization is obsessed with *problem solving,* equating it with 'performance.' And, management sponsors this mania, building its security on it, and then solidifying its comfort by over controlling... which, of course, leads to another crisis.

The essence of *worker comfort,* on the other hand, is built on *disenchantment.* Professional workers, in particular, seek education as the vehicle for attaining freedom and satisfaction in work. Management, instead, offers money (sometimes in ludicrous amounts) for what is essentially non-work or counterfeit work—what some might call 'make work.' This only adds to professionals' resentment and sense of being trapped—imprisoned by their dependence on money.

The spirit of the *Culture of Comfort* pervades the educated who, incidentally, are not educated at all; nor are they more highly skilled for having stayed in school longer. Since the 1950s, education has been less a serious pursuit and more an end in itself... a hedge against working.

What we had–Paternalistic Management

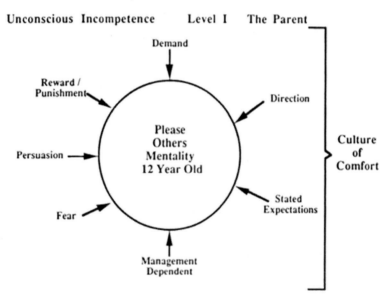

Figure 5-4: Culture of Comfort: Management as Parent – Profile of Management Dependence.

The result—*inflation* has invaded the job market. Work previously performed by a technician now takes a graduate engineer.

Work, at the same time, has been made considerably less challenging, becoming a clerical/administrative function... a lose/lose proposition for all concerned.

Given this scenario, what do professionals do? Do they empower themselves by seeking more challenging work? No! They seek more money—although they'll readily admit that what they're doing isn't worth the money they're getting. No matter. They see *money* as a means of self-protection; insulation from the ugliness around them. Besides, they say, "it gets management's attention," and "money's the only game in town."

What we had–Paternalistic Management

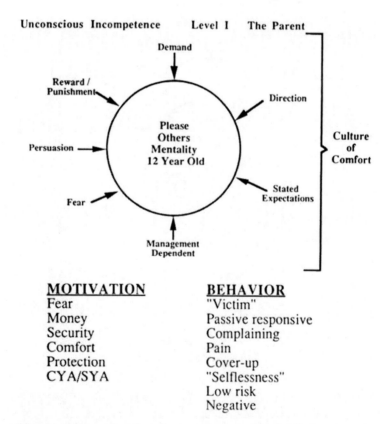

Unconscious Incompetence   Level I   The Parent

Demand
Reward / Punishment
Direction
Please Others Mentality 12 Year Old
Persuasion
Culture of Comfort
Fear
Stated Expectations
Management Dependent

MOTIVATION	BEHAVIOR
Fear	"Victim"
Money	Passive responsive
Security	Complaining
Comfort	Pain
Protection	Cover-up
CYA/SYA	"Selflessness"
	Low risk
	Negative

Note: All motivation is external to the individual

Figure 5-5: Culture of Comfort—Motivation & Behavior.

In the cynical 1990s, money is a hedge against personal commitment or communal involvement. Of course, if the money doesn't materialize, they are quick to retreat into the behaviors of *The Mad Monarchs*.

This finds professionals in a frantic search for status, place, and *comfort* (Figure 5-5). The higher the anxiety, the deeper the depression, which invariably spills over into their private lives. They are angry, unhappy workers without a cause, unaware of the basis of their anger or helplessness, seemingly incapable of extricating themselves from it. They label themselves *victims*, and then commence to play the role.

The Culture of Comfort and Management Dependence

Although the seeds of comfort were planted much earlier, this phenomenon gained momentum in the 1950s. Paternalistic management reigned supreme, playing the surrogate role of the strict parent to the worker's obedient child. Motivation was promoted by a fear-based rewards/punishment system. Hell's fire was put *under* the workers, not *in* them. The whole conditioning process was designed to please authority. The controllers of behavior were:

- Fear of Failure (failure to please)
- Fear of Discovery (shame of deviant behavior)
- Fear of Success (failure to sustain pleasing)

Most of us know of these fears. We sign up for them at an early age. Our culture conditions us to behave properly, to fit, to accept the confinement of organization. Individualism, also an American characteristic, becomes confused in these otherwise restrictive contradictions. The result is social instability and uncertainty of purpose, which leads to a *dependence* on authority, where *consistency* resides. In the organization, that is presumed to be with management. Thus, the *Culture of Comfort* is controlled by the phenomenon of *management dependence.*

With the perpetuation of the *should not's* and *don't do's*—the 1950s organization institutionalized the negative as a manifestation of parental wisdom and caring. This sponsored a disconnect between 'what we could be' and 'what we were'; between 'what we wanted' and 'what we needed'; between 'what we thought' and 'what we felt.' If you feel little has changed in the organization in terms of perpetuating this *self-estrangement* you are probably right. Despite all the words to the contrary, *paternalism* has not relinquished its hold on our minds nor our bodies, resulting in the most persistent behavior in the organization being that of an obedient twelve-year-old child in the fifty-year-old body suspended in terminal adolescence.

In any case, the *Culture of Comfort* looks for the exception, not the rule; for what is wrong, not what is right. *Comfort* is motivated more by failure than by success; more inclined to look for what is not working, than what is. The *Culture of Comfort* is addicted to problem solving, and therefore problem producing. *Comfort* will never run out of problems. 'Problems' are its most important product.

This spills over into relationships. There is a dread of giving compliments, for fear people will take advantage of us; a refraining from making too much of our own success, for fear we might lose it (or people might expect too much of us). "Think the worst," the comfortable say, "and you won't be disappointed." And then, of course, "If it feels good, it must be wrong."

Comfort inclines us to see ourselves as *victims* of paternalistic control. *Comfort* also finds it easier to complain than to do something creative; to take criticism personally than as a means of self-improvement. The comfortable take others' opinions of them more seriously than their own. The comfortable also wear physical pain as a badge ('see my scar!'), while avoiding the hazards of psychological pain, which is a mark of character. The comfortable always see everyone better off than themselves; having more money, better looks, advantage of education, etc.

Paradoxically, the comfortable have a fear of *letting the group down* (e.g., family, church, school, club, gender, race, country, company, friends), but never themselves, which compels them to do just that. The comfortable must always have the answer to everything, because they have an overwhelming *fear of not being smart.*

Against this cultural umbrella *of comfort,* a privileged few (paternalistic authority) orchestrate the demands of the organization to the passive many—that knowers (management) know what *doers* (workers) think and need. This worked reasonably well when the *educated minority* was responsible for the contribution of the essentially *ignorant majority.* That was then; this is now.

Today, the roles have been reversed, but with little change in organizational behavior. While paternalism continues to advocate its 1945s belief system (its same old *cultural bias),* it is management that has become the facetious minority, while professional workers have become the enlightened majority. This paradox, and our refusal to acknowledge it, is the main reason we can't get from here to there.

The Army of the Night

When the 20th Century was young, when things were simpler, and time moved more slowly, paternalism was reasonably effective. As surrogate parent to the workers, management made demands, gave direction, stated expectations, controlled rewards and punishment, while capitalizing on the fears of workers and their conditioned *Need to Please.* The workers—basically children—went from *familial* (parent) *dependency* to *paternal* (management) *dependency.* Children, as we know, exercise little responsible behavior without direction. Peter Drucker spoke of this when he said, "The only things that evolve by themselves in an organiza-tion are disorder, friction and malperformance." [9] Management holds to this as if it were a Commandment from Moses.

By the mid-1950s, however, an *Army of the Night* was qui-etly positioning itself for its dominance in the twenty-first cen-tury. Tens of thousands of spirited management trainees, engi-neers, and other technologists—with fresh diplomas under their arms—marched into American organizations to seek positions, not jobs; security, not opportunity; comfort, not challenge. More incredibly, they found it all waiting for them. America was boom-ing, and by the accident of their birth they were coming of age when nothing was impossible.

This *army* was politically naive and spiritually indifferent; seekers, not searchers. While most failed to find true purpose or happiness, they had no trouble stumbling into *comfort*.

These new professionals, although not behaving exactly as obedient 12-year-olds, were—in a subtle manner—wrestling with a need to please others. They were unconsciously rebellious. This was exhibited in such popular films of the time as *Rebel Without A Cause* (1955), starring James Dean, Natalie Wood, and Sal Mineo as teenagers dissatisfied with a world they didn't cre-ate. They didn't know what they wanted; only that they didn't want to become *boot lickers,* as were their parents.

This *Army of the Night* was also turned on by the *Beat Generation,* reading William Burrough's *The Naked Lunch* (1954), Allen Ginsberg's (1950's) poetry, and Jack Kerouac's *On the Road* (1958). Scatology was 'in' because it was brash, and a painless sub-stitute for action. Likewise, J. P. Donleavy's chaotic humor caught their fancy in *The Ginger Man* (1959), as did J. D. Salinger's con-tempt for the status quo in *The Catcher in the Rye* (1951).

Comfort found them essentially timid souls; spectators to the real, but devotees to reckless indulgence, consequences be damned!. They were into escape, not pain; vicarious adventure, not risk. This army carried in its soul the American spirit of enterprise, but found no safe place to put it. So, rebellion was mainly whimsical, vicariously expressed through books, films and irreverent thoughts.

This *army* marked the end of America's innocence and also the end to its safety. Yet, it would continue to seek comfort; only to increase its distress. Erich Fromm saw this mass social movement as going from the dependency of home to the dependency of organization. These 'seekers' sought psychological and physiological sanctuary without the necessity of encountering uncertainty. Yet, Erich Fromm, in *To Have or To Be?* (1976), cautioned that freedom demands embracing uncertainty, not *avoiding it,* for freedom can be realized in no other way:

"Not to move forward, to stay where we are, to regress… to rely on what we have, is very tempting, for what we have, we know; we can hold onto it, feel secure in it. We fear, and consequently avoid, taking a step into the unknown, the uncertain; for, indeed, while the step may not appear risky to us after we have taken it, before we take that step it appears very risky; and hence frightening. Only the old, the tried, is safe; or so it seems. Every new step contains the danger of failure, and that is one of the reasons people are so afraid of freedom." [10]

Management understood this *army,* and was ready to employ it. Explosive growth was in the air, and management had an appetite for empire building. 'More is better' became the accepted practice. Promotion and remuneration were based on the size of one's staff, with only token reference to performance. As the organization swelled, so did the titles. An enterprising supervisor could build his organization, successively acquiring the appellate of section head, then department head, then manager, then director, then vice president—even president of an operation—in a relatively short time. Such supervisors could doubtlessly carry an army of *organization men* with identical belief systems to their own to the top. With this progression, the organization grew into *unconscious incompetence.*

Meanwhile, forces were at work to disturb *Camelot*. Women failed to leave the work force in the numbers expected after WWII, and in the 1960s were coming back in droves. Automation, which was the labor union's greatest fear, was changing work requirements. Labor unions argued that automation would destroy the American work force. It didn't; merely changing the color of its collar from blue to white. Also, after dominating world markets with American products since the war, the surge was over; product demand had peaked, and was declining. Suddenly, Japanese products started to appear in the American marketplace.

Yet, there was little evidence anyone recognized that the bonanza was over. In fact, inflation and optimism continued to command the cultural landscape. In retrospect it seems incredible, but:

- Wages soared, even as productivity declined.

- In schools, grades escalated, even as student performance bottomed out at embarrassing levels, with socially promoted high school graduates who couldn't read, write, or handle simple computations.

- The standard of living ceased to be a function of productivity, but instead was based on borrowed optimism, as America moved from a creditor to a debtor nation.

Against this reality, management continued fainthearted practices advocated by a plethora of motivation and productivity books, including Saul Gellerman's *Management by Motivation* (1968), Frederick Herzberg's *Work and the Nature of Man* (1966), David McClelland's *The Achieving Society (*1961*)*, Douglas McGregor's *Human Side of Enterprise* (1960), Rensis Likert's *The Human Organization* (1967), Kurt Lewin's *Field Theory in Social Science* (1951), and Abraham Maslow's *Motivation and Personality* (1970). Yet, pick up any business journal today, and the same malaise that tormented the American cultural landscape those many years ago persists—even more so. [11] This finds Drucker lamenting, "We know nothing about motivation. All we can do is write books about it." [12]

Even so, management, over this period, has persisted in considering money the biggest motivator. This belief endures, despite the fiasco of Bethlehem Steel and ALCOA; despite experiences in the automotive industry; even despite exorbitant salaries now paid professional athletes. As many of the latter's private lives break into print, it is obvious money has not produced *Nirvana*.

True, money succeeds in getting workers' attention, but the *psychology of pay* is quite another matter. When its symbology is translated into satisfaction, money is not a motivator. In the end, if work is not satisfying, money only aggravates the dissatisfaction and does little to assuage this. From steel workers to baseball players, there is a pervasive echo, "I want the organization to respect me as a person, and to recognize me for my contributions to it." Money is never enough, and certainly not a substitute for being treated with dignity and respect.

Apparently, it is:

- Easier to increase wages than to yield to workers' demands for *control* of their work and for *freedom* to operate in a *trusting* environment;

- Easier to replace workers than to provide them with challenging assignments;

- Easier for management to serve their seniors than to support workers' requirements for appropriate tools and training to do their jobs;

- Easier to remain parochial than to adapt to a changing competitive world;

- Easier to focus on profits than on people.

The consequence of this fixation with 'things' and 'results' is *unconscious incompetence* and the *Culture of Comfort:*

Unconscious because all motivation of the employees is derived from external stimuli, as an animal might be conditioned. There is no sense of individual responsibility.

Incompetence because 'non-doing doing of non-thing things' and 'pleasing of others' are central to operations, as opposed to real work and genuine exchange. Once a job is learned, there is essentially a behavioral fix, rather than continuous learning.

The pain of new experience is avoided because the price is too high: that is, the risk of failure is greater than the reward for trying. *Safety, security,* and *comfort* dominate motivation, producing behaviors akin to the *victim.*

Regrettably, this has resulted in cultural drift and institutional collapse. Technology has exploded, with more change in the past 30 years than the previous 300. Yet, sustained by paternalistic authority and institutional rigidity, the *Culture of Comfort* continues to foster *learned helplessness,* and has paralyzed the American working population at a low maturity level.

In the organization, consequently, it remains more important to fit than soar; to impress than produce; to be passive than assertive; to follow than lead; to make one comfortable than to challenge; to sacrifice than to enjoy; to meet others' needs than to meet one's own; to go with the flow. Superiority is celebrated, but mediocrity is invariably rewarded.

About 30 years ago—deep in this dilemma, and fighting a phantom challenge (the *Culture of Comfort)*—management turned to *Human Resources,* 'the people's advocate,' for extrication. This was the poorest choice possible. Management had again abdicated its responsibility, delegating what it did not know or understand—its people. This violated a fundamental management principle: "You only delegate that which you know and understand."

Heady with its newly acquired power, *Human Resources* set out to achieve the *Culture of Contribution*—only to fall deeper into the embrace of the *Culture of Complacency*.

THE CULTURE OF COMPLACENCY

"In place of the traditional ethic of self-denial and sacrifice, we now find an ethic that denies people nothing."

—Daniel Yankelovich (1981),
American statistician

It has taken America 30 years to wake up, only to discover that it wasn't a nightmare after all… but a catastrophe. On the dawn of Independence Day, 1976, America awoke with an economic hangover. For 30 years America had been intoxicated with the spirit of invincibility. It had ignored the ominous signs of economic collapse, reassuring itself with characteristic optimism… and making rich celebrities of authors who preached optimism as their credo. [13]

The slide into economic and psychological decline seemed gradual… the buffer was that great. It wasn't until the shame of Vietnam reached our consciousness that reality started to break through. Staggering out of Vietnam, platitudes could no longer cover our embarrassment.

What we have created— Permissive Paternalism

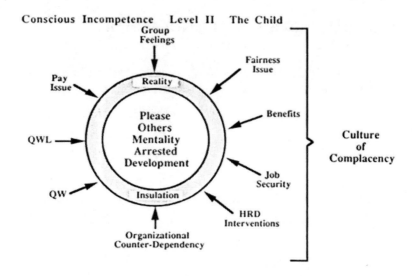

Figure 5-6: Culture of Complacency—all attempts to change the culture lie outside the individual.

No accident that the economic collapse coincided with a sudden withdrawal into personal searching and self-absorption. *Introspective psychology,* an enigmatic invention of the East, became a mainstream parlor game... from E.S.T. to Gestalt therapy; from psychoanalysis to reality therapy; from Rolfing to biofeedback and bioenergetics. A conspiracy of madness-as-normalcy (more appropriate to a Jean Genet subterranean novel) became a $3 billion business with 29,000 psychiatrists (M.D.'s) 26,000 clinical psychologists (Ph.D.'s) and more than 31,000 mental health social workers (both degreed and non-degreed) ready and willing to probe America's narcissistic psychic fixation. Suddenly, America lost its confidence as well as its *way.*

Social chronicler Daniel Yankelovich noted a perceptive shift in American values. He found that—from the mid-1960s to the mid-1970s—positive responses to: "Hard work always pays off," dropped from 72 percent to 40 percent for college students, and only from 58 to 43 percent for the general public, suggesting college-educated workers had grown more cynical. [14]

Interestingly, the roots of cynicism lie in the ancient Greek school of philosophy (fourth century, BC), which held that virtue is the only good, not just the highest (as Socrates asserted). To these early cynics, virtue meant a life of self-control, self-sufficiency, and suppression of desires. The Cynics made nuisances of themselves, parading their poverty, hostility to pleasure, and indifference to others; thereby gaining the reputation for fanatical unconventionality.

Where are our cynics today? In the Jeffries's and Boesky's, the Siegel's and Bakker's, the Hart's and North's… the Darsee's? These people differ little from the rest of us, except in their intensity. American workers and managers alike tend to hide behind the facade of cynicism. It doesn't matter. The point is, we have lost our way to *contribution*. We have caved in to *complacency*. A growing number of us are indifferent to what we do, what we make… what we have become. Cynics or not, we have retreated into the protective clime of the *Culture of Complacency* (Figure 5-6). We can explain this situation away, or do something about it. But first we must know where we are, and how we got here.

Human Resources: Pied Piper of Permissive Paternalism

When the American organization could no longer ignore or deny the economic/psychological collapse of American enterprise, it turned to its 'experts' in human engineering—Human Resources (HR) management.

Originally designated as 'personnel' management, HR was an unplanned, unforeseen, out-of-necessity development. Basically

245

a post WWII—even post-1960s—phenomenon, HR represents a hodgepodge of eclectic disciplines, from personal counseling to organizational development; from wage-and-benefits administration to management development. HR is traditionally stuck with the clerical-administrative functions relative to personnel that management prefers to avoid.

Employees have been schooled to see HR as their advocate, but a consensus of employees in most organizations—whatever the business—would likely challenge this designation... and for good reason. HR has been—and continues to be *management's union.*

While the organization has, over the past several years, attempted to find a simple solution to its dilemma, HR has used the opportunity to build its empire with a tissue of bromides satisfying to its client, management... but not to the general population, nor to the collective will of the organization.

In fact, these bromides have further isolated workers—and, by projection, the organization—from the reality of experience. Moreover, HR has sustained the *Please Others* mentality by holding employees in arrested (adolescent) development.

This was a *conscious process,* so the culture of permissive paternalism that grew out of it can be viewed as *conscious incompetence.* The *Parent,* which dominates the *Culture of Comfort,* producing management dependence, now yields to the dominance of the permissive *Child,* generating organizational counter-dependency. Let us now examine how this has happened.

The Pay Issue

Research continues to show that it is not pay, per se, but the symbology of pay that is important. Workers want to be paid fairly. They want to derive an adequate income from what they do to satisfy their financial obligations. They become obsessed with pay, however:

- Out of a personal pathology that contributes to their economic woes (e.g., gambling, living beyond their means, failure to save, etc.);
- Due to management's obsession with it.

Ironically, the two most time-consuming management practices vis-a-vis employees—pay programs and performance appraisal reviews—create more problems than they ever solve.

Although Human Resources knows better, it continues to acquiesce to management's view that pay is the prime motivator to productive work. To management's obsession that pay is the issue, workers obligingly respond by demanding more money for doing less. Workers know money is the 'language of management.' If workers can't get the attention they need in any other way, at least they can hurt management in its pocket book. And therein lies a great fallacy:

On one hand, workers act as if the company belongs to management. On the other, they resent management playing Santa Claus to them, doling out meager increases after 'Santa Claus' performance reviews.

What will motivate workers, if money is to be the currency of value, is productive work. This can take the form of a *gain-sharing* system, in which workers receive bonuses, as management does, based on the organization's performance. Forget performance appraisal! Forget salary increases!

Put the *Pay Issue* on a *real* basis—organizational performance. Take this trump card out of management's hand, just as grades should be taken back from teachers (originally, grades were meant to measure the teacher's performance, not the student's). If performance appraisals are to be given, workers should appraise their managers.

And as for workers not being able to handle a reduction in salary due to a bad performance year, it is high time they faced that possibility. As Drucker says, "We may now be nearing the end of our hundred-year belief in *Free Lunch.*" [15] What workers are actually saying with their money demands is, "I want to be part of the action; money tells me the company takes me seriously; pay me more, and you have to pay more attention to me and my ideas."

Workers talk in the currency of 'money' because it translates (for them) into a sense of worth and usefulness. And management complies because it is easier to give coin than compliments:

- Compliments are subjective and qualitative, subject to personal bias, and management would rather pay than deal with ambiguity.

- Consequently, pay is a major contributor to *Mad Monarch behavior.*

Money remains an ineffective ploy, sponsored by management and promoted by HR, because both are afraid to tackle the broader issue of ownership and control. By circumventing this imbroglio, however, they garner complacency rather than contribution.

Group Feelings

Groups have feelings. And when HR discovered the 'touchy-feely' approach, worker manipulation began. Manipulation is a process by which 'group feelings' are uncovered in sensitivity sessions and redirected to support management's agenda. Most managers are poor listeners, but good at using key words that approximate employees' concerns. Consequently, management is seldom aware of how little the group's concerns actually surface in these sessions. A typical session might conclude with:

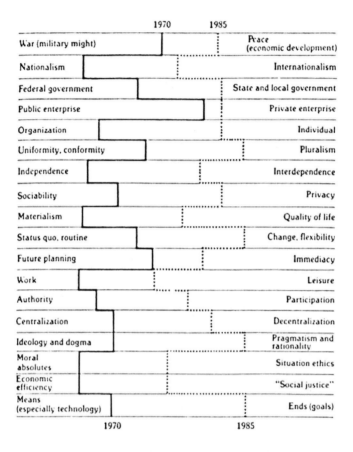

Figure 5-7: Changes in Value System—1970 to 1985
(The Technical Manager by Bruce F. Baird, 1983).

Management: "I get the feeling you are concerned about a possible layoff. Yes, well, we have had to cut back 120 people since last quarter. But that is it. We should hold steady the remainder of the year, with a modest employee increase in the fourth quarter.

Employees: (No comment)

Management: "As to a freeze on promotions. Well, Henry (CEO, always designated by his first name) just issued a *management bulletin* (a bulletin which concerns everyone but only managers get) indicating that it is off. The salary forecast calls for 80 percent of all employees to be considered for merit increases." (Appropriate smile)

Employee: "On what basis?"

Management: "Pardon?" (Smile fades)

Employee: "What is so magical about 80 percent? Why couldn't it be 90 percent or 60 percent?"

Management: "I don't think you appreciate what Henry is trying to do here. We have just come through a difficult financial period. To be able to release funds for distribution among 80 percent of our population is almost a miracle when you think about it."

Employee: "I don't think you've answered my question."

Management: "I'm sorry you feel that way. Are there any more questions?"

Employees: (no comment)

Management: "If not, thank you very much. Check with your HR representative for our next sensing session. Now let's all get back to work." (Grimace for smile)

Literally thousands of such sessions are conducted and ended thusly. They reflect management's agenda, not that of the workers; they function as ends in themselves, not as means to a mutually satisfying end, which would be *a more informed, responsive, worker-centered work force, integrated into a fuller understanding of where the organization is and where it is going.*

With management near panic at the thought of not being in control, the chances of spontaneity and frank exchange during such sessions are remote possibilities. It falls to HR, then, to ensure management that nothing unforeseen occurs. HR dutifully responds by preparing an *insider's agenda,* which management follows devotedly, to nobody's profit. It is a contrived exercise and viewed as such by all involved.

Somehow, *enabling*—which Carl Rogers advocates in *On Becoming A Person* (1961)—got lost. *Enabling* is a *person-centered* approach aimed at uncovering a person's agenda and assisting that person in dealing with it. If change is to occur, it is initiated by the person—not the manager. Enabling does not necessitate brilliant diagnostic skills on the manager's part. It merely involves treating people as authentic human beings, on their terms, enabling them to get in touch with themselves and their own experiences, and assisting them in making choices on that basis. An extraordinary instrument for accomplishing this is 'active listening,' as out lined by another Rogerian—Thomas Gordon—in *Leadership Effectiveness Training* (1977).

Human Resources, largely adapting Rogerian psychology to the organization, bought into the concept of sensitivity training as the vehicle for improved *group feelings*. It makes good copy on HR's 'action register,' but has a history of primarily negative impact on the organization. This is because it acts as an 'end in itself,' with little demonstrable change in the organization or managerial behavior.

A number of theorists on managerial performance, including Robert Blake and Jane Mouton in *The Managerial Grid* (1964), emphasize the 'relationship' aspects of Rogers' model. Such models attempt to appreciate managerial performance in terms of tasks and relational considerations. For more than a decade, HR—with Rogerian zeal—has plaintively emphasized management style… to the consummate confusion of management everywhere.

Suddenly, such words as 'employee involvement,' 'empowerment,' and 'participative management' fill the air like fireworks on the Fourth of July. Rather than creating a balance between 'tasks' and 'relationships' (the so-called *teaming approach)*, management seems immobilized by a cacophony of intimidating demands. "You will change your management style, or you're out of here!" has become a not uncommon declaration.

Quite frankly, no one explains what 'management style' is, or isn't, because nobody actually knows. As sketchy as the research on style has been, HR has swallowed the concept whole, and proceeds to talk in 'psychobabble' to managers… to the confusion of everyone. No matter how noble the intentions, this is what many managers hear:

"You can no longer kick ass and take names to get things done. You must treat employees with kid gloves."

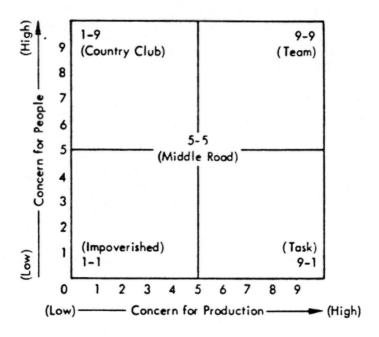

Figure 5-8: Blake & Mouton Managerial Grid.

On the other hand, senior management, while demanding this change in management style, continues to manage with the same old heavy-handed, autocratic tactics. Somehow, the whole thing 'doesn't compute.'

And as a consequence, many managers, visibly flustered, have ceased to manage at all. By not making demands on their people, they have discerned, they can stay out of trouble. 'Management by abdication' has thus become common practice.

Meanwhile, the emphasis on *Group Feelings* has led many workers to become immersed in socializing. They join an organization because it has *groovy people* and great *country club-like rec-reational facilities,* not because it provides them with challenging work. Remember:

The predominant culture of the organization dictates what motivates new members to join.

If socializing and leisure activities are driving behaviors sponsored by the culture, then complacency is the principal outcome—not contribution. The culture cries out, "Being friendly is more important than being functional."

Selection to the 'complacent' organization is based on the following criteria, and in this descending order of importance:

Do I (interviewer) feel comfortable with this individual?
Will this individual fit in my (our) organization?
Is this person qualified (to do the work required)?

If the answers to the first two questions are positive, the interviewer will probably find some way to justify the third despite the fact the candidate falls far short of desired standards. Conversely, if the candidate is highly qualified, and causes the interviewer to feel uncomfortable (even intimidated), there is absolutely no chance the candidate will be selected in a *Culture of Complacency.*

Carl Rogers advocates that relationships go from a management-centered to a worker-centered orientation; from focusing on position power (authority figures) to knowledge power (authentic doers). *Work* remains the constant focus, but on a different fulcrum. The Rogerian model is a good idea that deserves a better champion than Human Resources.

Fringe Benefits and Entitlement

At the end of the twentieth century, typical fringe benefits in most Fortune 500 companies included:

- Medical and dental insurance

- Life insurance
- Sick leave and paid vacations
- Retirement programs
- Paid holidays
- Incentives on savings
- Preferred stock option plans
- Day care allowances
- Maternity leave allowances
- Credit union banking
- School tuition reimbursement

A study of the Fortune 500 (1988) indicated fringe benefit and entitlement programs cost these companies (1988 baseline), $3 trillion—equivalent to then United States national debt. This cost today (2014) is unsustainable for these mega-corporations if they plan to stay in business.

To illustrate, a division of one Fortune 100 Company, employing 4000 people, saw medical costs escalate from $780,000 in 1978 to more than $8 million by 1982… with no significant increase in personnel.

To pay for these increases, without dipping into profits, would require an increase of more than $70 million in new business for a $200 million operation, or a growth rate of over 35 percent. Not realistic! Consequently, what most companies did was cut personnel and not always wisely.

[We are now in the era of Obamacare, which is the law of the land. It is designed to provide healthcare for most Americans, but it is off to a rocky start in 2014 with critics from the left as well as the right.

Regarding acceptance of Obamacare, corporate response has not been promising. It is apparent that a number of major companies are holding back on hiring full-time workers until they see the actual impact of the Affordable Healthcare Act.] [16]

Fringe benefits have proven successful in recruiting and retaining workers. Operationally, however, they have proven a motivational disaster. They are taken for granted and are out of control.

Because benefits and entitlement are not seen in terms of hard currency, and because they are not included in taxable income, they are not considered as *real money* costs. Yet, they can cost a company as much as 50 percent more than a worker's actual taxable income.

With his 'Two-Factor Motivation Theory,' Frederick Herzberg introduced the concept of *hygiene factors*. According to Herzberg, fringe benefits and entitlement are hygiene factors:

Having these benefits does not necessarily mean workers are satisfied.

But take these benefits away, and workers become intensely dissatisfied (Figure 5-9).

Thanks largely to HR's leadership, benefits and entitlement have put the organization in a difficult position. How do you maintain organizational stability when you are fiscally bleeding to death?

HYGIENE FACTORS	MOTIVATORS
Environment	*The Job Itself*
Policies and administration	Achievement
Supervision	Recognition for accomplishment
Working conditions	Challenging work
Interpersonal relations	Increased responsibility
Money, status, security	Growth and development

Figure 5-9: Herzberg's Two-Factor Motivation Theory.

Cost control is one of the 'quick fix' strategies now at work, and, in fact, has become a recycled *new* discipline—'cost control management.' It is easier to reduce costs than to generate new business; less painful to cut benefits than to increase productivity or establish new markets. And, of course, it is hard to argue with the logic that shows that a $1 million reduction in benefits represents the equivalent of generating $10 million of new business.

Because most American workers have never worked for themselves and have little appreciation of the cost of time (vacations, holidays, etc.) or the cost of things (medical/dental insurance, etc.), they resent these *takeaways*. This, too, often translates into *Mad Monarch* behavior. But why?

Management continues to waffle when it comes to *leveling* with workers. Instead, it has attempted, in many cases, to package the 'take-aways' as 'increased flexibility' in choosing benefits... as if they are not what they often are—*take a ways*. This is camouflaged as 'buying' and 'selling' vacation time, 'taking' or being given 'credit' for long-term medical insurance, etc. This condescending treatment of employees is as if they are too 'slow' to see through the deception. This is not to say that it is not a grave problem; only that a little honesty—even if it is painful—could build bridges to understanding.

The cost of fringe benefits to Fortune 500 companies in 1988 averaged out to 40 percent—or an additional $16,000 fringe-benefit income for a worker making $40,000.

What does a company get for this? Not much! At best, counter-dependent workers who are increasingly out of touch with reality. Such workers complain about having to pay 20 percent of their medical bills, while the company picks up the other 80 percent. Yet, if these workers don't find their way to increased productivity soon, they could very well be paying 100 percent. If this isn't a wakeup call, consider this. It's only a matter of time before benefits and entitlement will be taxed as real income.

This means workers making $40,000 will have to pay taxes on a $56,000 income. Rather than waiting for their refund checks, they'll be wondering where to find the money to keep Uncle Sam off their backs. This will be a 'come to Jesus' time, and it's right around the corner.

What we have created–Permissive Paternalism

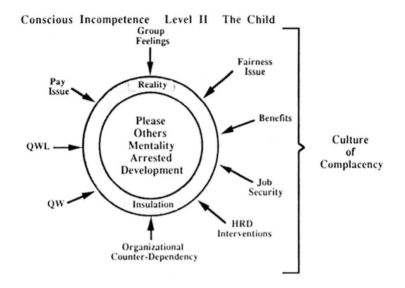

MOTIVATED BY
Security
Group feelings
Good time
Caring management
Perks
Cosmetic effects

BEHAVIOR
CYA & SYA games
Crisis
Confused priorities
Passive defensive
Non-responsible
"We"/"they"
No risk
"Selflessness"
Appearing busy

Note: All attempts to change the culture and strategies "outside" the individual

Figure 5-10: Culture of Complacency—Motivators & Behaviors.

The Fairness Issue

Fairness is an interesting issue, largely because there is no such thing. Whether we are *winners* or *victors, losers* or *victims* is, to a considerable degree, a function of how we see ourselves. Not how others see us, but how we see ourselves. Workers who are obsessed with finding *fairness*, consistently find instead, the lack of it. What they fail to see is that they allow unfairness to happen… not always, of course, but most of the time. It's the true 'bad break,' however that they cling to—labeling it unfairness.

When destiny is tied to someone else's rainbow, life is forever a disappointment.

Peter Drucker is emphatic: "To predict the future, one must create it."

William Jennings Bryan adds, "Destiny is not a matter of chance, it is a matter of choice; it is not a thing to be waited for, it is a thing to be achieved."

In that same connection, Percy Shelley adds, "As to us—we are uncertain people, who are chased by the spirits of our destiny from purpose to purpose, like clouds by the wind."

And, finally, Robert Louis Stevenson submits, "Wherever we are, it is but a stage on the way to somewhere else, and whatever we do, however we do it, it is only a preparation to do something else that shall be different."

Incidentally, the *Fairness Issue* is generally viewed in terms of deprivation, rather than excess. Yet how often we read of the children of celebrities who fail to cope with the excess of privilege… from Dianne Barrymore *(Too Much Too Soon,* 1961) to Lindsay Crosby *(Parade Magazine,* February 25, 1990). Death comes to them at an early age because of alcohol, depression, debauchery, and failure as men and women. Once the support system of family is removed, they see themselves as worthless because they cannot face the future without money… and so they either slowly commit suicide by drugs and drink, or more quickly with the gun.

Read the biographies of Drucker, Bryan, Shelley, and Stevenson, and you will learn that adversity was their constant companion. And like a mad bull, they rode it to achievement.

Life and work were not always fair, but their focus was on making the most of their respective situations; of taking charge of their respective destinies; of looking for opportunity, rather than justifying complaint; of making things happen, rather than waiting for them to occur. We do not find steel in our spine by filling it with Teflon.

Yet, having said this, Human Resources has been successful in making the *Fairness Issue* a predominant factor of work for the majority and the minority; for professionals and skilled tradespersons; for men and women alike. As such a dominant issue, *fairness* confirms the thesis of *worker counter dependence* on the organization. Thus, the organization's debility is a function of the dependence of the workers. Rather than taking control of their destiny, many workers suffer from a sense of being controlled— and therefore subjected to the will and caprice of management.

Rather than sensing their own empowerment, they find solace in comforting each other by whining about how unfairly they are being treated. They take consolation in playing the 'victim of the system,' which insulates and isolates them from the *Culture of Contribution.*

Lost in this preoccupation with *fairness* is recognition of *worker power.* In the *Information Age*—where knowledge holds most of the trump cards in this game of Bridge that links the past with the future—workers hold a finesse hand, while continuing to play the dummy. It would be comedic if it weren't so tragic.

It is an endless battle of control, with those *exercising control* (management) not having it; and those *having control* (workers) not exercising it; with productive work falling between them. In *praise of fairness,* it is reduced to a *praise of folly.* Who orchestrates this scenario? Human Resources. [16]

To be fair an oblique explanation of this development can be traced to the rise of college educated blue-collar workers. Many of these college graduates have gone into the "helping professions," which includes human resources. These first and second generation professionals came from families used to taking orders, not giving them; to subscribing to the agenda of management, not participating in its design; being influenced by the whim and fancy of management, not influencing its bona fides; following, not leading. In the end, life is what we make of it, not what others make for us.

Job Security

In *Wisdom of Insecurity* (1951), Alan W. Watts explains that insecurity is a given, and once we accept it as a fact we miraculously overcome it. We are then able to act; to do; to be; to take the initiative. Insecurity, Watts discovered, is actually a mania for control.

The American culture has a fixation for 'nailing things down'—for having people, events, and situations behave predictably. We don't like surprises. We desire some divining device to take the suspense and risk out of things; something that will cut through ambiguity to make sense of things… but without pain or discomfort, effort, or involvement. Something magical!

This finds many Americans, who live from pay check to pay check, religiously participating in the state lottery at the rate of $20 or more per week. This is not an investment. This is looking for something for nothing. Even if the person should win, it isn't earned, and so does not contribute to an improved sense of worth… or of a sense of control over one's life. It is feeding an endemic disease, rather than alleviating a mania for control; a mania for *security*.

This mania finds us, in both our personal and professional lives, compulsive planners and impulsive implementers. We are obsessed with order and standardization, which, paradoxically, create the chaos that intimidates us. We like manicured lawns and dent-free automobiles, but throw debris from our cars and behave in public places as if we are savages. We are terrified of confusion and public display of emotions, yet if data fail to fit our preconceived notions, we have no problem refuting or changing them. On balance, this mania for security finds us *victims of insecurity.*

From our earliest days as workers, the rationale for staying where we don't want to be, and doing what we don't want to do, is the company retirement plan. This is part of the recruitment, hiring, and orientation strategy. But it doesn't end there. Periodically, thanks to Human Resources, expensive slick brochures are published, reminding us of how good we have it. The symbology is on what we will collect, not on what we could be contributing; on our benefits, not on our usefulness.

Obviously, the *Security Issue* is an attention grabber. Mention *job security*, and workers' ears perk up. American workers associate *security* with *money*, justifying staying in a job they hate because they can't afford 'to take a chance'—to do what they like for less money. This is because:

If I have money, I will be secure; if I have money, people can't hurt me;

If I have money, I will be loved; if I have money, I will never be lonely; if I have money, I need never grow old. [17]

Yet, due to the precipitous drop in the productivity rate of American workers vis-a-vis those of other Western and Far Eastern nations, money is no longer a buffer to our insecurity. Workers in those parts of the world... because they are far more productive... now make more than American workers. Worse yet, Americans are not habitual savers, which puts them even farther behind their more frugal international competitors, who are big savers.

Due to their belief that security can be purchased, if not won in a lottery, many Americans conduct careers parallel to their principle occupations. They give little thought to living within their means, or challenging the status quo of their current jobs. It is almost a helpless belief that they are stuck in their job, and incapable of living otherwise. This produces a *double bind* between themselves and their work, diffusing their attention, energy and effectiveness, while making losers of both them and the organization.

Job security is predicated, first, on the survival of the organization, and, second, on workers remaining skilled and industrious in relevant technologies. The workers can't succeed if the company fails, and the company can't succeed without the workers. The word is *interdependence.* Alas, what will it take to convince workers that *they are the company*? It isn't something 'out there'! It's right where they live—and work.

Granted, this is the 'Age of Uncertainty,' in which the stability of the job, or even the profession, is transitory, finding workers obsessed with the future. Meanwhile, in the agony of waiting for stability to arrive, and frustrated with what they are doing (or have become), many workers disdain the company for its hold on them—*organizational counter dependence* personified.

What's more, their insecurity translates into inaction, or passive behavior. They sense the prevailing norm as being 'not messing up; not stepping out of line; not stepping on toes.' So, they justify being passive. Yet, few get into trouble for taking the initiative, which they ignore. Security consciousness is a way to practice conspicuous *conscious incompetence.* The paradox is that the more security promised or promoted, the less capable workers are of dealing with the reality of *insecurity.*

We are in the midst of an economic war for survival. You don't give soldiers guarantees that they won't be lost while protecting the common interest. Nor do you distribute neat computer printouts telling your soldiers 'what isn't' in the hopes they won't be bothered by 'what is.' You don't play Human Resources 'Russian Roulette' with their insecurities, but design ways to embrace them. [18]

Quality of Work Life

Working conditions, especially in the factory, once varied from grimy to abysmal. There were blatant, even criminal abuses of worker health and welfare. Now with exotic chemicals, breeder reactors, and the like, the hazards go beyond the ambience of work to the community. This provokes public anxiety and palpable concern for *Quality of Life*—an issue that, in the organization, centers on the *Quality of Work Life (QWL)*.

The ecology of environment, in both the community and the organization, has made necessary (if not sufficient) progress. It is the *Ecology of Mind*, however, where the situation is as abysmal as it was early in this century. Consequently, what negatively impacts workers is not so much the physical climate, as it is the psychological. Sins of commission and omission regarding workplace health and safety are being addressed and rectified, but scant attention is being paid to workers as the persons they are today. Note well! You cannot forget about workers as human beings… ever!

The 'psychobabble' continues to resonate from the ivory tower of *mahogany row* to line operations on *the floor,* but there exists little evidence of attention to QWL in terms of such psychological abuses as:

- Being asked to do more with less resources;

- Being asked to work overtime and on weekends because there are fewer people to do the work;

- Seeing the ranks of individual contributors shrinking while management creep continues unabated;

- Contending with redundancy exercises, wage freezes, and reduction in benefits, while seeing top management acquiring million dollar bonuses [19];

- Dealing with the uncertainty of takeover, and the frustration of almost constant reorganization and reallocation of resources;

- Discovering that loyalty and seniority no longer count for much;

- Feeling you are always the last to know about something that affects you personally and professionally;

- Being promoted, then demoted—not for performance deficiency, but due to organizational restructuring;

- Being asked to keep copious records that nobody reads and to report continuously to superiors who know little about what you do.

It's a bureaucratic nightmare that perpetuates demotivation. Meanwhile, the problem is resolved by periodically repainting the workplace walls and ceilings.

These psychological abuses contribute to low morale, representing pollution of the worker's mind, heart, and spirit. They suffocate pride, and crush the worker's dignity as a human being. This is truly unfortunate for, as Cyril Northcote Parkinson says, "My experience tells me (after nearly eighty years of living) the only thing people really enjoy over a long period of time is some kind of work." Incidentally, Parkinson's Law anticipated the post-WWII corpocracy disease: "Work expands so as to fill the time available for its completion." [20]

In any case, with more emphasis placed on QWL in terms of the physical, many workplaces resemble shopping malls more than places of employment. This is particularly true of post-industrial high-tech facilities, with robotics, lasers, computer-aided design and manufacturing; where the ambience of the sweat shop is a vestige of another era.

Indeed, these 'shopping center' workplaces feature piped in music, soft colored walls, indirect lighting, soundproof cubicles, sparkling-clean rest rooms, game rooms, full-line cafeterias, coffee break rooms, and even outdoor 'rest centers' for smokers. They seem as tranquil as a college campus framed in tree-lined symmetry, with picnic areas embroidering the lake-front landscape... giving the impression that the workplace is home—in all its idyllic splendor.

This festive atmosphere is not without a conscience with Special Olympics, 'wellness' days (free physical examinations), and carnivals for the disadvantaged. And, there are 'shutdown' parties and weekly 'TGIF' beer blasts. In short, workers in such places have never left home. They simply have acquired a different mother.

Despite this grandeur, ask workers if they are happy in their work; if they feel challenged and utilized to their fullest; if they are appreciated; if they have the resources to do a good job; and if they have freedom and control of what they do... and you will discover that QWL is still at issue. The smoke and mirrors have solved little.

Quality of Work

Quality of Work (QW), too, has misfired. It is inextricably linked to *QWL*—they are as integral as Yin is to Yang. Yet, job stagnation has been treated with job enrichment—with little worker involvement. It is apparent that neither management nor workers understand the problem. While work continues to change with improbable speed, management attempts to isolate work from this dynamic flow—to freeze it in place, and then treat it as a stationary thing. Conversely, workers view the exercise with disturbing amusement, taking little responsibility in the process.

Management does this with *job descriptions*—among the more archaic documents of our time. Job descriptions had some validity when workers were essentially trained orangutans, but this is no longer true. With thinking, more than doing, the product of modern work, *role identity* and *role relationships* are much more valid. But this requires a clear understanding of:

- The function and purpose of work;

- Worker relationships—how they render support to the function and to each other;

- The expected outcome.

If this bears a striking resemblance to the 'guild-like' relationship of management to itself, it is not accidental. Management and the professional worker occupy the same territory, and herein lies both the problem and the opportunity, which we will discuss in Chapter 6.

Broadly speaking, a *functional group description*—stating expected performance outcomes—would be more appropriate than job descriptions. Individual members of the function would then create, manage, and control the process. They could then vary the process as you would any *quality control process.*

As for the *performance appraisal system*, it is the antithesis of QW in today's society. Performance appraisals are not only irrelevant and counterproductive to organizational goals, but they attempt to impose an objective, quantitative system on an essentially *subjective, qualitative process:*

- Where *thinking* is the primary product, *QW* requires subjective standards.

- Where *manual labor* is the primary product, *QW* dictates objective standards.

Because it continues to be ignored, this simple difference has caused more problems than it can ever solve. With the professional, productivity is more a matter of attitude than activity. A professional in the right state of mind can save tens of thousands of dollars by gaining insight into why a process doesn't work, or can cost an organization its 'competitive edge' by becoming just another bureaucratic fixture.

Supposedly, *performance appraisal*—a Human Resources cornerstone, is intended to manage employee development. Because it is designed to serve management and not the worker, however, it has become more an opportunity for management to 'play God.' It represent s a *subjective* process treated as an *objective* review. Yet, employees who are liked, and 'toe the mark,' receive good reviews, while employees who 'make waves' or prove to be too 'individualistic' receive less favorable reviews. Almost no one, however, receives poor reviews. Those with less favorable reviews know that they will 'get theirs' when management triggers redundancy exercises. [21]

Modern *performance appraisal* versions have workers making self-assessments and comparing theirs with their management's. This supposedly encourages joint problem solving, with employees invariably being the issue when, in fact, the problem may very well be that of the manager. Small wonder the process is more symbolic than real. What is *real* is that performance appraisal is relatively inconsequential in employee development and has little significance in influencing behavior.

Discontinue performance appraisals across the nation, and there will be an immediate productivity increase:

As workers and managers focus on something else—hopefully work.

As the artificial worker-to-management dependence connection (which the process encourages) is disembodied.

While the role of the manager gravitates to where it belongs... that of *the facilitator*—the processes of productive work may be activated, enhanced, and maintained.

This could instantly prune the organizational tree down to size, because managers can facilitate many times the number of workers they can manage in the traditional, bureaucratic way. Is management necessary? Again in the words of Peter Drucker,

"So much of what we call management consists in making it difficult for people to work." [22]

Job descriptions and performance appraisal create a climate of *management dependence* and *organizational counter dependence*. They also establish a low threshold of trust between workers and managers because, as matters now stand, neither of their functions are authentic. More importantly, they promote alienation between workers and their work and between workers and themselves.

Quality of Management

We've seen a seismic shift in values within the organization and without an appropriate managerial response (Figure 5-7). There is not an organization in America that has truly restructured itself to align with these value changes. If this were not true, organizations profiled in such works as *In Search of Excellence* (1982) would demonstrate more consistency. But, as reported by *Business Week* two years later (November 5, 1984), many of these organizations experienced roller coaster economic cycles since being profiled as models of excellence.

An organization fully aware of these subtle value shifts would do well to consider the following before attempting to restructure itself:

- Individual behavior always follows that of the organizational structure;

- Organizational structure generates unique cultural biases, which translate into collective behaviors;

- To change individual behavior requires giving attention first to cultural biases and then to the organizational structure. You cannot change the structure *(system)* before you change the predominant way in which workers think and feel *(cultural bias)* about work, management, the organization, and themselves.

- Attempts to change behavior by ignoring either the cultural biases or organizational structure contribute to, at best, a temporary remedy.

Such temporary remedies, of course, are consistent with 'aspirin management.' In order to restructure for *Quality of Management*, however, the manager's role for controlling performance is verbatim that of Pope John XXIII:

"See everything. Overlook a great deal. Correct a little."

For management's actual role with an essentially professional work force is to serve workers by listening and encouraging them to manage themselves. This is the basis of *Quality of Management,*

The term *organization culture* is being tossed about with the careless glee of a carnival barker. Even so, it is an important expression because no human group can exist without a culture. To define it:

Organization culture is merely the integration of the predominant patterns of the human group. It includes their thoughts, speech, actions, and the products of those actions. But it also depends on the capacity of the organization for learning and for transmitting new information and knowledge from one generation to another. More directly, culture is the way things get done, overtime, in a given organization.

Much like some individuals, organizational cultures can deny or resist change. They can stubbornly ignore all the indicators that suggest their survival is in jeopardy.

Moreover, it is difficult to read the culture of an organization from the outside. And, workers in the organization, those who are experiencing the culture, are largely unaware that it exists. This contributes to the confusion of what it is and how it works.

What is significant here is that organizational cultures change, but organizations don't necessarily change with them. When organizations fail to change as they experience cultural shifts, strong cultures can become weak, fragmented, and obsolete.

Take the culture of *Company A*, which is structured to promote stability, predictability, consistency, politeness, obedience, loyalty, harmony, hard work, provincialism, and a parochial perspective. In business for more than a century, *Company A* has grown from a modest product base to a sophisticated high-tech systems line of products. It has established a reputation for service and reliability, with more than 80 percent of its management coming from engineering. Business has grown moderately, but consistently over the years. Return on investment, however, has been disappointing, as have other financial indices. Demographically, the working population is represented by a bimodal curve (i.e., under 25 and over 45 dominate) skewed towards the 'over 45' work group. *Average* 'service to the company' is more than 20 years. Most workers have spent their entire careers at a single facility and in a single function.

Company B has been in business nearly 25 years and has grown at the rate of 30 percent per year since its founding. It is on the NYSE, with active trading and ever-improving financial indices. *Company B* has limited fixed resources and few factories—subcontracting most of its fabricating and manufacturing to specialized contractors. It is heavy into R&D and marketing, with state-of-the-art technology central to its operation and marketing thrusts. The longest life-cycle for a product to date has been 18 months which, incidentally, matches the average 'service to the company' for employees. Few employees have more than fifteen year's continuous service. Intensely marketing driven, with nearly all its top management coming out of this discipline, the organizational culture is dynamic, but unstable, with a 30-percent attrition rate and a 40-percent churn (i.e., changing jobs within the organization) per year. Entirely performance driven, it accepts—

even encourages—aggressive, sometimes volatile behavior as a norm. Its peculiar rallying call is "There is an enemy and potential customer behind every tree!" Workers are not permitted to rest on their laurels nor to become comfortable. Movement is the motto. Improvement is the game. Job security and role security are foreign to their experience. Demographically, the average age is slightly more than 29, with the present CEO barely forty.

No two companies are ever in the same place at the same time. A 100-year-old company is not where a 25-year-old company is. Nor is any product history the same. Therefore, each company faces a different reality. When they are in the same competitive market, however, as are *Company A* and *Company B*, they must have a clear understanding of what has worked for them and why; and what has not worked for them and why not.

On balance, it is warfare in which they must structure their respective organizations and adapt their respective cultures to the needs of the marketplace:

The business environment should be the single greatest influence in shaping an organization's culture.

Company A concentrates on selling, being a 'work-hard/play-hard' culture, depending heavily on its history of past successes and loyal customers. *Company B* spends twice as much of its budget on R&D than *Company A*, even before it knows if the final product will be successful. *Company B* is a 'bet-your-company' culture, but risk is closely tied to a liaison between R&D and marketing.

Which company do you think has *Quality Management* in today's environment?

Company A	Company B
Quality of Work	
Control	
It was clearly the responsibility of managers.	It was the responsibility of the person closest to the work.
Teamwork	
Workers worked essentially alone.	Organize work in terms of teams.
Measurement	
Managers kept and tracked records.	Thought everyone was contributing to the customer's satisfaction and should measure themselves in that regard.
Professionalism	
Only managers and selected specialists were considered in these terms.	Considered everyone as having a "customer" and therefore was a professional.
Communication	
Top management makes the statements required.	Everyone should be talking about customers and their requirements.
Organizational Economy	
Exclusive domain of its managers.	Everyone should be able to track their own impact on the bottom line.
Environment	
Saw the work place as a place of work; essentially sterile.	Saw the work place as a workscape. Everyone to "paint" the right climate for getting the work done.

Figure 5-11: Values Differences—Quality of Work.

Company A	Company B
Quality of Worklife	
Individual Respect	
Only senior people accorded this treatment: senior people are "indispensable."	Esteemed every person because it valued their unique skills.
Personal Challenge	
Reserved to high-level people it considered had to be kept operationally sharp.	Everyone is challenged to the level of their capacity or desire; sharpness is critical to organizational success.
Personal Growth	
Had little patience with the concept, seeing growth as a benefit of being employed.	Saw learning as a constant requirement for growth; as people learn new things, the company prospers.
Enthusiasm	
Saw it as a nice word, but not a requirement; that is why people call it "work."	Believed people who are not turned on to what they do, will not be happy at work or effective in it.
Ethics	
Believed one should run a company as fairly and honestly as can be effectively done.	People must feel they are working for an ethical company; ethics is fundamental to company success.
Work/Life Balance	
One's personal life comes after the job is done...whatever that is.	Employees feel best when their life and work mesh in a harmonious balance.
Rewards	
Pay and promotion are the biggest factors in people's expectations of rewards from working.	There are as many possibilities for rewarding people as an organization can discover.

Figure 5-12: Value Differences—Quality of Work Life.

The *Culture of Complacency*, under the auspices of Human Resources, has 'stolen the worker's mind.' This culture has isolated the individual from the pain of real experience, instead fostering 'learned helplessness.' Workers exposed to such conditioning are essentially robotic, programmed to breathe, sleep, digest, and excrete, with an instinct for reproduction and protection of their children. Beyond that, their minds are largely mechanical, for they are living and working on automatic pilot. T. S. Eliot once asked:

"Where is the life we have lost in living?"
"The robot has stolen it," he answers.

But nowhere is it written that we cannot steal it back.

The Culture of Contribution

"Every one has been made for some particular work, and the desire for that work has been put into his heart."
—**Julal al Din Rumi** (1207-1273), Indian Master

"If you wish to work properly, you should never lose sight of two great principles: first, a profound respect for the work undertaken; and second, a complete indifference to its fruits. Thus only can you work with the proper attitude."
—**Swami Brahmananda** (1863-1922), Indian Master

"The Work Ethic Lives! Americans labor harder and at more jobs than ever." This attention-grabbing *Time Magazine* caption (September 7, 1987) was the lead-in to an article that, curiously, insisted that hard work is ennobling... that people 'forced' to work two and three jobs to 'live in the style they have become accustomed to' is proof positive that the American work ethic is alive. Actually, it suggests quite the opposite, for 'hard work' is scarcely relevant, much less to be exalted.

Granted, there is a growing community of displaced workers in conventional jobs. They must be retrained or retired; they cannot have it both ways. If they refuse to learn new skills, they represent a 'casualty of war.' *Conscious competence* demands reality be acknowledged and that moralizing be put on the shelf. We are under siege, and this is no time for half measures.

On the other hand, there is a jaundiced appetite in the American consciousness for a strenuous schedule. As mentioned elsewhere, Americans take pride in boasting how hard they work;

how 'tough' their schedules; how many jobs they have. They prefer this self-deception to committing their minds and hearts to the real challenge of work today—mental gymnastics, not menial diversions. This is evident in virtually every demanding technological discipline in the graduate school curricula of America's finest universities… they are dominated by foreign students, primarily Oriental, with Americans too busy chasing the buck or the basketball to bother.

Is Work A Process Or A Product?

American society has become 'soft' by working hard. As our society has embraced automation and computers, our lagging American culture has insisted on behaving as if still on the Western prairie. We have taken the 'cowboy' out of the frontier, but we have found it impossible to take the frontier out of the cowboy.

A society which attempts to solve its predicament by working harder manages only to exist, barely finding time to live. Living requires concentration on process, on profiting from experience and making the most of opportunity; existing represents preoccupation with results, with the product of process, with working for the sake of working.

Some refer to living as 'existential'—a philosophy of life that has time for beauty, daydreaming, contemplation, for 'smelling the roses'… for experiencing the multi-dimensions of human existence that are the legacy of the society of man. How is it that one of the richest societies in the history of mankind can never find much time for living for it is too busy existing?

Company A	Company B
Quality of Management	
Business and Organizational Understanding	
Only top management needs a sense of the "Big Picture."	Everyone should understand that they are a piece of the "Big Picture." No work is done in a vacuum.
Relating Job to Society	
Saw this as essentially a senior management concern.	Believed that employees should see that the work of all accumulates to a final product or service, for which all should share in the credit.
Trust	
Earned by each person over a long period of time.	Should be assumed that each person is credible unless proven otherwise.
Recognition	
Recognition should not be overdone. Only when people separate from the company can their contributions be recognized.	People should be recognized as often as possible.
Relating Past, Present and Future	
A sense of history can only come with tenure, an association over a long period of time.	History is an excellent way to stress traditions or the need for changes in the future, which ought to be fully shared.
Leadership	
A manager is essentially commanding an army and he must provide marching orders for the direction to which he wants the troops to march.	Believed that leadership requires vision. Vision relies on inspiration to become reality: thus, a leader should work on iterating the dreams of the people.
Spirit	
It is nice if something "magical" develops, but one can reach goals without it.	No enterprise is exactly like another; that is what provides the competitive edge. Spirit must be found or created.

Figure 5-13: Value Differences: Quality of Management.

Conscious/Unconscious

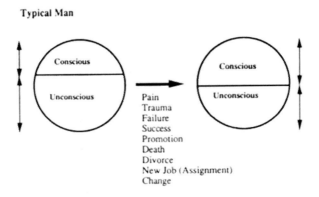

Figure 5-14: Path to Increased Consciousness.

To quote Sigmund Freud, "It is only through pain that our level of awareness, our conscious mind increases."

Therefore, if anything, comfort reduces our awareness while increasing the problem of cognitive dissonance–that is, we see what we want to see, hear what we want to hear, feel what we want to feel, think what we want to think.

Existence is focused on performance, on results, which is actually anticlimactic. In the *Prison of Panic called NOW,* workers spend eight, ten, even twelve hours a day fighting through scrap and rework activities in search of the problem, as the focus is primarily on the three R's: redesign, rework, and reschedule. Work is essentially lifeless and pathetic, floating on a sea of uncertainty and red ink. Meanwhile, little investment in time or money is focused on the process, where the seat of the chronic problem lies:

- Manage the process, and the product will take care of itself;

- Manage the product, and the process will give you nightmares.

Working harder, in such instances, makes work a negative coefficient.

In the context of this discussion, work and workers have changed dramatically, while management and measurement of work has remained fixed in antiquity… as have rewards and recognition. American workers are not performing, because they are not being treated with the *trust, respect, freedom,* and *recognition* to which they are entitled.

Unfortunately, many American workers would rather work hard than take risks. Being results oriented, they want guarantees; to know what they will get for what they give. They have no desire to 'study their butts off if all it means is an assistant professorship 'somewhere,' making the equivalent salary of a police officer with a high school diploma. Nor are they likely to bid on a demanding assignment if 'failure' is a strong possibility. Chances are they don't know what they want, because they have spent their entire lives trying to *Please Others.* They exist… they don't live. Their cover-up is the shroud of hard work, which America finds ennobling, for it respects someone who is 'trying,' even if the activity is pointless. With such a mindset:

- It is more acceptable to be a grind than great;

- Only 'geeks' would love what they do, regardless of pay;

- Arrogance personifies those who value what they think (about themselves) over what others think about them;

- Only those 'full of themselves' put 'Pleasing Self' ahead of 'Pleasing Others.'

Yet, the mindset of *Pleasing Others* at the expense of *Pleasing Self* comes out of the cultural landscape *of comfort* and *complacency,* not *contribution.* The *Culture of Contribution* is a very different place. It is the land of giants—giant achievers and giant 'pain-in-the-asses.' It's the land of giant contradictions, giant inconsistencies, and—giant breakthroughs.

Topography of the Culture of Contribution

Because it is the land of pain, risk, uncertainty, and limits, the *Culture of Contribution* represents a new landscape; a new visage. It is the land of growth and purposeful performance.

It is easier to talk about contribution than to test the measure of our potential. The *Topography of Contribution*, therefore, is enchanting from afar, but threatening when approached... for it is easier to complain than contribute.

Yet, this topography is the next American frontier. Obviously, it is not as mysterious nor as far reaching as a space probe to Mars. It is right here—under our very feet. It is ours if only we have the sense and the will to claim it.

Given the fact that the organization has cut individuals off from facing their own reality, this is no small challenge. Indeed, corporate behavior has neither sponsored growth nor encouraged purposefulness. Despite all its attempts at remedial programs and processes, it has, instead, directed the organization into the land of *comfort* and *complacency*.

By sustaining the *Need To Please Others*, as a condition of employment, a servile and lethargic culture is inevitable. Such a culture is not honest, avoids pain, and contrives to be what it is not. As Sigmund Freud asserts:

"It is only through pain that our level of consciousness increases."

If anything, *comfort* and *complacency* reduce our awareness of reality... for we see what we want to see, hear what we want to hear, feel what we want to feel, think what we want to think. *Yet, it is only through consciousness that we can manage change.*

For this to happen, we must experience pain, discomfort, dissatisfaction, and, possibly, even trauma. Do not misconstrue this as 'pain for pain's sake,' or 'no pain, no gain.' There should be no glory in our ability to endure pain. We are discussing primarily *psychological pain*—the pain of embarrassment, inadequacy, failure, rejection, or social exclusion. Think about your own life. What has made you, or failed to make you, the person you are or could become?

[Here in 2014, young people are coming to me, highly qualified young people, people in their late twenties and early thirties, professionals, who are being treated in a cavalier style by potential employers. Why? Because they can.

These employers, insensitive to their plight, in this stagnated economic climate that they did not create, hire them as resource people or contract consultants, not as persons or permanent employees.

These young people went into debt to be educated, postponing their livelihood. In other words, they paid their dues.

They write hundreds of resumes, submit them on line, and if lucky talk to a machine when they make a phone call.

Then when it appears that they are being hired, they wait, and wait. They check back and are told more checking has to be made on their references. Then they wait some more.

And if fortunate, they are hired for a project—without benefits—and then dispatched again to the unemployment lines. The process is then again repeated, with interminable time spent writing and resubmitting resumes on the Internet, and talking to machines.

This is psychological pain elevated to psychological abuse. And it has become all too common in this second decade of the 21st century.]

Chances are it involves embracing, as opposed to resisting, the *pain of experience,* for we learn so little from success. Actually, when things are going well, we move about almost robotically. But let something go wrong, and we are painfully aware of it.

Admittedly, the pressure to conform, to wax insincere, is sometimes overwhelming. Unconsciously, we desert our thinking and feelings to behave as others would expect us to behave. When the rewards for such behavior are so great, as in the *Culture of Comfort* and *Complacency*, we become strangers to our authentic selves. This plays havoc with our health and, by extension, that of the organization, because contribution is a counterfeit game.

It is this bogus culture that produces low productivity, high accident rates, time and attendance problems, misused or misplaced equipment, higher production costs, more procedural errors, breakdowns in communication, we/they polarity, spontaneous conflicts, listless responses to crises, clock watching, grabassing, denial or cover-up, inappropriate dress or language, and, ultimately, failure to meet the payroll.

An organization can be drunk with its success and choose to rest on its laurels. Back orders tell it business is good, but new business tells a different story. Selective memory can hide the truth from an organization as well as an individual. This can lead to the circular argument of *what* it is, *where* it is, even *why* it is. An organization can thus easily become the victim of its own deception… as was the case with American automobile manufacturers from 1954 to 1979. Thirty years later we had the total collapse of the automotive industry, necessitating the bailout by the government.

In essence, the organization's performance structure is dependent on its *cultural biases*. Do these biases enhance its capacity to respond to ever-accelerating environmental demands? If it does, it has the *Topography of Contribution;* if not, it is playing a pretentious game of Monopoly. Let us now examine why.

Proving the Culture of Contribution

Proof that *contribution* is the viable culture is in behavioral indicators:

- Workers in this climate are *purposeful.*
- They are *not afraid to 'fail,'* for they have ample opportunity to succeed.

- They move with confidence, not arrogance.

- They are *available*… to help, to listen, to advise.

- They *express their opinions* with spirit and challenge those who differ with them in good humor.

- The atmosphere is *collegial and respectful,* without being pretentious.

- These workers are *not always agreeing.* In fact, they may appear to be arguing, but being right is not as important as being effective.

You sense that it is *fun* to be at work. Problems occur, but there is *no panic.* Nor is there evidence of finger pointing. The focus is on *what is* wrong, not *who* is wrong. Everywhere there is evidence of *creative vitality*—from the way they dress, to the layout of their work stations. Homemade signs abound (e.g., *Six Sigma Quality Saves On Excedrin*) chiding fellow workers to *prevent problems,* not correct them.

To an outsider, immersed in such creative chaos, it might seem people are goofing off—but this could not be further from the truth. These workers are completers, not complainers. They know their complementary roles and move with happy fluidity.

Motivation is *knowing your role* and performing it in a relaxed fashion. Challenge is a game played by learners, not knowers. They are performers, not personalities. They anticipate trends and deal with them accordingly. Crisis management represents embarrassment, if not failure.

The climate is positive, with a great deal of freedom 'to do your own thing,' which is seen as a privilege, not a right—and so is not abused. Admittedly, workers are 'selfish' in the sense that they clearly have a high need to 'please themselves,' but they are much less *self-centered* than those of the 'please others' mentality. Their *enlightened self-interests* create an enthusiasm that is 'catching' and directed toward the service of others, not themselves. In that sense they are the antithesis of narcissism.

They see management far differently than management sees itself:

- Management's role is seen as being there to serve them, because they are the *organization's first customer.*

- They are frustrated and growing impatient with the timidity of management's leadership, which fails to see them and their role vis-a-vis management as complementary or to see the challenges ahead with clarity.

Where we want to be–Interdependent Management

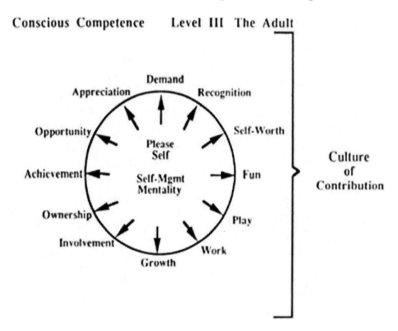

Figure 5-15: The Culture of Contribution.

Consequently, several eclectic actions are underway simultaneously:

- There are concerted efforts (but without much success) to *educate management* into recognizing the mutually supportive roles of management and professionals in shaping the new paradigm of organization.

- Those of a more enlightened nature are pressing forward with the concept of a *common guild* of management and professionals, in the interest of solidifying organizational leadership through integration of these disciplines (to the bemusement of many in management).

- Failing this, there is evidence that management is being increasingly *ignored,* with as much as 90 percent of the business of the organization being conducted around it.

Cases where attempts are being made to bridge the gap between management and professional workers are evidence of *Level III* behavior and the highest level of organizational consciousness—*conscious competence.* It is the level of the consummate adult, in which separate realities are understood, accepted, and then put aside for a higher level of awareness (see Figure 5-15).

There is no anger at this level because nothing is taken personally. The driving concern is the organization—and its effectiveness. Here, the Adult Ego State has little interest in what ought to be, but much in 'what is'—and what can be done.

Conscious Competence:
The Importance of Embracing Resistance

Conscious Competence (Level III) can best be experienced through *embracing resistance…* to pain, discomfort, and dissatisfaction… and then soaring on to new heights because of this embrace:

"The dove, as she speeds her way through the air, may marvel at the resistance to her flight by the atmosphere," once wrote Immanuel Kant (1724-1804), "but we know that but for that resistance she could not fly at all."

Consider all the posturing that goes on as organizational behavior vacillates between *independence* and *dependence,* while, simultaneously, open cooperation is vigorously resisted. "That didn't happen in my department"… or, "We got our reports in on time. *We* did *our* part!" And on and on. Incredible resistance is manifested… until one day, resistance is embraced, and *there is breakthrough.* Then, the realization of the interdependent nature of everything comes crashing through our consciousness.

Suddenly, we realize *nothing can be accomplished alone!* We soar above the arrogance of our 'separate reality.' No matter how good we are at what we do, we now understand that we need others to compensate for what we do poorly. As Peter Drucker observed, "People of great strengths have great weaknesses."

Recognition of this paves the way to interdependency and a successful organization. Yet, our culture often views resistance quite differently—seeing it as something negative and, therefore to be avoided. Darlene Goth-Neuman sees it most positively:

"Resistance is a positive and powerful force. When you understand that resistance has a purpose in assisting us to create, the habit of resisting resistance will be changed. Resistance enhances our ability to learn and adapt to varying sit nations. We must not change the object of our judgment, instead we must change the judgment of our object." [23]

With the pressure to change an unrelenting fact, there is a tendency to resist change consistent with that pressure. Alan Watts suggests that is why *we have both the accelerator and brake to the floor.* But do we accept the absurdity of this? Of course not. Instead, we invent macho colloquialisms to describe reality as 'when the rubber hits the road,' a reality that finds us 'burning up rubber'—and going nowhere. Is it not an indicator of madness when the culture we have created and the organization we have preserved burns us out?

The *Tyranny of Technology* has turned most things inside out and upside down, finding that which is alleged to be rational instead quite mad. Until recently—before *glasnost* and *perestroika*—there was a growing union between productivity and destruction; what Herbert Marcuse calls, "the brinkmanship of annihilation."

Yet, despite this glimmer of light, the horizon remains darkened by technology serving to institute new, more effective forms of social control and cohesion (e.g., multimedia scientific management of opinion; telling people what to think and why to think it). None of this is done with malicious intent, for if it were, it would be easier to identify and eradicate. Regardless, there is resistance to suggesting the ominous consequences of too much technology.

Actually, the swirl of technological splendor has changed everything, while changing nothing at all. For example, a case could be made that modern medicine has had little to do with prolonging life—that diet and health care deserve most, if not all, of the credit. Modern medicine, despite all its horn tooting, has had only a very modest impact on society. But someone who does not follow this closely could find this an absurd statement (which the American Medical Association counts on very heavily).

We're certainly not getting better as human beings. And the organization, which we have created to serve us, continues to perpetuate the false need for toil at the expense of pleasure; aggressiveness at the expense of community; competition at the expense of cooperation; misery at the expense of joy; and injustice at the expense of human rights equity.

In short, most of us work in sick organizations that arrest our development as individual achievers by their failure:

- To embrace our individual differences by harnessing our energetic spirit in diverse enterprise;
- To embrace our collective contributions by their insistence on uniformity of effort;
- To confront the real issues of organization, which relate to *cultural biases* and *counterproductive work climates.*

Consequently, American professionals are trapped in their own design, lost in the swirl of the magic of the day, going backward as they move forward and, therefore, not moving at all.

It is precisely for these reasons that the *Culture of Contribution* is, at this moment, so critical to organizational life. Individuals are needed who think for themselves with real thoughts and confront real issues that affect the organization's health and wellbeing. These individuals march to their own drummer, responding to a 'beat' that originates deep within themselves... not to the manipulative 'tweets' of a B. F. Skinner like pigeon.

But the organization is weary of these individuals who see and serve according to their own music, rather than the cacophony of the organization. Because *comfort* and *complacency* can be controlled, and *contribution* controls itself, there remains a primitive *cultural bias* that wants to maintain comfort and complacency—at the expense of contribution.

As the American organization zooms toward entropy, and the inevitable disintegration of traditional structures, contribution—emanating from a *Please Self* mentality can be seen rising out of the chaos and ashes. The paradigm is evolving, founded on communal support and collective contribution.

Obviously, there is strong resistance to this rebirth, for it places *Pleasing Self* ahead of *Pleasing Others.* Yet, *Pleasing Self/Pleasing Others* is a pivotal concept which confronts the organization as the attitudes of workers change towards everything—themselves, management, and the organization—and work itself.

The 'Pleasing Self' Mentality

There is no single tendency in the American psyche that causes more frustration and loss of purposefulness than the insane drive to Please Others. This is an indication of a disturbed psyche. People who spend an inordinate amount of time worrying obsessively about what others may think of them demonstrate an unhealthy preoccupation with the self. A product of our upbringing, this obsession is the curse of our thinking and our times.

And, because we grow from the 'outside in' and become everyone within our experience before we become ourselves, it is a process of self-imprisonment; of victimization. Put even more directly, for those afraid to think their own thoughts and please themselves before they attempt to meet the needs of others, it compromises all efforts to be productive and to lead productive lives… for it confines them to a veritable cage.

So many roadblocks exist to self-appreciation and self-discovery that many of us never have the pleasure of knowing ourselves. One reason is our *cultural bias* against rebellion. Yet rebelling is *essential* to healthy growth and development and absolutely our first sign of freedom. Disobedience, which is so frowned upon, is an integral part of this process. As a result, many good little girls and boys remain arrested in their development—never becoming truly men and women of the first rank. Take the reflections of a middle-aged executive of a multinational corporation:

"I've spent too many years doing exactly what was expected of me; being a good son, a good husband, a good father. In my company I'm known as a 'good soldier.' When I ask myself what I am about, I'd have to say I don't know anymore. I've tried for so long to fit in; I've held back for so long; I don't know what or who I am." [24]

People have purchased millions of self-knowledge books in a desperate attempt to deal with their *arrested development.* No subject has been treated with greater seriousness or more willful mischief than this genre. As a consequence, we seem never able to get enough of these palliatives. Alas, these books have become a bottomless source of 'pearls without wisdom.'

There are, of course, some exceptions. In *The Act of Love* (1985), for example, Erich Fromm is helpful when he suggests that love and understanding of self cannot be separated from love and understanding of others. Before we can love another, we must first find our way to loving ourselves. There is no short cut; no off ramps, or excursion fares.

Now, if we substitute 'accept' for 'love,' it reads:

- Before we can accept another, we must first accept ourselves as we are.

- If we accept ourselves as we are, we are more likely to accept others as we find them.

The key to unleashing incredible power and energy… first as an individual and, then, collectively, as an organization… lies in this brief declaration of intrapsychic awareness.

Think about it. In our culture, we continuously try to change others so they conform to our artificial standards. This obscene act degrades *others* 'as they are,' and—in the process—diminishes us 'as we are'. It is a 'no-gain game,' and it has become an American sport. Put otherwise, many of us find ourselves:

- Taking on other people's problems as 'ours'; then

- Projecting our problems on them as 'theirs'

- And then… in a game of compulsive projection… trying to make them 'right' with what is wrong with us, when we—not they—are the problem.

- Finding it impossible to say "no" when we don't want to hurt someone else's feelings when they make demands on us, demands that put us at risk or disadvantage, jeopardizing our security and well being.

It is a very rare individual, indeed, who looks at another, and sees, feels and experiences what that individual senses. That is why *acceptance* is so key to organizational health. And it starts with self-acceptance.

When there is self-acceptance, there is no need to lie to ourselves. We can look at ourselves as products of experience, knowledge, education, and socialization, and recognize what assets and limitations are apparent. With such clear vision of ourselves, then, we can see others more clearly—without the need to look at them as if looking into a mirror. This permits self-accepting people to truly pay attention and thus mobilize their resources to accomplish the possible.

Paradoxically, the greater our acceptance of our own behavior, the easier it is to change. The greater our tolerance for different behaviors, the easier it is to deal with others... as they are. What's more, when these differences are *accepted*, people of different perspectives are more inclined to respond positively to requests to modify their behavior.

Conversely, denying our own behavior makes changing it nigh impossible. The denial, in fact, reinforces our intolerance not only of 'the behavior in question,' but the behavior when it is personified in others. Take the person who denies they 'cut corners' to get things done, only to criticize someone else when they are seen doing precisely that. One's credibility, then, has a false echo, and we are seen to have a double standard. Forcing others to act as 'we would act,' therefore generates resistance, dissension, and, ultimately, dysfunctional behavior. Significant contribution is clearly the loser.

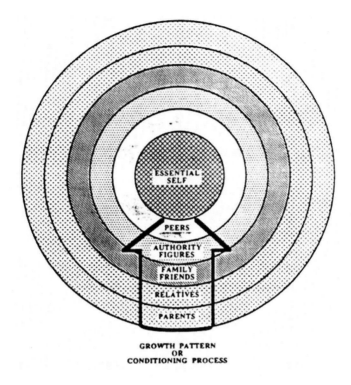

Figure 5-16: The Pattern of Growth or Conditioning Process.

There is a simple three-step approach we can take to realizing *conscious competence* in the interest of behavioral change. It is used by *Gamblers Anonymous, Weight Watchers International,* and *Alcoholics Anonymous…* so, it is not new:

- Awareness—being aware of our *separate reality* and what triggers our undesirable behavior;

- Acceptance—accepting our behavior and finding no need to become defensive about it; then choosing to consider the option of changing the behavior to promote our own self-interests;

- Action—being disposed to executing a plan designed to deal with our undesirable behavior in the interest of being more effective, healthy, and happy.

Choosing to reject a behavior is different than denial. For example, people may suddenly admit they have a drinking problem *(awareness)*—accepting it as part of their lifestyle. And, they may even go the extra step of tracing the symptoms to the apparent causes *(acceptance)* contributing to this life style, without anger. They might even consider entering a chemical dependency unit, or perhaps decide to quit drinking 'cold turkey'—because psychological resolution precedes the chronological commitment *(action)*.

Notice that, with *acceptance*, subjects rise above the imprisoning confines of their *separate reality*. There is no need to take the situation personally—to resort to defensiveness. Anger, too, is impossible when one rises above the situation. The higher the consciousness, the greater the tolerance for human foibles. Human frailty is taken in stride and appreciated with good humor, still realizing human beings are imperfect, but perfectible.

As powerful as acceptance is in dealing with self, it is even more powerful in dealing with others. *By accepting others as they are, you never own their problems.* You can be empathetic, but you never have to carry their monkey on your back. They may resent you for this at first, but 'that's their problem'—not yours. Nobody makes another human being stronger by carrying their burden. As simple as this truism is, many continue to carry others' burdens—to every one's disappointment.

Actually, *self-acceptance* is exactly the same as liking oneself—the two are synonymous. There is less self-delusion with self-acceptance, because it is not necessary. Genuine feedback is appreciated, while… because the person is not self-ignorant… the insincere is distinguished from the helpful with little difficulty. Criticism is taken at face value in terms of what is learned.

In any case, there is no 'cave in' to criticism, for it is weighed on its merits—not on the pedigree of the critic.

Incidentally, sincerity of feedback is a function of trust. The higher the trust level, the more genuine the feedback is likely to be.

Obviously, when a person with a strong *Please* Self orientation is employed in an organization with a strong cultural predisposition to *Please Others*, it is likely to be a hostile environment. This is not because the *Please Self* person is not motivated to perform. More likely, it is because such a person's focus is too heavily on performance and not seriously enough on personality... the principal game of *Please Others*.

Realistically, the individual inclined to *Please Self will* have to submit to the predominant culture, or leave. There is little chance persons of this orientation can survive the hostility of a *Culture of Comfort/Culture of Complacency,* which they doubtlessly will encounter. Retreat, then... to a more supportive climate... is the prudent strategy.

A high need to *Please Self* is a weighty responsibility, especially in a breakdown culture in which opposing camps are created on every issue, and finger pointing substitutes for dealing with problems.

Contribution may one day be the dominant culture, but that is little solace to today's pioneer in the trenches, trying to make a living. What is curiously incongruous is that many otherwise traditional organizations tolerate a small contingent of *Please Self* personalities. This is deceptive tribute. Some may even be given 'celebrity' status, although they defy organizational pomp and circumstance.

Be careful! This is less likely 'tolerance' than a concession to their extraordinary contributions (e.g., outstanding scientists, salesmen, even renegade engineers). Due to their peculiar flair, they are given wide berth and permitted to flex their idiosyncratic genius without recrimination. But let the business move away from their expertise, and one faux pas, and they are gone.

This uncharacteristic attention distracts these unique individuals from realizing their real power. While being treated as luminaries, of course, they are neutralized from being a threat to the organization's status quo. Legions of otherwise brilliant men and women have been so finessed by this simple, but effective stratagem. Ironically, managers, given to displaying similar behavior, are sacked quickly as a wink. The organization has little sense of humor for managers who display idiosyncratic individualism.

Pleasing Self vs. Selfishness

The organization would like to promote the idea that the *Please Self* mentality is the ultimate in 'selfishness.' Quite the contrary—on closer examination, the ultimate in selfishness is likely to be found in 'the unselfish.' Typically, they permit themselves to be exploited in a masochistic fashion by being taken for granted, taken advantage of, given faint praise, and then treated as 'gophers.'

When people permit others to bankrupt them emotionally and psychologically, they do nobody a favor. Instead, they redistribute their pain, agony, and self-pity where it is least deserved—on their family and loved ones—causing deep unhappiness. Ironically, in this 'zero sum' game, those who are the 'takers' from these 'givers' are actually the unhappiest of all. They never get enough, always demanding more. Worse yet, they have little respect for those who allow themselves to be so dominated.

There is only one way to be truly 'unselfish,' and that is through 'total selfishness'… through first meeting one's own personal needs before attempting to meet those of others. To meet the needs of others at the expense of one's own needs, admittedly, is applauded as virtuous. However, it is psychologically self-abusing, narcissistic, wasteful, and dishonest.

More virtuous, by far, is to assert oneself by meeting one's own needs, and then—out of the generosity of one's spirit—the needs of others. To submit to social conformity at the expense of one's free choice does not engender a kind heart.

Where we want to be–Interdependent Management

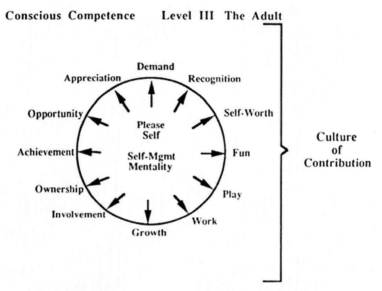

Conscious Competence   Level III   The Adult

Culture of Contribution

Motivated By	**Behaviors**
Challenging work	Victor
Opportunity to fail	Purposeful
Right to an opinion	Confident
Right to be wrong	Cooperative
What is wrong (not who is wrong)	Pleasure
Problems	Creator
Work Itself	Completer
Creative License	Bottom Line Responsive
Owning what he does	Pioneer
Calculated risks	Proactive Responsive
Doing	Positive
	"Selfish"

Figure 5-17: The Culture of Contribution… Motivation and Behavior.

Because *saints* tend to defy the human condition—placing themselves above its vanities while reinforcing their culture's vagaries—they might be considered the most ethnocentric of human beings. Albert Schweitzer was perhaps not a saint, but he lost patience with the 'jackass' society that pervaded Europe in his time—not only among his fellow bourgeoisie, but also within the intellectual community to which he belonged. He was surrounded by wasted lives and retreated into a womb of his own making.

Schweitzer, it could be argued, brought the arrogance of Western culture to West Africa, setting up a hospital and clinic. On the other hand, his *'reverence for life'* confused the natives, for he couldn't kill the smallest of insects. His hospital, as a consequence, would never receive the *Good Housekeeping Seal of Approval.* Conceivably, he probably went there to find himself. It is questionable he went there to learn. Perhaps a sense of life's futility drove him there to pay a humanistic debt to compensate for these misgivings. Perchance by 'saving' the natives from themselves, he felt he could find his own salvation.

Whatever the motivation, it is interesting that the European society he rejected celebrated him as an altruist and painted him a humanitarian. Was Africa bettered by the incursion of this Westerner... is it better now? What is most remarkable about this man is not what he did, but that he had the courage to 'do it'... the courage to *Please Self* by serving others.

Perhaps the most significant characteristic of the *Please Self* mentality is the need to focus on purposeful engagement. The world outside can be totally 'out of control,' but the individual operates on a separate dynamic—chaos synergizes his efforts, as he thrives on the dynamics of change.

Meanwhile, those in charge who deny the reality of the evolving disorder move further from being in control. Denial, as if nothing has changed, only accelerates dysfunction. This is manifested by:

- Decisions not made;

- Risks not taken;

- Actions not followed through... because the *Please Others* contingent is still trying to 'mind read' their superiors who, remain equally ill-informed. Everyone assumes the guise of control, while running out of control.

Panic pervades the breakdown culture. Everywhere *Please Others* pervades the ambiance: managers are trying to please customers, corporate bosses, stock holders, suppliers, subordinates, peers, immediate bosses, community leaders, even their confessors, and ending up pleasing nobody. They are at the end of their wick, but still smile through clenched teeth.

So, what do they do? Do they say, 'Damn it? Enough already!' No—they open another a pack of cigarettes, and have a couple of martinis at lunch... or they go on a health kick, giving up one 'narcotic' for another, punishing themselves into a condition they never had when they were half their current age. They acquire younger 'significant others,' while carrying a pack of *Rolaids* in their briefcases, alongside a deluxe container of *Extra Strength Excedrin.* They drink gallons of coffee, looking forlorn and perplexed. And then they have a cerebral hemorrhage, myocardial infarction, peptic ulcer, kidney attack, liver complaint, or simply retire on the job.

Were these same people inclined to *Please Self,* the outcome would be quite different, but they are not... and that's the problem.

The Price of 'Pleasing Self'

The *Please Self* mentality in today's American organization stands out in isolation:

- Fellow workers stay away from them as if they have the plague.

- They are punished at performance appraisal time for being different being seen as "not cut out for this industry."
- They are the subject of conversation by the herd.
- The herd is intimidated by those who have the audacity to be *productive;* and *focus on performance.*

The *Please Self* person is an 'inside outsider.' He must resign himself to this fact in order to contribute, while wondering why 'contribution' is rated so low, and conformity so high. Alas, this is not likely to change anytime soon unless we witness precipitous decline.

Like Stephen Jay Gould's *An Urchin in the Storm* (1987), we are programmed to survive only when we are threatened with extinction. The sense of danger precedes activation of the survival mechanism. The human species has a herd mentality that must be frightened into action. The herd is slow to learn, to react. Actually, if human beings could survive as well without each other as they can survive with each other, they would.

In *The Selfish Gene* (1976), Richard Hawkins sees 'selfishness' as indigenous to survival. He develops an interesting marriage of the concepts of biology and social theory, suggesting that selfishness is inherently robotic. Evolution, he claims, has been always selfish, and we are a *survival machine*—on both a molecular (genetic) and mechanistic (human) scale.

Selfishness is inevitable, as the organism or social system senses that its survival is in jeopardy. So, there is little profit in punishing ourselves for our inevitable selfishness.

Watch video of former American athletes Jimmy Connors and John McEnroe play the 'game' of tennis. With them, it wasn't a game but the frame of survival. What superb athletes demonstrate is an understanding of the importance of an 'ecology of mind.' They put their full being into the contest at hand. To be distracted would keep them from their appointed task—victory. The outcome may be 'victory,' but the focus is on process.

There are, and have been, more gifted athletes on the tour. But most relate with envy to these two men's persistent intensity and purity of purpose. Spectators 'love to hate' them because they display temperament and selfish determinism, both of which are discouraged in our culture. Few fans would risk such conduct at home, much less at the office. These athletes, therefore, provide them with a bold experience... while fans remain in safety and vicarious comfort. So, they watch as much for what these athletes are, as for what they do.

Meanwhile, fans slip more securely into unconscious incompetence *(Comfort)* or conscious incompetence *(Complacency)* as the tennis ball goes back and forth. Connors and McEnroe epitomize conscious competence *(Contribution)* in a most American way, but for these fans it is only a movie in their heads.

What Connors and McEnroe symbolized is the new direction of the American professional. Like a growing cadre of professional workers, they understand the game the organization has played on them, and they will have none of it! They are taking the power away from the tour management and the American Federation of Tennis, and putting it in the hands of the truly powerful—the playing professionals. Without the likes of Connors and McEnroe, professional tennis would have become as interesting as a polite hand of Bridge. Corporate life resembles this card game with the tennis match metaphor rumbling under the surface.

We have entered the age of restless, energetic Americans who want to put America back on track. They are tired of the 'silly putty' games that management and the organization have been playing on them. In the same way that Connors and McEnroe want competent officiating, qualified coaching, and appropriate facilities and equipment, these new Americans want quality standards in all aspects of their work and life.

Should you be inclined to stereotype Connors and McEnroe as 'brats,' be advised these are the new American values steeped in personhood. Not only do these athletes believe in America, but their public utterances and conduct off the court indicate that there is no danger they will be less resolute in their future undertakings. They are part of the 'spoiled brat' generation, but they have gone beyond self-indulgence to meaningful contributions. They are a part of the promise of the new breed and the restless edge of the professional class.

Today's professionals are demanding more control of their lives and more freedom and opportunity to express their will. They are flirting with the same risk-taking of a Connors or McEnroe. Clearly feeling they have a better idea, they refuse to buy into 'the way it is.' They want to define their situation in terms that make sense to them. They are tired of hearing growth advocated, while budgeting cuts; hearing individual initiative proclaimed, while demanding conformity. They are moving toward an 'ecology of mind.'

Ecology of mind is purity of purpose without intervening confusion. Guilt has been a big contributor to making *Pleasing Self* synonymous with self-indulgence. Soren Kierkegaard (1813-1855) understood our anxiety regarding pleasure. He saw pleasure as our greatest fear. Pleasure and sin, thanks to ascetic Saint Paul, are seen as one and the same. Paul made pleasure toxic to the human spirit and our immortal soul... and we have been trying to sustain his conviction ever since. Guilt is the 'social sin' encountered when one places *Pleasing Self* over *Pleasing Others*. This is the disposition of composers, painters, writers, and artists of all persuasions. Now, it must be the disposition of professionals... who must listen to the wisdom of their own hearts and play the music of their talent in concert with kindred spirits. This is my hope and their salvation.

If there need be guilt, have it be only when one is not making a *contribution*. It is time process serve the individual and the organization alike. Not only does this support *conscious competence*, but, paradoxically, it dissolves 'turf wars' between managers and professionals as survival is not somebody else's job.

Endnotes

(1) Source: Kathy M. Kristof, *The Los Angeles Times* reported this in *The Tampa Tribune-Times*, May 27, 1990. Dr. Hammer, a trained physician, died December 10, 1990 at the age of 92. Although he is best known for his Occidental Petroleum empire, and his "citizen diplomacy" about the world in the interest of his businesses, ordinary householders know the name "Hammer" best for "Arm & Hammer" baking soda.

(2) Anthony Ho, Marissa Mayer On Yahoo's Fired COO: De Castro "Not A Fit," January 28, 2014, the Internet. He was not replaced.

(3) Susan C. Faludi, *The Wall Street Journal* as reported in the *St. Petersburg Times*, May 27, 1990.

(4) Fisher, James R., Jr., "America Is Dead: A Time To Begin," *St. Petersburg Evening Independent*, January 1, 1976.

(5) Heilbroner, Robert, "Seize the Day," *The New York Review*, February 15, 1990, pp. 30-31.

(6) 1988 U.S. Statistical Abstract Table No. 1397, 1985.

(7) Rifkin, Jeremy, *Entropy: A New World View* (New York: Bantam Books, 1981). Read Rifkin's "Diminishing Returns of Technology," pp. 95-97 and the twentieth century just completed, pp 135-199 and see how little we seem to have learned.

(8) *Business Month*, November, 1988; p. 39.

(9) Tarrant, John J., Drucker: *The Man Who Invented The Corporate Society* (New York: Warner Books, 1976), p. 311.

(10) Fromm, Erich, *To Have or To Be?* (New York: Harper & Row, 1976), p. 95. See *Escape From Freedom* (Rinehart & Co., Inc., 1941) where this is the main topic.

(11) Typical evidence of this is "Desperately Seeking A Dose of Productivity," by James C. Cooper and Kathlene Madigan, *Business Week,* February 19, 1990, pages 27-28, where the

authors state, "The sad performance in 1989 has already lifted the cost of doing business, because wages and benefits of workers grew much faster than productivity."

(12) Tarrant, op. cit. p. 312

(13) Kennedy, Paul, "Fin-de-Siècle America," *New York Review*, June 28, 1990. Kennedy covers the debate between those who see America in decline and those who foresee a new millennium for America.

(14) Yankelovich, Daniel, *New Rules: Searching For Self-Fulfillment In A World Turned Upside Down* (New York: Random House, 1981), pp. 38-39.

(15) Tarrant, op. cit. p. 318.

(16) Kathy Kristof: According to Duke University/CFO Magazine, nearly half of the United States companies said that they are reluctant to hire full-time employees in the present business climate, MoneyWatch (December 11, 2013).

(17) Obamacare and the Affordable Health Care Act came in for much criticism as it was implemented in 2014. One can imagine what it was like in 1933 when President Roosevelt was promoting social security. It was advertised as a "short term" policy, which is now an economic staple of American society. In 2014, Zachary Goldfarb and Amy Goldstein in "Politics," referring to Affordable Health Care, write that it will prompt over 2 million to quit their jobs or employers to cut hours. Kathy Kristof in Moneywatch (December 11, 2013) writes that according to Duke University/CFO Magazine that nearly half of US companies are reluctant to hire full-time employees.

(18) Warner, Samuel, *Self-Realization and Self-Defeat* (New York: Grove Press, 1966), p. 37.

(19) Sinetar, Marsha, *Do What You Love, The Money Will Follow* (New York: Dell Trade Paperback, 1987).

(20) To illustrate this point, General Motors Board of Directors voted (June, 1990) to double the pension for retiring Chairman Roger Smith (from $550,000 to $1.1 million a year), whose company lost 11 percentage points (from 46 to 35) in market share during his leadership, not to mention the tens of thousands who lost their jobs on his watch (from 1981 through 1989).

(21) Parkinson, Cyril Northcote, "Parkinson's Law," *The Economist Magazine,* September, 1957.

(22) In fairness to this issue, see Mall, Douglas T., *Career Development in Organization* (San Francisco: Jossey-Bass, 1986).

(23) Tarrant, op cit. p. 312.

(24) Goth Neuman, Darlene, *Writings* (Anaheim Hills, CA: Goth Neuman, Inc., 1980).

(25) Sinetar, op. cit. p. 19.

CHAPTER SIX

SO WHAT!

"Transformation of American style of management is not a job of reconstruction, nor revision. It requires a whole new structure, from foundation, upward... Transformation must take place with directed effort... Failure of management to plan for the future and to foresee problems has brought waste of manpower, of materials, and of machine-time, all of which raises the manufacturer's cost and that the purchaser must pay... The inevitable result is loss of market, loss of market begets unemployment. Performance of management should be measured by potential to stay in business... not by the quarterly dividend.

"It is no longer socially acceptable to dump employees onto the heap of unemployed. Loss of market, and resulting unemployment, are not foreordained. They are not inevitable. They are man-made.

> *"The basic cause of sickness in American industry and result-*
> *ing unemployment is failure of top management to manage."*
>
> **—W. Edwards Deming** (1900-1993),
> American statistician

T IS TASTELESS, colorless, and odorless, and neither felt nor feared. But it is poisonous nevertheless. It has been attacking the vital organs of the American organization and making it quite ill. While the poison's cumulative effects have not yet killed the organization, it has severely limited the organization's ability to see itself clearly—much less deal with the challenges ahead. And the cause?

The American organization can be observed to be 'sucking up its own exhaust fumes.' Were it more a conscious act, it would be considered an attempt at suicide. In any case, should the toxicity persist and the will to survive as a first-rate nation continue to fade, the point is moot. A more pressing concern is this:

Does the American organization, as is, have the capacity to survive if it rediscovers its will?

Work Without Managers is directed at that question. Although this book is a diagnosis of the disease rather that a prognosis of the cure, an analysis rather than a solution, its theme has a bearing on a course of action. It is my view of all types of organizations—from the trenches. Organizations, from that vantage point, differ little one from the other. Here is my analysis of this cultural landscape thus far:

The need for a new organizational paradigm **(Chapter 1)** was discussed in terms of the changing values, relationships, and educational backgrounds of the majority of American workers, and how the current organization fails to support or adapt to those changes. This failure has punished professional workers especially, who are now in the majority, and who have little sense of the shift in power from management to them.

Using René Thom's *catastrophe theory* **(Chapter 2)**, the relationship of continuity, discontinuity, and subsequent catastrophe was illustrated. According to Thom's theory, no matter how zealously or conspicuously continuity is supported, incremental discontinuity (albeit concealed) eventually triggers *incipient catastrophe*. Given the continuous buildup of tension between management and professionals, the relationship between continuity, discontinuity, and catastrophe was examined in terms of process by which catastrophe occurs suddenly (and without warning) in the organization, particularly after long periods of apparent calm.

The current situation suggests that organizational control may collapse at any moment and give rise to dramatic changes. When, or in what form that may occur is impossible to predict. The most optimistic possibility of catastrophe avoidance is an integration of management and working professionals into a common leadership guild. But, as time passes, that possibility seems less hopeful.

What is forcing this 'final solution' on the American organization is the echoing footsteps of economic competition **(Chapter 3)**, largely from Europe and the Far East, but also from the noticeable economic footprints of Brazil in South America. As America's market share shrinks and many leading American industries are threatened with extinction, there is disheartening evidence that, while competition is 'eating our lunch,' many Americans continue to presume it is free.

The combination of a 'free lunch' mentality that rides on repressed management 'panic' has resulted in the American organization more resembling a madhouse **(Chapter 4)** than anything else. Six silent organization killers are considered in depth, noting that the organization, oblivious to these threats, continues to operate essentially as it has since WWII, with, at best, only cosmetic changes. You would think, from this madcap behavior, that America's WWII victories were only yesterday and that the world was still 'America's oyster.' Clearly, due to the persistent poison of euphoria, there is little sense of impending danger... The war changed our values and relationships to each other, as well as to the rest of the world. We had markets, products and profits we never dreamed of—a standard of living beyond our most optimistic desires. We went off to college, got good jobs, and became owners (no longer renters). We lived well, and all was right, for 'God was on our side.' We helped rebuild Europe and Japan, and felt good about ourselves. When those we benefited started to become self-sufficient, we smiled at their resurgence and continued to feel good about ourselves. After all, America made it happen! We even bought their quality products, while reflecting that the price was right 'because they work cheap; Americans don't.

Not to worry—we went off to war in Korea to police the world and to Vietnam to show we were still made of the 'right stuff.' We put a man on the moon, took most of the Nobel Prizes in Science and Technology, and continued to feel good about ourselves.

So the balance of trade was in bad shape, so the national debt was 'out of control'; so our basic industries in steel, coal, paper, petroleum, and textiles were in trouble; so hundreds of thousands of workers in key industries would never get their jobs back; so our streams were becoming increasingly polluted, and our air threatened to be unbreathable; so our bridges, highways and railroads were crumbling; so our kids went to school, got their diplomas, and still couldn't read or write; so the rate of productivity per worker was falling precipitously; so American manufacturing was being called a 'hollow industry,' with more and more manufacturing done for American producers abroad; so what!

We were Americans, and everybody wants to be an American—the envy of the world—and that was that!

There was no sense of urgency, only panic. Panic denotes hysteria: urgency denotes seriousness. Panic finds the organization pressing and management fresh out of ideas. The workers—now, mostly college-trained thinkers, no longer factory fodder—aren't buying into the panic. Worse yet, they aren't buying into the urgency or anything else. They are off playing *Mad Monarch games*

(**Chapter 4**) with reckless abandon, deriving satisfaction mainly outside of work. They go to work to support a lifestyle, to complain, to socialize and to make busy, not to make a contribution.

Enter Human Resources (**Chapter5**) with its "gosh-do-we-care-about-our-employees" hyperbole—from employee benefits to executive bonuses—which has little relationship to purposeful performance. The workers (now mostly professionals) retreat into passive behaviors, cut off from the reality of their own experiences by a potpourri of ill-conceived interventions of Human Resources.

As a result, we have the *Culture of Contribution* displaced by the cultures of *Comfort* and *Complacency*, where work is either an accidental or counterfeit activity and workers are either management dependent, or counter dependent on the organization for their total well being suspended in terminal adolescence.

The American organization is 'sucking up its own exhaust' and getting sicker by the minute. At a time when it should be thinking most clearly, it can hardly think at all. About the best it can manage is to go through the motions, and slowly, at that. The imperative now is to know where it is, how it got there, and what it needs to do to get out of this crippling zone of comfort or complacency.

When the Simple is Complex

There is a difficult, protracted struggle ahead for the American organization. The process of purposeful performance is a simple one, but the requirements to 'make it happen,' unfortunately, are not equally simple.

Mere reform, as W. Edwards Deming reminds us in *Out of the Crisis* (1986), will not be enough; nor will 'aspirin management.' The American organization must be rebuilt from scratch, with different thinking and values, a more appropriate infrastructure, new leadership, and a new sense of what constitutes purposeful performance.

The organization must change the way it sees reality, and abandon the way it thinks and processes information in its problem solving.

Nobody ever did anything just because they knew. Knowledge must he operational. To operationalize knowledge it must be felt. Values are 'felt knowledge,' which shape the cultural bias of organization. Cultural bias is the mechanism that governs behavior. The organization tends to resist change, preferring to sustain the values that it knows and understands—that it feels. To ignore this fact spells doom for organizational change. The sooner this is understood the sooner the change process can begin. Value change is a slow, painful process for everyone, and there are no short cuts or negotiable detours. Cosmetic changes—saying 'change has occurred'—do not make it so. Time, patience, and experience are its only determiners.

The structure of organization is pathetically out-of-date with the relationship of managers to workers, and to work itself as work, workers and the workplace are structured for another time and place. The organization must be formatted to accommodate the changing skill mix of employees, the changing technologies of organization and—most directly of all—the changing requirements of work. As matters now stand, the organization is unresponsive to ever changing and accelerating demands because it insists on substituting activity for action, deliberation for decision-making, comfort for contribution, quantity for quality, and panic for patience.

Leadership of the organization is wrong for the requirements of the organization and its people. Leadership is 'seeing where the organization is and where it is going,' versus where it intends to go, and then 'serving of all of its people,' starting with its first customers—the workers. Not only is the professional work force a hedge against the pusillanimity of leadership—it is the source of light in this otherwise bleak picture... yet, it continues to be ignored. Meanwhile, this professional work force is lost in its own confusion—wailing at the system for not showing it 'the way,' when 'it is the system,' and cannot hand 'that way' off to management.

Work today is much less tied to activities and contributions of the individual, more to synergistic processes that involve teaming or group contributions; much more self-actualizing than conforming to arbitrary standards. [1]

In the absence of a foundation-in-understanding of these implications, workers and managers reared on precise worker/manager roles do not appreciate the shift in emphasis and power.

Even the teaming concept is confusing. The fluid dynamics of operations in the current climate call for behavior more akin to that of a basketball team than of a baseball team:

A baseball team is nine individual contributors who happen to be on the same team. Baseball is called 'the Great American Pastime' because it is obsessively and statistically driven by individual effort, with little interdependent behavior required. Cricket is a similar game for the British, and we know where they stand in the world of commerce. [2]

A basketball team, on the other hand, is five interdependent players irrevocably involved in the fluid dynamics of a process in which success depends on them working together. Moreover, basketball is intuitively and situational driven, while baseball is cognitively and strategically driven. Notice, too, that the leader in basketball is called a 'coach,' a facilitator of the action; while in baseball, he is called a 'manager,' or a 'caller of the shots.' Now let's examine these points in more detail.

No. 1: Thinking Differently On Purpose

Perhaps the only way to realize *purposeful performance* is not to seek it.

The rationally trained mind might have trouble with that statement. "Give me the facts," it would demand, "and leave out the B.S." After nearly a century of 'facts' cascading into the fathomless void of American enterprise, you would think Americans would challenge this philosophy.

But the American culture is deeply impaled in a deterministic approach, or the 'Blitzkrieg School of Problem Solving' (i.e., exercise an all-out assault on 'it,' and spare no money or resource to claim a victorious solution). Being only comfortable with nitty-gritty deductive reasoning, we expect the effect to follow the cause:

- "Find the cause for AIDS," so the logic goes, "and we will eliminate the effect."
- "Find the cause for America's industrial collapse, and we will once again regain world dominance of the marketplace."

Rest assured, medical science will spend most of its resources on trying to isolate the AIDS virus through research, and then develop a miraculous vaccine to prevent it. Yet, the cause does not lie exclusively in the subatomic world of microbiology, but also in the social psychology of human relationships. The disease lies as much in the mind as it does the body (the two are part of the same whole, but we treat them as strangers to each other).

Ironically, once the AIDS virus is identified, and the miraculous vaccine applied, the virus is likely to mutate to a new, more impervious strain... and thus the vicious cycle continues. Only the medicine of behavioral change will complete the miracle.

Analytical thinking is the religion of the modern mind. It is the wholehearted push in the direction of 'Artificial Intelligence.' 'AI' enthusiasts hold that all human thinking, whether conscious or unconscious, is merely the enacting of some complicated computation. There is no room for the mystical or the spiritual. Indeed, the theology of that religion is *logical positivism*, the dominant philosophy of the 20th Century American mind. [3]

There is a dogmatic belief that logical positivism (also known as *scientific empiricism*), can solve anything. This fuels the belief, "Don't worry about pollution—science will come up with the answer one day."

Medical science, for instance, has created the most sophisticated toys to reinforce this belief of infallibility, including 'CAT scanners that direct X-ray beams through the skull from multiple directions; computerized blood analyzers with impressive printouts; cardiac pacemakers; renal dialysis machines; lasers surgery, and 3-D software replications of structural maladies.

It is clear that 'Nuclear Man' has gambled almost everything on a mechanistic approach to his dilemma. This has been done in the belief that the 'Heart of God' resides in science; that man can ravage his environment in wanton glee, or abandon his mind, body and spirit to senseless pleasure, and 'Science as Superman' will be there at the most critical moment to rescue his mortal flesh from his reckless abandon.

What is paradoxical about science is that the cleaner the methodology, the more abstruse the ramifications. Take nuclear power plants. How dangerous is the waste of this 'cheap' energy source? We haven't the foggiest notion! Barges of nuclear waste roam the American continent in the dead of night like 'vessels without a country,' looking for safe havens to dump their dubious product. Scientific reassurances notwithstanding, each reactor annually produces tons of radioactive waste that remains toxic for thousands of years. With no truly safe way to dispose of this waste, it represents a horror story beyond comprehension.

Then, do advocates of 'logical positivism' favor another possible energy source? Of course not. They focus instead, doing what we all do in our rational approach to problem solving—ignoring the real problem (nuclear as primary energy source), and concentrating on a solution to a solvable problem (more efficient production of nuclear energy).

What we need is an energy source that is renewable, economical, efficient, and safe. Eureka… we have it! Solar energy meets all these criteria. The main obstacle is not technical, but political. [4] The shift from nonrenewable to renewable resources involves dealing with a stubborn *cultural bias* favoring the use of coal and oil. So, it is not a rational, but an irrational dilemma based on conventional wisdom and greed.

Obviously, logical positivism would hold no store with this assessment referencing the technical and scientific achievements over the last century, failing to mention that science created most of the problems it ultimately solves.

Scientific empiricism arrogantly denies the spiritual component of man. It holds the view that if it cannot be measured, validated and replicated it does not exist. Empiricism is a logical progression from the works of three men, René Descartes (1596-1650), Isaac Newton (1642-1727), and Ludwig Wittgenstein (1889-1951):

- René Descartes' *Cartesian Philosophy* formed the basis for the division between the mind and the body; between the spiritual and material worlds of man. Descartes' famous proclamation, "I think, therefore I am," overlooks emotions as the source of a persons true being (see Antonio Damasio's "Descartes' Error," 1994).

- Isaac Newton, better known for Newtonian physics, also formed Newtonian psychology, which described man as essentially a machine personified by a well-made clock.

- Ludwig Wittgenstein, and his dedication to empirical observation, believed man could maintain a value-free and scientific perspective.

Each man contributed to building a more persuasive argument for the division of man:

- Descartes between behaving (material world) and believing (spiritual world);
- Newton between thinking and feeling;
- Wittgenstein between subjective and objective points of view.

What is fundamental to purposeful performance in the workplace is the recognition that:

- We are both subject and object;
- We are never 'value free';
- Thinking and feeling are part of the same process;
- We live in a world that is both abstract and concrete. Both are parts of the same essential whole. To deny the one is to deny the other.
- We are both a cognitive and intuitive thinker. Our subconscious mind plays an active albeit not an obvious role with our conscious behavior.

Difficult as it might be to grasp, purposeful performance grew out of chaos and confusion—not out of order and consistency. To strain for order, then, is to embrace disorder.

Purposeful performance is a dynamic process that may reflect chaos from a segmental view, but order from a holistic one. That is because we are an integration of these diverse parts:

- Mind-body-spirit;
- Subject-observer-object;
- Thinking feeling-behaving.

So, to deny one part at the expense of another is to intensify the conflict within us and between us. Conversely, to accept this diversity, and to work toward full integration, is to establish wholeness, which is identity.

Identity is the beginning of understanding and accepting ourselves as we are. And, therefore, making us ready to accept and understand others as we find them. This—looking at the individual as a system—is what J. Krishnamurti meant when he wrote in *You Are the World* (1972):

"In oneself lies the whole world, and if you know how to look and learn, then the door is there and the key is in your hand. Nobody on earth can give you either that key or the door to open, except you."

The current popular jargon—especially in the business and professional world—is 'the systems approach.' This holistic view is consistent with identity and purposeful performance. Systems researcher Russell Ackoff puts it poetically:

"If you take a system apart to identify its components, and then operate those components in such a way that every component behaves as well as it possibly can, there is one thing of which you can be sure. The system as a whole will not behave as well as it can. Now that is counter-intuitive to Machine Age thinking, but it is absolutely essential to 'systems thinking.'

"The corollary to this is that if you have a system that is behaving as well as it can, none of its parts will be."

These new ways of thinking have tremendous implications for the organization. When a department is trying to outperform all others, it means it is not supporting other departments as well as it might. Or, it is doing well at the expense of other departments. Likewise, when an individual is not accepted on the basis of his or her peculiar characteristics, attributes, and talents—instead is force-fitted into a job—the results will surely be discouraging for all.

A systems perspective requires recognition and acceptance of differences—different skills, different attitudes, different dispositions, and different personalities. The current climate in the American culture, however, has room for words that denote 'differences,' but little room for the requisite behaviors.

The organization continues to 'kill' itself trying to make workers fit the job and its preordained expectations. The more the organization fails in this obstinate course, the harder it tries to make it so. Linear logic is its guide, and no one seems to notice that, like a horse with blinders, it plows directly straight ahead—missing opportunity after opportunity with employees who have a range far beyond its expectations. And, once again, everybody loses.

Putting Our Macho Complex to Rest

We must rethink much of what we have been taught to think and blend the possibilities of the Western mind with Eastern maturity. This involves marrying the left brain with the right brain and uniting our ability to think rationally with our ability to think intuitively. The left brain is the home of technology; of science and industry. The right brain is the home of art, music, and religion—where the symphony of the human intellect paints the landscape of life.

The left brain resists the intuitive hunch because it is not founded on facts. The right brain resists the left brain because there is little display of sensitivity. It is a war, more damaging and ubiquitously threatening than the destructive power of thermonuclear weapons. It is a war that's been waged since the dawn of man, continuing now in the afternoon of his experience.

We know so much about so many things, and so little about ourselves. We establish societies and nationalities; create languages and cultures to support them; and then we maintain our splendid isolation from ourselves and our reality.

What is germane to this discussion is that the *Religion of Technology* has created a new dogma that forms a *cultural* barrier between the left and right brain, the worker and work, the worker and manager, and the Western and Eastern world of thinking.

Workers and managers are struggling with each other. The results today are lower productivity and less purposeful performance in America; tomorrow, in the world. Now, with the globalization of economic interdependence, it has grave consequences. Find the answer to individuals and their relationships with themselves, with each other, and with their respective organizations, and you are well on your way to finding the answer the whole world is seeking.

The left brain is associated with the male; the right brain with the female. In human biology, of course, masculine and feminine characteristics exist in everyone. Sex roles are learned, not genetic behavior. Nobody has a predisposition to act 'male' or 'female.' Yet, all men are supposed to be masculine, and all women, feminine (Figure 6-1). This has meant giving men leading roles and most of society's privileges.

The rational mind is linear, focused, and analytical. It belongs to the realm of the intellect, whose function is to discriminate, measure, and categorize. Thus, rational knowledge tends to be fragmented.

The intuitive mind is based on direct, nonintellectual experience of reality arising out of a state of expanding awareness. Intuitive knowledge tends to be synthesizing, holistic, and nonlinear. Holistic, incidentally, is from the Greek 'holos,' whole, and refers to an understanding of reality in terms of integrated wholes whose properties cannot be reduced to those of smaller units.

EXPECTATIONS OF MEN	EXPECTATIONS OF WOMEN
Active and Productive	Passive and Receptive
Rational and Cognitive	Irrational and Intuitive
Aggressive, Competitive, even Ruthless	Responsive, Cooperative, and Consolidating
Conscious of Themselves	Conscious of Environment
'Thinkers'	'Feelers'
Inclined toward Science	Inclined toward Mysticism

Figure 6-1: American traditional societal expectations
of men and women

Looking at the list of opposites in Figure 6-2, it is easy to see that American society consistently favors the 'masculine brain' over the 'feminine brain,' rational knowledge over intuitive wisdom, science over religion, competition over cooperation, exploitation of natural resources over conservation, etc. This emphasis, well-supported by our paternalistic system of management, has led to a profound cultural imbalance. This imbalance lies at the root of our current crisis—an imbalance in thoughts and feelings, values and attitudes, and our social and political structures.

In the Eastern view, there appears two kinds of activity:

- Activity in harmony with nature;
- Activity against the natural flow of things.

The Eastern mind prefers the former to the latter. The Western mind, on the other hand, has been determined to conquer and exploit nature; to make nature conform to the requirements of man. A recurring misconception is that the Eastern viewpoint is, therefore, passive, while the Western view is active. This is misleading.

LEFT BRAIN	RIGHT BRAIN
Masculine	Feminine
Demanding	Contracting
Aggressive	Responsive
Competitive	Cooperative
Rational and Cognitive	Intuitive and Affective
Analytical	Synthesizing
Concrete Orientation	Conceptual Orientation

Figure 6-2: A Framework of Reference for Exploring American Cultural Values and Attitudes

The Eastern view seeks a balance between man's needs and the requirements of nature. Conversely, the Western view sees us retreating from polar opposites, rather than integrating them into a cohesive strategy. For example, the American culture takes pride in being scientific. Our time is referred to as the 'Scientific Age.' Science is used to making nature submit to its will. Clearly, nature has been seen as the enemy, and all the guns of science have been trained on this adversary.

Consequently, the natural has all but disappeared in our foods, with chemical additives and preservatives robbing us of Nature's natural flavors. There is no telling how much damage science has done to ecosystems and their ecological balance. Incidentally, in Europe they still use natural fertilizers and refrain from adding chemical preservatives to milk and bread. This means the shelf life of these products nil. And you must shop daily for these staples. The taste, of course, is well worth the inconvenience.

Unquestionably, America is dominated by rational thinking and scientific knowledge (which is frequently considered the only acceptable knowledge). This 'Macho Complex' finds little room for intuitive knowledge, or awareness, which is just as valid and reliable. Generally speaking, intuitive knowledge is not recognized at all. We are mesmerized by the near magic powers of science, unwilling or unable to consider the costs of this adulation. This attitude is widespread, pervading our educational system as well as our commercial, social, religious, and political institutions.

Since the celebrated statement of Descartes, "I think, therefore, I am," we have, as Fritjof Capra puts it, "retreated into our minds, forgotten how to think with our bodies, how to use them as agents of knowing." [5] In so retreating, we have cut ourselves off from the natural environment; have forgotten how to commune with nature and cooperate with man.

What left-brain 'Macho' dominance has meant is that virtually everything gets thrown out of proportion. A simple example is the idea that 'more is better,' or if something is good, more of the same will be even better.

As another example, we have expected intellectual power, scientific knowledge, and technological skill to go hand-in-hand with wisdom, ethics, and spiritual well-being. But you can see from this discussion that there is great disparity between wisdom and knowledge. As noted here, the vast majority of our leaders— whatever their profession or discipline—are close to bankrupt when it comes to wisdom and ethics. And this has nothing to do with how knowledgeable they might be.

From yet another perspective, it is unfortunate so much emphasis is placed upon sexual preference. When you think of how little of our actual life is sexual, and how much more our preoccupation with it dominates our thinking, one can puzzle at this misdirected energy.

This obsessive compulsive behavior has made a major industry of a fantasy product, sex. As the preeminent sociologist, Pitrim Sorokin, has written, it is when we are least sexual that we are the most preoccupied with sex. [6]

321

People of a particularly gentle persuasion, for example, are frequently well acquainted with 'right brain' thinking. They have a different perspective (and perception) than their 'Macho Male' brothers. They have made meaningful contact with their feminine nature, which we all possess, and have learned from it. They often demonstrate a subtle awareness of things cultural, showing a natural affinity for the aesthetic, from poetry to painting, from drama to didactics. And we desperately need minds of this kind in the boardrooms across America, as well as in every other walk of professional life. We need poetry in commerce, government, and industry. Engineers, economists, and political scientists have done about all the damage we can stand... perhaps more than we can absorb. [7]

America's one-sided, one-dimensional progress has reached the alarming stage. This situation is so contradictory that it borders on insanity:

- We can control a soft landing of a space craft on distant planets, but we cannot control the polluting fumes emanating from our automobiles and factories.

- We propose Utopian communities in gigantic space colonies, but we cannot manage crime in our cities.

- The business community salutes the terrific growth of the pet food and cosmetic industries as signs of progress, but we cannot afford to feed the homeless or to provide health care for the needy. Obamacare is meant to ameliorate this shortfall, but Affordable Healthcare is yet to be proven the remedy to this pervasive societal problem.

- We are among the 'best educated' of Western nations in terms of per capita high school and college graduates—with arguably the best university system in the West—but fewer Americans read books, are multilingual, or are familiar with the culture or geography of other nations, much less their own. In fact, some see the American educational system as 'killing the spirit' of the American student to learn.

Regarding the latter, noted historian Page Smith in *Killing The Spirit* (1990) leaves no doubt on the failure of America's great universities to educate. He sees these universities divided into departments which compete against each other for funds and students and speak in jargon comprehensible only within their ranks, forming a modern Tower of Babel. Indeed, the problem is pervasive throughout the American culture.

No. 2: Recognizing and Dealing with the Ambivalence of American Values

Some 300 years ago, America broke away from the confining shackles of European society to establish its own identity. Some 200 years ago, America produced an incredible body of men who were multidimensional and dedicated to establishing the individual American spirit. They were not afraid to be different, to be *Outsiders*, not afraid to cultivate the inner world of expression as they sensed it.

Walt Whitman captured this spirit when he proclaimed with innocence and exuberance:

"I am larger and better than I thought. I did not know that I held so much greatness."

Yet, we bristle when someone makes such a proclamation. We think greatness is rare, whereas Whitman knew that the seeds of greatness are in all. Where are the Walt Whitmans of today? Where are the voices of *The Outsider* who march to their own drummer as did Henry David Thoreau?

Many of the giants of our republic lived in the late 18th and early 19th Centuries, including John Adams, John Quincy

Adams, William Cullen Bryant, Aaron Burr, John Calhoun, James Fenimore Cooper, Ralph Waldo Emerson, Benjamin Franklin, Horace Greeley, Nathanael Greene, Alexander Hamilton, Nathaniel Hawthorne, Oliver Wendell Holmes, Andrew Jackson, John Jay, Thomas Jefferson, Abraham Lincoln, James Madison, Herman Melville, James Monroe, Henry David Thoreau, George Washington, and Daniel Webster.

These men were essentially aristocrats in temperament and democrats in spirit. They had a quiet reverence for things mystical, but a consuming passion for living life to the fullest. America was young and had not yet succumbed to debilitating mediocrity. Nor had it been consumed with self-conscious self-approval. Henry David Thoreau's *Walden* (1854) and Ralph Waldo Emerson's *Self Reliance & Other Essays* (1844) were expressions of man in a new 'Transcendentalism.'

Transcendentalism flourished briefly in New England during the first half of the 19th Century. Never a systematic philosophy, it held the romantic view that individual intuition was the highest form of knowledge and that God was immanent in nature. Much influenced by Eastern religious teachings, many of these early American thinkers held a mystical belief in individualism in harmony with all things in nature. In a word, these early Americans displayed 'balance.'

It was during this same period that Alexis de Tocqueville captured this nuance in his *Democracy in America* (1835). He outlined the advantages and shortcomings of democratic political and social systems providing his assessment of the values and hazards to the democratic way of life that are still pertinent today.

Richard Reeves relived Tocqueville's journey in his book, *American Journey: Traveling with Tocqueville in Search of America* (1982). Reeves reaffirmed how right Tocqueville was when he could see the nation moving away from greatness toward comfortable indifference. Put otherwise, a case can be made that America has been trading off on its early greatness for the past 150 years. [8]

Look at any organization in America, and you will find the same arid landscapes Tocqueville warned could develop due to laxity under an indifferent democracy. Education is an excellent example:

Even at our most prestigious universities, Page Smith proclaims in *Killing the Spirit* (1990), there is not an opportunity for a decent education because teachers are not personally involved with their students. Students get instruction, not education, in the form of information transfers, communication techniques, or impersonal and antiseptic phrases to cover 'non-teaching teaching' to facilitate 'non-learning learning.'

Interaction between professors and students is minimal or non-existent because professors are preoccupied with scholarly research and publication. Career minded faculty, Smith notes, cannot afford to spend time with students. They must 'publish or perish' by having their 'scholarly' tomes appear in the 'right' journals. This helps them win promotion and tenure, which means they stay employed.

The results are what Smith calls a 'cult of dullness,' in which clear writing and inspired lecturing are deviant and suspicious behaviors. Nothing is done to challenge the system—the prevailing mode of thinking or 'doing.' This, incidentally, fits nicely into the industrial model of 'non-thinking to do non-doing of non-thing things,' because what these professors have to say, according to Smith, amounts to practically nothing at all.

This has been the curse of such acclaimed American writers as John Updike. Granville Hick's *Saturday Review of Literature* critiques Updike's early works, and laments, "he writes like an angel, if only he had something to say."

'Style has come to eclipse substance; impression to take precedence over making a difference.' Smith calls this 'scientism,' a devotion to the scientific approach to all fields of study, including the humanities. This has driven the spiritual values out of our universities, leaving a desert like arid climate.

This dedication to research would be defensible, Smith admits, if it involved purposeful performance in the sense that the product of the research had some value to the classroom or to greater society. "The vast majority (of scholarly works)," he writes, "are mediocre, expensive and unnecessary."

And who pays for all this 'non-teaching teaching and non-learning learning'?

You might think it is borne by the parents who make the sacrifices for their sons and daughters—now as high as $240,000 for a four-year degree. However, it is American taxpayers who ultimately foot the bill, as major universities are heavily endowed with government contracts and concessions.

What Tocqueville predicted about America 150 years ago has largely come to pass. What will it be like 150 years hence?

Cut across American society, from the academic community to the government, from industry to commerce, from religious institutions to charitable organizations, and without exception, you will find there is no place for greatness to exist, or to be cultivated. These organizations appear instead to be obsessed with internal politics, which often are so vicious there is little energy left for coping, much less for excellence.

The paradox is that the only hope for America is with the rising aristocracy of professional/technical workers. The burgeoning professional class must take hold of its power and celebrate differences and diversity as 'aristocrats in temperament and democrats in spirit.' Obviously, the traditional formula for organizational continuity and succession planning will never get us there. Indeed, it has succeeded magnificently in giving relevance to the Baron Macaulay refrain:

> *Was none who would be foremost*
> *To lead such dire attack;*
> *But those behind cried "Forward!"*
> *And those before cried "Back!"*

We need leadership as we have never needed it before. We need greatness as it once existed when we were relatively new as a nation. We need changes; real changes. We need balance and humor and love and industry. We need thinking that is inter disciplinarian and holistic.

What we don't need is an organization of 'like-thinkers and-doers' who have rarely experienced an original thought, but know how to get promoted. You know the type:

- They buy the 'company line' lock, stock, and barrel.

- They research the company etiquette and then teach the course.

- They 'get results,' and the results they get are the results expected.

- They epitomize the corporate value system, from the way they dress, to how they walk and talk and carry the company torch.

- They have the kind of family they are expected to have (preferably two-children, a boy and a girl, who are bright, good looking, and a credit to the family and company).

- They belong to the right religion, and they go to the right church in the right congregation, on a regular basis.

- They volunteer for the appropriate causes and become involved at the level expected.

- They live in the right neighborhood, with the right type and style of house, which has appropriate architecture and landscaping.

- They shop at the right stores, buying the appropriate brands of merchandise, supporting the products of customers and vendors alike.

- They prepare the right kinds of meals, entertain at the appropriate time excepted of them for their function and level in the organization, and with the right kind of decorum.

- They spend the expected number of hours at work and at home with their family. Outside of work, they pursue familiar pursuits of someone like them in their station and career.

- They vacation in a manner appropriate to their level of compensation and consistent with what others like them have done in the past.

- They are friends with their colleagues on the basis of invitation and approval.

Men and women of this description are running America... into the ground.

On the other hand, Americans of a 'different persuasion'— who live, breathe, and understand what is actually going on in the organization, and who have all the appropriate skills to do the job—would have little chance to be candidates for promotion, much less accepted members of this group if they were any of the following:

- A 40+ year-old bachelor or spinster
- A confessed lesbian or homosexual
- Openly promiscuous
- Suspected to be chemically dependent
- An AIDS patient
- Too short, too fat, too tall, too thin, too old, too young, too experienced, too inexperienced, too stupid, too bright, too obsequious, too independent, too secretive,

too candid, too gregarious, too reclusive, too aggressive, too passive… too extreme

- Openly disenchanted with company policy
- Openly opposed to the bureaucratic 'games'
- Bored with 'motherhood' pontifications of the CEO and openly expressive of that fact
- Too self-righteous and individualistic; 'not a team player'
- Too theoretical, conceptual, abstract—too literate
- Too prone to 'tell it like it is'
- 'Not for sale!' 'Can't be bought!' 'Nobody has a line on them.'

Many young men and women enter the organization with their idealism and values clearly on display. From that point forward, they give in or give out, because most American organizations have a low tolerance for diversity of opinion and behavior… and, again, everybody loses.

Throughout our history, greatness has come in strange packages. Walt Whitman, an acknowledged homosexual, would tail President Lincoln as if obsessed with capturing a glimpse of him. A strange, wonderful man, today many critics consider him America's greatest poet. Whitman proclaimed the freedom and dignity of the common man, and he sang the praises of democracy. He had an incalculable affect on later poets, inspiring them to experiment in prosody as well as subject matter. Indeed, he celebrated himself: "I did not know that I held so much greatness." But could he function in today's American society? Would his genius shine?

The One-Dimensional Society

To discover the source of this aversion to greatness, you need to look no further than our educational system. Romantic formalism, and its quest for egalitarianism have placed 'skills training' above 'knowledge building' or content learning. And so, instrumental education has taken precedence over classical education.

Consequently, the managers of most American corporations and government bodies have received vocational training at the expense of the classics. Page Smith sees Ivy League education being reduced from thinking to technique, and from teaching to instructing. And, because you deal with what you know, that is what the organization and its people get—vocational leadership and vocational training.

This represents a problem for the organization. If its management thinks mainly in terms of utility (e.g., from a vocational education perspective), or what it can get out of the individual, the individual will logically think in like terms—or what can be gotten out of the organization. This equation contains no interest in 'giving,' 'sharing,' or, for that matter, in 'purposeful performance.'

At another level—similar to what we learned about the behavior of professors at our great universities—vocational education puts the emphasis on doing only what makes people successful in their careers. "That is what America values," they say to themselves, and they gravitate toward an America that is increasingly becoming a 'One Dimensional Society.'

In this context, a MBA degree is merely a vocational degree. It is as vocational as learning a trade in trade school. Essentially ignorant of their world, many MBAs scoff at the mere mention of the cultural implications of their work. Moreover, being trained in a set of skills (finance, management, information systems, computers, digital electronics, etc.), they are unlikely to be acculturated to the background reading listed below. This reading, incidentally, might prove useful to them for a truly multidimensional, international perspective of the competitive world they have joined:

- Homer's The Iliad: The Odyssey
- The Bible

- The Trojan Wars
- The Torah
- Aristophanes (*The Birds)*
- The Koran
- Euripides (Cyclops)
- The Bhagavad Gita
- Sophocles (Oedipus Rex)
- The Holy Crusades
- Plato (The Republic)
- Alexander the Great
- Julius Caesar (The Gallic Wars)
- The Epistles of St. Paul
- Mediations of Marcus Aurelius
- Edward Gibbon's Decline and Fall of the Roman Empire

As the French say, "The more things change, the more they remain the same." This tip of the cultural iceberg would probably surprise novice readers, reflecting as did Solomon, "There is nothing new under the sun." After all, we are the product of thousands of years of acculturating experience, which makes knowing something about our cultural heritage a good deal more consequential than being obsessed with our family genealogy. The 'family of man' is technically and culturally a family, making us all brothers and sisters. The better we understand this, and the more we know about how to use it the greater the possibility we can live and work together in harmony throughout the world.

Chances are this discussion of the 'one dimensional' character of American society has made you anxious, perhaps angry, or even bored... all indicators of the deterministic bent of our American minds. Most of this type of reading has been excised from high school and college curricula, being placed under the rubric not applicable information.

Look at the leaders of our government and the major corporations of American business and industry. Most have little time for reading and less inclination to acculturating experience, for where is the instrumental value? Read books written by these 'no nonsense' government and corporate leaders, and you will find few if any references to their ancient counterparts. They are essentially men and women with vocational mindsets and perspective, playing 'quick and easy' games with America's future. If that seems harsh, it is meant to, for there is little evidence that we can be reassured otherwise.

The Hunt for the American Character

Given this 'one dimensional' mentality, it should come as no surprise that we have sought the answers to the American Dilemma with a one-dimensional approach to the problem. We have placed all our trust in the 'rational solution' to purposeful performance by using half our brain and, as a result, have come up 'half empty.' We have attempted to solve the problem with the same type of thinking that caused the problem in the first place.

Over the years, the deficiency of this approach has been acknowledged with *'Reader's Digest*/McCult-type' systems for closing the cultural gap between the left and right brain:

- There is the 'Aspen Institute,' catering to executives in a rather picturesque distracting clime.

- The Great Books Club, which caters more to professionals who feel they have been educationally 'short changed.'

- Then there are such corporate-sponsored *Learning Centers* as those exemplified by Xerox and General Electric, which are sometimes 'on' again and 'off' again.

- And, across the continental United States, we have 'not for profit' and 'for profit' satellite cultural-fix operations, such as *The Center For Creative Leadership* (Greensboro, NC.) and *The Tom Peters Group* (Silicon Valley, CA.), which genuinely attempt to make a difference, but mainly make an impression.

All of these efforts are 'instant pudding' attempts at developing more integrative thinking in promoting cultural awareness, leadership and value change, which, given the most generous of resources and the time allotted to attack the problem, should take at least 50 years. You cannot overcome a century of progressive neglect by the miracle of laudatory enterprise.

Only time and attention will overcome the *cultural bias* of the American character. It will be decades before the American psyche will routinely:

- Reestablish the sanctity and stability of the American family;
- Advocate creativity over conformity;
- Champion cooperation over competition;
- Celebrate greatness over mediocrity;
- Honor students with original ideas over students with good grades;
- Award high school diplomas only to students who are minimally bilingual and pass a comprehensive basic skills examination;
- Prize making a difference over making an impression;
- Mobilize and utilize diversity and difference in organizational effectiveness;
- Sponsor, recognize and reward teamwork over individual performance;

- Encourage a cosmopolitan perspective over a parochial point of view;

- Find parents willing to support their offspring's school debate or piano recital over their athletic achievements;

- Support the arts equivalent to that of professional sports today, including comparable compensation for artists to that of athletes;

- Support making teachers the highest paid of all professions, rather than, now, being nearly the lowest paid.

If this sounds ambitious, compare it to what our main competitors are doing right now and then give pause.

No. 3: Changing the Organization Structure from a Physical to a Psychological Climate

If the organization knows what it wants to accomplish and is structured to accomplish it, it will succeed because it will experience purposeful performance. On the other hand, if the organization knows what it wants to accomplish, but is not structured to accomplish it, it will fail because it will experience dysfunctional performance.

Structure should be designed to facilitate the organization's function. Likewise, structure should facilitate three-way communications, vertically and horizontally—up and down and across functional lines. It is imperative everyone who needs to know, does, preferably before, not after, changes are made.

In any case, the information explosion has made quality communication more important than ever. 'Quantity' communication, which is somewhat in vogue, springs from the belief that employees should know about everything that is happening. This is not only impossible; it can be highly counterproductive.

The *Information Requirements of Employees* follow the rules of common sense:

- Employees want information to do a good job.
- They want to make the right decisions in their work.
- They want to have the information that affects them personally.
- They want information that ensures their personal growth and development.

The four commonsense Principles of Communication are:

- How does the information affect me personally?
- How does the information affect me professionally?
- How does the information impact on what I am now doing?
- How does it 'sound' (i.e., is it believable; does it make sense)?

The organization's structure should facilitate decision-making at its lowest levels in order to expedite real time response to changing work demands. The criteria for truly effective decision-making:

- Occurs at the right level;
- Involves the right people;
- Takes place at the right time.

Structure must clarify *roles* and *resources* available for carrying out the intended strategy. In the same sense that job descriptions have become meaningless, concerns about responsibility and authority are passé' in this context. It is *role identity* that is critical to organizational success—*role identity and the relationship of roles.* Once these are understood, authority and responsibility flow naturally to the requirements of the situation.

Using our basketball analogy, one player's role may be 'to penetrate the defense as point guard and create the offense,' while another's role may be 'to screen the weak side guard to set up the small forward in three-point range,' etc.

Pat Riley, the successful former coach of the Los Angeles Lakers, and now president of the Miami Heats, tells a story on himself as a player, which illustrates knowing your role and the relationship of roles.

The Lakers were playing in the NBA championship game, and only seconds remained on the clock. The ball came to Riley at the top of the key. He was wide open and took the shot. He missed. The Lakers lost. In the dressing room after the game, trying to console himself on the missed shot, he said, "I was wide open," to nobody in particular. "You were wide open," Wilt Chamberlain, the great center declared, "Because nobody was guarding you."

It was sharpshooter Jerry West's role to take the shot. Riley's role was to get the ball to West. But he didn't because—momentarily—he forgot his role and tried to assume the role of another. This happens every day in the organization and with similar consequences.

Role identity should be based on special skills and the knowledge to do a particular job. Each person contributes to the process on the basis of well-defined, complementary roles—not on position power. A particular role, however, may find an individual 'taking charge' when his expertise is demanded. On another occasion, his role may be that of supportive player.

Many organizations are exploring 'self-management work teams.' Understandably, these are experimental pilot programs, and they must create *the psychological climate* necessary for the role identity to work as it does on athletic teams.

That said the organization continues to play one of its favorite games—*reorganization.* Since reorganization is recurrently an act of frustration, devoid of patient deliberation, this seldom works and more restructuring follows. Constant restructuring is a good sign the organization is 'out of control.' Missing in this understanding is that structure today is:

Far less a mechanistic or physical activity and
Far more a psychological climatic condition.

Such activities, as relocating personnel; moving offices and furniture; redefining functional responsibilities; and feverishly updating organizational charts, have little positive impact on the organization—perhaps no more than 20 percent.

Meanwhile, in direct contrast to this inconsequential activity, the appropriate *psychological climate* can produce an improvement in organizational effectiveness as great as 80 percent.

Management—playing its 'worry beads' of reorganization—may placate itself temporarily, but such activity has little permanent impact. On the other hand, cumbersome as an organization might be (even with too many levels of nonfunctional management), if the organization's psychological climate:

- Advances an easily, identifiable *mission statement,* which all employees can understand and buy into, along with a set of guiding principles supporting that statement;

- Cultivates a *common language* reflecting the shared values, which all workers support and believe to be true;

- Presents a *consistent message* in all its communiques that is in tune with this mission, these principles and values; and

- *Walks its talk* in virtually everything it does, recognizing that symbolic interaction and managing perceptions are critical to the success of its leadership; then, *people have the will* to overcome seemingly insurmountable deficiencies.

Remember, it is not 'the perfect' organization that succeeds, but the happy and healthy one. Such an organization has a sense of humor about itself, along with the wisdom to balance risk and opportunity with prudence.

This is not to suggest that 'tree trimming' (see Figure 1-3) is not advisable, but simply to point out how powerful the *psychological climate* can be in creating purposeful performance. Far too frequently, it is ignored as more of that soft stuff when it produces consistently hard data.

By the same token, once the 'psychological climate' is established, managers who are dysfunctional will wither away like dead branches on a tree, eventually falling off of their own accord, thus strengthening the organization. Once again, a reminder that purposeful performance is realized largely by not seeking it directly.

The Structure A Psychological Entity

One American automotive company has made a major turnaround in a ten-year period. So remarkable was this resurrection that an acquaintance, in a consultant's role, called on this company to learn more about this success. The morning of the visit, when he tried to start his rental car, it wouldn't start. Thirty minutes late for his appointment, he expressed his embarrassment to the security guard at the information desk upon arriving at the company's international headquarters.

Looking the consultant in the eye, the guard asked, "What kind of car are you driving, sir?" He breathed a sigh of relief when told. "I would have been very surprised if it were one of ours," he said. "You see, our mission is to make the best automobiles in the world. We are all dedicated to that purpose."

The consultant smiled, put on his visitor's badge, and proceeded to the elevator. There, while waiting, he engaged in conversation with two engineers, bringing up his recent car problem. Their response was quite similar to that expressed by the security guard. Intrigued with this coincidence, when the consultant reached the appointed office, he checked to see what the secretary's response might be. Again, it was the same. Without fanfare, each person clearly and simply repeated *Ford Motor Company's* 'mission statement.'

This was not an accident. Nor was it coincidental to learn that everyone spoke the same language or that considerable effort had gone into circulating a consistent message. Clearly, the psychological climate here made a deep impression on the consultant. As one United Auto Workers union official put it, "We've always had these banners around 'Treat People with Respect.' Now, it is clear that we mean it."

This visit was made in 1989. Ford was thought to be a goner in 1980, but by 1989, it was the top American competitor in the automotive industry. What happened?

Ford got smart about people. Small wonder that in 2008 when General Motors and Chrysler had to ask for a bailout by the federal government, Ford was able to manage its operations through that cataclysmic business downturn without participating (see "Beverly Geber's "The Resurrection of Ford," Training magazine, April 1989).

Mixed Messages

This caused the consultant to look more closely at some 'mixed messages' that had been advanced in other organizations—organizations that were finding it difficult to even decide what business they were in, to the confusion of many employees. In conversations with these employees, here are some typical responses:

"We are told, on the one hand, that we want to grow the business and, on the other hand that we need to cut costs."

"We are encouraged to be innovators—even entrepreneurs—and then they define our jobs, responsibilities, and activities so absolutely that we have no room to move, much less think."

"We are advised of the importance of performance, and then the emphasis is put on conformity."

"We play psychological games with each other—nothing gets spelled out in behavior."

"We verbalize about building trust and use the words like empty calories out of the vending machines."

"We speak constantly about 'team work' as if you can get anywhere if you are a team player. Come on!"

"We talk about 'planning our work' and 'working our plan.' In 30 years here, I've seen only one kind of management rewarded—crisis management."

There is a perverted consistency here as well, for these remarks came from a diverse group, including senior managers, engineers, administrators, and custodial workers.

The 'psychological climate' is pervasive in any organization, driven by its 'cultural bias,' and can be either positive or negative, managed or out-of-control. People are not bricks, mortar and cement. They need special cultivation and attention, but the payback is many times greater than any other physical asset.

Psychological Forces Within The Organizational Structure

Getting a grasp of the situation starts with recognizing that employees are organizations within themselves. They are the nucleus from which the organization builds itself to purposeful performance—or to relative dysfunction:

- You can't treat some employees with respect and not others.

- You can't favor some employees and expect other employees to applaud your efforts.

- You can't share 'company secrets' with some employees and put other employees in the category of 'not needing to know.'
- You can't make demands on some employees and treat others with 'kid gloves.'

MISSION

To win the proposal and dedicate all our energies to that purpose. We are a single team in which the focus is always on what is best for the team to win.

VALUES

How we accomplish the mission is as important as the mission itself. Fundamental to our successes are:

- People—team members are the source of our strength, their skills the core to our winning.
- Results—the quality of our results will be the result of our joint efforts, the differentiator.
- Winning—winning as a team is the ultimate achievement. It secures everyone's future.
- Fun—a spirit of fun surrounds this opportunity, giving everyone room to express their talents.

GUIDING PRINCIPLES

- Quality of the proposal comes first—to win, the quality of our joint efforts must be top priority.
- Members of the team are our first customers—our work must put our team members first in order to do a quality job.

- Continuous improvement is essential to our success—we must create a climate for innovation and doing things differently to make this a unique and winning proposal.

- Total involvement is a key to our success—we are a team with everyone participating. We must treat each other with trust and respect.

- Integrity is never compromised—we must conduct ourselves in a responsible and ethical manner.

Figure 6-3: An Aerospace Proposal Team Mission, Values and Guiding Principles.

All employees must feel that they are special; that they are important; and that they are making meaningful contributions to the success of the organization. Three basic psychological forces within the infrastructure of peoples' make-up determine whether they are in control of their lives and in a 'readiness' mood to make a meaningful contribution:

The forces within the *self* and between the *Ideal Self* and the *Real Self*;

The forces within the *situation* determines how the situation will be defined;

The forces within *others* and between *Self-Demands* and *Role Demands*.

If the organization fails to communicate a *clear mission*, to develop a *common language*, and to resonate a *consistent message*, there is likely to be a constant battle of individual employees with themselves (between 'the *Ideal Self* and the *Real Self*).

We are not very accepting of ourselves as we are and look for reasons to justify this conflict. On the smallest pretense, we can move away from seeing things clearly, to reading all kinds of negative implications into organizational communiques, or the behavior of others towards us.

Self-deception plays an important part in poorly *defining the situation,* whereas self-acceptance plays an equally important part in seeing things 'as they are.' When things are seen clearly, *The Mad Monarchs* have no place in the equation (refer to the "Fisher Model of Conflict and Stress," Figure 4-5, page 157). When the organization and the individual are in tune with each other, these six silent killers vanish and purposeful performance takes their place.

Paul Hersey likes to use 'maturity' or 'readiness' to describe purposeful behavior in his *Situational Leadership Model.* Maturity is a useful term for this discussion. When the organization treats its employees with maturity (i.e., as adults), their *readiness* to act responsibly improves significantly. They are more apt to respond positively to otherwise negative situations, including occasional ambiguities, chaotic developments, or even sporadic crises. The key here is:

How the organization views workers terms of maturity and the type of climate it creates for them.

They are more prone to be flexible and able to meet unforeseen challenges, if their minds and bodies are healthy.

If the forces within the 'situation' and the individual's 'self' are in a healthy state, then the individual should have little problem balancing *self-demands* and *role-demands.* If not, the individual's behavior may be erratic to the extreme of paranoia. Once again, there is a natural conflict between these two demands, which depends largely on the maturity of the individual. The more mature ('ready') the individual, the more appropriate their actions will fit the situation (see Figures 6-4).

SELF DEMANDS

- Need to protect fragile ego;

- Need to let people know 'how important you are'; 'how experienced and good you are'; and 'how lucky they are to be working with you';

- Need to identify with people who personify your 'ego-ideal,' by name-dropping, etc.;

- Need to project personal bias and build power base around it.

ROLE DEMANDS

- Perceive situation in order to focus on facilitating group in interactive behavior;

- Demonstrate competence and caring in earning group's trust and respect by serving them and meeting their needs through leadership;

- Show an easy grace in contributing to the self-confidence and self-esteem of others;

- Assist others in discovering and using their own unique capabilities.

Figure 6-4: Some personal reactions to demands.

What a difference people make when their personal systems (i.e., their values, beliefs, expectations and perceptions), are working toward the same purposeful performance. Likewise, when the forces within the organization are in balance:

- The structure facilitates carrying out the organization's mission.
- Everyone knows what is expected of them and why.
- Work is congruent (it is organized to meet a common goal, not structured to create conflict and confusion among functional disciplines).
- The structure supports its stated function.
- The structure fosters cooperation, collaboration, and open communication.
- Work is fun, and everyone enjoys what they are doing.
- The structure supports a creative climate of purposeful enterprise.
- The structure supports individual growth and development.

Thus, the problem with structure is less a physical phenomenon than a psychological one. It should not start with 'flattening the pyramid.' That will come in due course, as role identity, role relationships, and teamwork evolve, thus fragmenting and eventually dissolving inappropriate *cultural biases.*

Even 'management creep,' which is certainly a concern, will first stagnate and then drop off precipitously, as the psychological climate is created and sustained... for professionals 'to show their stuff.' There will be little reason or no motivation to encourage pyramid climbers. As this climate pulls the organization in the direction of contribution, purposeful performance will eventually eclipse dysfunction, driving out many of the dreaded symptomatic organizational problems of today, such as a winning personality (making an impression) taking precedence over doing the job (performance). Again, it is indirection that is the answer. The best way to realize purposeful performance is not to seek it.

Ford Motor Company has shown what a giant can do. But even Ford admits it is involved in a revolution that will take at least a generation or more to reach its appointed objective.

Figure 6-5: The Cry of the Future [9].

No. 4: Coping with Leaderless Leadership

The 'paradoxical dilemma' of our times is that professionals cannot lead and do not want to follow.

Do you want to lead? Probably not. Does that mean most of us want to lead? Again, probably not. Now, here comes the rub. Why is it most people don't like to be led? They want to believe they are in charge. Then, why don't most people lead? *Because they simply don't know how to lead.* And so, most American organizations have a management system and call it *leadership.*

Leadership is in a state of retreat bordering on confusion. Not only is leadership out-of-date, but also out-of-touch with the reality of work and workers. Because the leadership culture programs the way workers behave, corporations get the leadership and behavior they deserve (see James R. Fisher, Jr.'s "Leadership Manifesto: Typology of Leaderless Leadership," AQP Journal, Winter 2002).

The central issue of leadership is understanding what is meant. Does it mean 'strutting your stuff'—does it mean compliance, coordination—does it mean management?

Compliance suggests some arbitrary constraints to affect behavior, such as coercion and manipulation, neither of which connote leadership. People follow leaders, not because they have to, but because they want to. When there is *coercion,* it is 'leadership' of a most finite duration. People will only take so much coercion and then they rebel by resisting. Before they rebel overtly, however, they'll sabotage operations via the *six silent killers.*

• Cooperation is voluntary and given freely. • Compliance is involuntary and coercive.

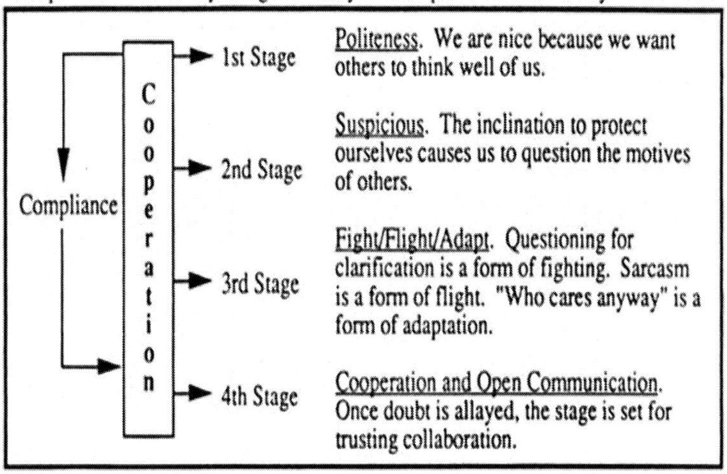

Figure 6-6: Sequential Chronology of Interpersonal Relations.

Obviously, there has to be some *coordination* in order for the followers to effectively follow. But when 'coordination' is the central thrust of 'leadership,' it becomes simply management. Management is a mechanistic, maintenance function which secures and perpetuates the *status quo*. It is the comfortable home of *logical positivism* and *scientific empiricism*. Management was invented to sustain the 'secular religion' of technocracy. When the German philosopher Nietzsche proclaimed, "God is dead," the religion of materialistic scientism was born, and nascent management, in all its bureaucratic splendor, followed soon after.

We, as followers, want an opportunity to express our ideas, to be appreciated for our contributions, to give vent to our aspirations, and to demonstrate our unique individualism. We yearn to display our talents, to show our form. In brief, we want to manage ourselves with an acceptable level of freedom, control and trust:

- *Freedom* to give individual expression to our work;

- *Control* of the work we do;

- *Trust* that we will be successful, but with empathetic support if we should fail.

Given a supportive work climate, we will follow with exuberance as long as the leadership leads us to improvement on the job and in our capacity to control our lives. But this is also where it becomes a somewhat 'sticky wicket':

If we follow at the expense of *Pleasing Self*, deluding ourselves that we are happy and fulfilled, or that we have 'no choice,' we are moving toward *management dependence* and the *Culture of Comfort*.

If we get caught up in "what a great job I have—benefits and all," or "what a great place it is to work here—all the people are so wonderful," forgetting about improving our skills, growing our talent and making a significant contribution, being as "snug as a bug in a rug," chances are we have stopped challenging ourselves altogether and are securely ensconced in *arrested development* in the *Culture of Complacency.*

A Difference of Perspective

There is a certain amount of *moral courage* to followership which somehow gets displaced as we move up the organization. Take the case of the woman who was working at her station when the CEO of a major multinational corporation, and his executive entourage, stopped at her work station to chat during a ceremonial plant tour.

"And how are you feeling today, young lady," the smiling CEO asked. She turned, looked him full in the face, hands planted firmly on hips and said, "Horseshit!" And turned back to her station resuming her work. The stunned CEO, with caring in his voice, said almost in a whisper, "I'm sorry," and moved on.

Fortunately, one of the executives broke rank and talked to this woman for a few minutes. It turned out she was a single parent with two preschool children; that her set-up man didn't show, which meant she would have to work at least two hours overtime to meet the shipping schedule. She had no idea who could pick up her children at daycare, and so she was at her wits end to know what to do.

Now, this blue-collar worker had 'had it!' She wasn't fearful of her job, nor much impressed with the 'big shots' who were in the plant that day. She was full of her problem and when asked, unloaded. To the manager who stayed behind, she admitted no sense of courage or regret, nor did she feel anything but anger for her situation. It was an honest emotion, honestly wrought without malicious intent or dubious motivation. And it was accepted in that same sense by the CEO. You could even go so far as to say there was genuine compassion and concern in the CEO's voice as he expressed his regrets.

Change the scenario to an executive the CEO might encounter on a similar tour. Imagine one of them reacting in like fashion on a particular bad day saying, "Horseshit!" when asked how he felt. Imagine, if you will, the inevitable consequences.

The psychodrama which would surely unfold would find 'self-demands' and 'role demands' amalgamated into mortal conflict. Not so for the hourly worker. The frustrated or angered executive is not expected to have, much less show his feelings; certainly, not to 'lose control.' Only hourly employees have that privilege.

The CEO knows his power is largely symbolic with the work force; that the influence of leadership falls more on his ability to symbolically meet the humanistic needs of the majority than those of their top executive staff. You could even say the CEO feels a sense of 'ownership' of this staff, having purchased the 'rights of obeisant servitude' through executive compensation, bonuses, perks and privileges given. Hence, the executive staff is available largely at the CEO's convenience.

The Subtle Difference–Leadership vs. Management

Leaders are not concerned about leadership qualities or even charisma, but with purposeful performance.

Think in terms of their followers. Followers are the best guide to how leaders lead.

Understand the work climate and know the degree to which leaders can be open and trusting, or guarded and suspicious. Know the organizational culture must be open and trusting before it can tackle its problems.

Use the human resources they have. Invest in personnel development. Leaders know 99 percent of their people are capable. But, perhaps as much as 90 percent are either not challenged, or lack opportunity. Paradoxically, the more out- standing the employees, the greater the problem. Employees must be guided by their own light. Better that leaders get rid of good people than have them go sour, or become guilt rid- den for having to move on to greater challenges. The job of leadership is always development. Therefore, leaders should not punish themselves for doing a good job.

The subtle difference between leadership and manage- ment is in the psychology, not the functionality. If leader- ship and management were performed by a machine, they would be interchangeable. But they are not. Management does mechanical things well—planning, budgeting, organiz- ing, controlling through formal authority. Leadership, while doing these same things, educates its people to think differ- ently about work through inspiration and visioning.

Figure 6-7: Leadership is committed to Growth and Development

So, the higher one climbs the hierarchy, the more courage it takes to be oneself. Consequently, few muster such courage, succumbing instead to the seductive powers of comfort and conformity. Undoubtedly, they reason they have 'too much to lose.' And so they are bullied into obedience if not obsequious subservience to the CEO's demands, and call it 'loyalty.'

Indigenous to the American character is also an aptitude for taking risks and enduring the necessary pain that goes with growth. This is missing in these two cultures. More importantly, *there is no leadership in the Cultures of Comfort and Complacency, only management.*

Where there is true leadership, there is always a dynamic-tension and pull between leadership and followership. Indeed, they enhance each other. At the same time, leaders and followers are intimately connected in *interdependent* action. Surprise, disappointment, conflict, chaos, incredible levels of achievement, and continuous growth are part of the vigorous process. There is no comfort, little safety, no room for complacency, and no living off yesterday's achievements. Every day is a challenge and an embrace of the unexpected. Here the *Culture of Contribution* resides and the *Please Self* disposition flourishes.

"Leaders," suggests James MacGregor Burns, "represent the compleat follower." This is true. To lead you must first learn how to follow. Leaders learn how to lead by being ardent, passionate followers. Leaders and followers are indissolubly connected, but followership precedes leadership.

Peter the Great, who singlehandedly brought 18th century Russia into the modern Western world, would wander amongst his people in disguise to learn what they were thinking and feeling. In this manner he checked the pulse of his leadership, not through sycophants, but through direct contact. He loved his people and he wanted desperately to understand them so that he could more ably become their servant.

Something is wrong in the American organization today. Leadership covets leading but is disinclined to serve. Instead, it aspires to be served. Worse yet, having little knowledge of its followers, its perceptions are too frequently based on anachronistic stereotypes etched in 1945 nostalgia.

What's more, such leaders see themselves 'as the organization,' managing it thusly as if they in fact owned it. Likewise, they take it upon themselves to 'own' most of the organization's problems, sharing with their followers only what they deem necessary to execute 'the correct strategy.' Too frequently, this is done with limited information and knowledge. And so, not only are such problems insufficiently resolved, but they often exacerbate into major snafus.

More incredible still, these 'leaders' often think they are leaders because they are treated preferentially; that is, they have their own private bathrooms, executive dining privileges, special parking with free car maintenance and care, private club memberships, access to the company's private plane, interest-free loans, and so on.

Many managers would sell their most prized possessions to belong to such an exclusive club. Seldom do such incentives, of course, lead to the service of others. The message these perks generate is 'to be served,' not to serve. And so, today that is the 'leadership' the organization too often gets.

The Triangle of Growth

The remarkable feature of humanity is that everything begins with 'man' in the singular, progressing to 'collective man' in the plural, or in the sense of this discussion, the organization. With regard to growth, there is no static or safe period for either the individual or the organization. Once the individual or the organization attempts to play it 'safe,' it loses. Things start to fall apart. Likewise, when we or the organization stop growing, atrophy sets in… plants, animals, man, organizations… all the same. Eternal struggle is indigenous to all life without exception.

Struggle starts when we learn to talk, continues as we strive to walk, attempt to master a three-wheeler, try to roller skate… and beyond. Ever know anyone to look graceful the first, second, third or fourth time they put on a pair of roller skates?

Roller skating is embarrassingly difficult. The reason is, the 'center of gravity' changes as we negotiate the corners by a 'cross-over' of our legs, leaving us precariously off balance. If we avoid the 'cross-over' maneuver, of course, we never actually learn how to skate gracefully. To become a graceful skater requires enduring the *pain* of embarrassment and the near constant *risk* of falling on our tush, because we will fall many times before we perfect the maneuver.

If unwilling or unable to endure this pain, or to take the risk, we will never learn to skate. This could be one of our first encounters with 'embracing resistance.' It requires us to 'let go' of ourselves, trusting that our intrinsic psycho-motor skills will suffice to give us control of our balance.

And, of course, that is precisely what happens. Those who have mastered this maneuver have embraced their resistance to self-consciousness. They have given themselves a psychological edge for when the next challenge comes along.

But, alas, we tend to forget these successes. 'Embarrassing skills' are most successfully learned, as a consequence, when we are quite young; when we are not afraid to make a 'fool of ourselves'; when we are not intimidated by failure. Failure is not even relevant. Indeed, the young are open to diverse new experiences, taking risks, and possibly getting hurt.

Wake Up, America!

- Unconscious Incompetence — *Culture of Comfort* (Asleep)
- Conscious Incompetence — *Culture of Complacency* (Half Awake)
- Conscious Competence — *Culture of Contribution* (Fully Awake!)

Figure 6-8: Three Cultures in terms of being awake.

Incidentally, our aversion to physical pain seems to 'level off' at an early age, whereas our aversion to *psychological pain* never seems to crest. Since the pain we experience as we get older becomes more associated with 'psychological pain,' we tend to go to great extremes to avoid it. Because of past 'hurts,' we avoid certain relationships, economic opportunities and life experiences… such as the awkwardness of learning a foreign language in our mature years.

Young organizations differ little with this. Take the early days of *Apple, Inc. Apple* demonstrated an incredible capacity to take risks and court embarrassment. For a period, *Apple* was as cautious as *IBM*, then Steve Jobs returned and energized *Apple* into his image and likeness to be the successful company it is today. Once organizations get 'a little long in the tooth,' however, they tend toward conservatism. Likewise, if they have a traumatic experience, they tend to shy away from similar challenges.

'Success,' however you define it, is the outcome of careful attention to the *process*, nothing more. We learn precious little from success, the *outcome* itself. We experience it, may trade on it, and sometimes become consumed with it, but we seldom grow from success.

Real Road to Growth and Development

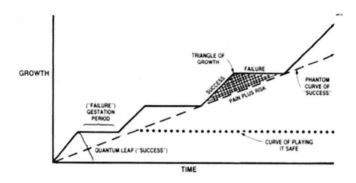

- **Growth is not in linear increments, but in strategic leaps**
- **Gestation period is period of real learning**
- **Gestation period is time of trauma, retrenchment, assimilation of failure; a time when the learner**

Please Self – Is not concerned about letting the group down
Mentality
     – Does not have to appear smart

     – Is Open to taking risks and enduring pain

- **Quantum leaps are periods of success, but of little real learning**

Figure 6-9: The Real Road to Growth and Development.

The essential component of growth is the part the American mind prefers to ignore, the inevitable 'plateau.' Every individual and organization experiences plateaus several times in their existence… if they are truly in a growth mode. If they play it safe, however, they can remain on a plateau for an eternity (see Figure 6-10), the plateau of arrested development.

Ideally, the period of static development might be called the *Plateau of Failure* in an effort to dramatize how important 'failure' is to our success and that of our organization. [10] Plateauing is a period when we finally confront ourselves and that reality. The processing of the knowledge gained during this period can then become useful in the form of invaluable insights. An added advantage to this phase is that we are likely to be given more 'room,' as we are treated as if 'failure' were a communicable disease.

Make no mistake, this is a remarkably meaningful stage of development. It is here the 'chemistry of being' in all its naked splendor reveals itself... if only we allow it to happen. All growth has an appropriate gestation period. This is ours.

It is the *place* and *space* where wonders can break through to our consciousness, putting us into a different strata of knowing, feeling and being. On the other hand, *we don't have to worry about letting the group down* because it is not likely to be around. And like an unassuming child, *we don't have to be smart,* being totally in a learning configuration.

We often think of individuals who have 'plateaued' as going nowhere. This is not true. Or if it is, it is because those individuals have misinterpreted their own experiences. The *plateau* is a period of incubation. Pregnant with past experiences—both successes and failures, we are inclined toward introspection, taking inventory of ourselves. It could be called a 'time out' period, much as athletic teams take 'time outs' in tense moments of competition to regroup and reassess their situation.

Attention is focused on *being,* not becoming. 'Being' involves us with ourselves, of finding out how to *Please Self,* as well as to discover what 'makes us tick.' This is a healthy form of self-involvement. *Becoming,* on the other hand, involves us with others, and our frantic efforts to meet their needs and live up to their expectations... in short, to find ways to *Please Others.* This is an unhealthy form of self-involvement.

Corporations, through their lack of leadership, can attempt to be all things to all people—employees, stockholders and customers, ending up being nothing to everyone. Instead of using a period of leveling off in the business as an opportunity to look at things differently, the organization, like the individual, can go through a period of denial, depression, projection (e.g., finger pointing), stress and strain, and ultimately, panic. It is moved by *forward inertia*, which displays its limited vision and contains its corporate self-doubt.

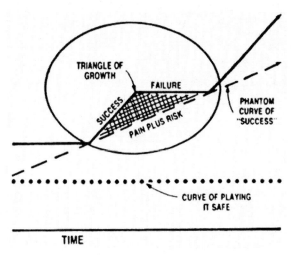

Figure 6-10: The Triangle of Growth.

Unfortunately, there is little learning in this process because the organization is attempting to 'appear smart,' or to look like it has its act together when it clearly doesn't.

Since plateaus are an inevitable phenomenon, no individual or organization escapes them, but everyone can contribute to using them as launching pads for 'blasting off' to new experiences. The American mania of 'action for action's sake,' however, is not the way. In other words,

"He who hesitates is lost," or "When in doubt, it's better to do something, than nothing, even if it is wrong," is not good executive action planning;

Acting now can actually exacerbate the situation and extend the time on the plateau.

This impulsive, impatient behavior describes a common American management practice. It is the expected action of someone in a state of panic, unaware or incapable of dealing with reality.

Survey of 900 United States Executives
• 93 percent said managers were not rewarded for developing subordinates for leadership. On the contrary, managers are often rewarded for killing off talented managers who are threatening their own jobs.
• 87 percent said it was impossible to make lateral moves in their companies, an essential for developing leaders who will know how the whole company operates, not just a portion of it.
• 80 percent said they had inadequate programs to identify what people needed in order to develop leadership skills.

Figure 6-11: A Call for Leadership: Managers Need Not Apply. [11]

Breaking the Loop

While our international competitors begin to live their economic dreams, America itself is stranded on a plateau, the nightmare of *comfort* and *complacency*. What got us there will not get us off. We must first encounter and admit to our doubts and inadequacies. This is not a time to complain, justify or rationalize. It is a time to learn. The internal dialogue of the American organization is a vicious cycle of delays and denials. This dialogue has become a closed-loop circuit which finds the American organizational psyche going *'round and 'round,* producing little movement or progress because it is fixed on fantasy.

[Universities and consultants are generating social research on what is presented here, twenty-five years after the fact when this was first published. This research is considered "social capital" or metadata

that was common knowledge to most workers in the trenches those many years ago. Where were the academics and consultants then?

You might say "better late then never," but one wonders as they are relying on this social capital at better perceiving the workers, when the leadership is where the focus should be.

Alas, in many instances, the development of this capital is in face-to-face virtual reality networks, then using these networks to target and tailor corporate responses to organizational needs.

This is the wrong focus. The focus should be on the leadership and why it is unable to perceive these organizational needs. Every worker in said organization has a good sense of what these are, and doesn't need to be involved in some virtual face-to-face assessment.

No surprise, they expect to tap into these metadata for better decision making, which as this book argues is getting it all "ass backwards."

Do you think this an exaggeration? A conference in Chicago at the Northwestern University in late 2014 has this precise format as its "strategy of leaderhip."] [12]

To break the loop, we must find our 'roller skating legs' and embrace our resistance to *right brain* thinking, for only our right brain recognizes and accepts a warped vision without defensiveness. It is our *left brain* that defends the circuit of cyclic thinking.

Ironically, the increasing importance of 'breaking the loop' places the *Outsider* in the mainstream. The *Outsider*, having no vested interest in the outcome, can be instrumental in convincing us to focus on the process. More significantly, the *Outsider* can surface our most painfully embarrassing concerns, issues the *leaderless leadership* would prefer to avoid. Leaderless leadership fancies itself riding the crest of economic advantage secure in the safety that "It didn't happen on *my* watch!"

The *Outsider,* lacking personal involvement, being neither a 'bleeding heart' nor a 'crusader,' has no investment in either anger or cause. More importantly, the *Outsider* is not interested in the concern 'to be free,' but is passionately committed to the ideal of 'to become free.' And herein lies an important difference.

Rejection of the *status* quo is the first step toward freedom, which is 'negative freedom.' This produces 'to be free.' Most criticism and rebellion is an expression of 'negative freedom.' With the *Outsider*, it is not enough to repudiate what is not acceptable. 'Negative freedom,' alone, will not put America back on track. We have been pushing 'negative freedom' for the past half century... and you can see what it has accomplished, *forward inertia*.

[Philosopher Isaiah Berlin developed the "Two Concepts of Liberty," or freedom as it is used here.

Negative freedom, as defined by him, allows the individual to be left to do or be what he is able to do or be without interference by others such as the government.

Positive freedom involves constrains and impositions that restrict freedom in the interest of harmony and support of individual needs that cannot be otherwise derived.

Berlin did not argue that positive freedom should be rejected, but be recognized as one human value among many others. His point was that the more positive freedom the less autonomy and control the individual has over his destiny. We are motivated to increase our positive freedom at the expense of our negative freedom for reasons of security, safety, comfort and stability.} [13]

To become free ('positive freedom'), on the other hand, recognizing the natural interdependence of the individual and the organization in dealing with situational forces as they develop. This means everyone accepts themselves as part of the problem and, therefore, as part of the solution. The problem is not outside anyone, but permeates all interests. To solve it together, as a single entity, is *to become free...* to become 'one organization.' [14] It overcomes *inertial isolationism*, which is seemingly endemic to the American character.

The bearing of 'to be free' and 'to become free' on this discussion is that the American organization is admittedly struggling against itself for survival. The best medicine it could possibly take, given this predicament, might be to manage a trade off between negative and positive freedom rather than to conflate either of them. We cannot get along, alone, and we do need group guidelines and the imposition of standards so that we all profit together. It is never a either/or proposition. Our desire for privacy and our need for interdependence do not need to be at cross purposes. True, there is risk involved and change cannot be expected to occur without difficulty or inevitable setbacks.

To change, in any event, requires the positive force of the faculty called 'imagination' to be brought into play. Colin Wilson in *Access To Inner Worlds* (1983) points out 'imagination' is actually "the ability to re-create experience, in all its complexity and richness. And the *right brain* is able to do precisely that." [15]

Meanwhile, the ranks of the disgruntled and disenchanted grow—that is, those who want 'to be free.' Well-intentioned professionals of all ages placed their confidence in a *system* that they now feel has betrayed them by imprisoning them or stultifying their development. Obviously, they are still not looking to themselves for the solution, but to 'management,' whatever management may mean to them. This has buried the dilemma only deeper in their subconscious and made challenge a greater phantom.

Gregory Bateson in *Steps to an Ecology of Mind* (1972), describes this as a *double bind* which causes these professionals "to feel lost in the labyrinth of roadblocks, detours, and new construction across the main thoroughfares of their minds." [16] Their perceptions have not held up well to reality testing. They are beginning to understand they cannot maintain their present high standard of living (S.O.L.), for example, without eventually paying. As matters now stand, the American government is borrowing money to maintain the *S.O.L.*, while it watches our per capita rate of productivity continue to fall.

Professionals are finding it increasingly difficult to separate themselves from the corporate problem of American society. The nice home, good pay, and comfort are all threatened... with the ominous signs over the horizon which they would like to ignore, if they could. But the evidence they see proves we cannot have it both ways:

We can no longer pretend we are the 'best and the brightest' when our performance deteriorates against world competition.

No matter what our association, chances are the organization is shrinking, and with it, our confidence.

Consequently, lost or alienated from what we thought we were, many of us have decided that if reality doesn't mean what we thought it meant, then there is no meaning at all; that we might as well 'pack it in.' [17] But America's decline is clearly a choice. It is not inevitable.

Consider this absurdity. What would we think of a man who lived out on the lawn in a tent, while he built himself a magnificent home, and then absentmindedly went on living in the tent and left the house empty? Colin Wilson sees that as precisely what we have done. [18] Perhaps we are trying too hard to solve our dilemma, and not taking the time to appreciate the vast richness of our magnificent country. With a predominant 'sense of panic,' we have slipped deeply into an insidious habit of anxiety, tension, and over-alertness. This is not to be confused with awareness. 'Over-alertness' is a legacy of the past. We need crises to keep us alert. The management of crises fuels 'over-alertness.' It leaves the house empty.

When we consider this absurdity more closely, we realize we already know the answer. We have chosen to retreat into *comfort* and the *status quo* at the expense of our *identity* and *reality*. Now, we may choose to move 'out of this tent' and into our magnificent home. *We may choose to be purposeful with intentionality. We may choose to put our lives in focus.*

No. 5: Finding Our Way Back To Purposeful Performance

"We have designed organizations which ignored individual potential for competence, responsibility, constructive intent and productivity," wrote Chris Argyris two decades ago. [19] Regrettably, it still holds true today. The organization pays close attention to every detail that enhances individual potential for *purposeful performance* except the workers themselves. They are left out of the equation.

The *psychological infrastructure of the organization* has not changed at all, permanently secured in the 1945 model. At a time when we need to think and behave differently in the workplace, we *reorganize* or move the furniture and call it 'change.' This only masks the problem.

Work as *purposeful performance* is both a structural/ functional and psychological problem. The difficulty with performance relates to the *structure of work* and the *function of work* as they both relate to the *organization culture*, on the one hand, *and the psychological perception of the structure and function of work* as it relates to the *worker*, on the other. The organization has paid conscientious attention to the structure and function of work as it relates to managerial authority, but has ignored the psychological perception of work, as it relates to the worker, with near disastrous consequences (See Figure 6-12).

Conventional wisdom of the organization equates *structure* and *function* with managerial *control* and *results*.

Professional workers equate *structure and function* with *self-control* and *process*. And this equates to their level of satisfaction.

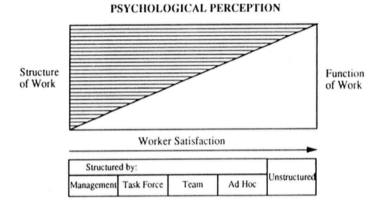

Figure 6-12: Control & Satisfaction as a Function of Structure.

Conventional wisdom can boast that work has been designed with the latest scientific ergonomics to enhance productivity and worker satisfaction. It can proclaim the structure of the organization is streamlined to pose minimal barriers to productive work. It can even refine the selection process to attract the most able, yet all is for naught, if it does not satisfy the workers' psychological needs in terms of the existing workplace culture. And what are these needs?

Professional workers today are not impressed with what management can do *for* them, or even *to* them if it does not include:

- *Freedom* to express themselves in work,
- *Control* of how work is accomplished,
- *Trust* that the work will be done correctly.

This is the *symbolic currency* that makes a difference—currency, to date, conventional wisdom shows little inclination to advance. It sees such currency as surrendering traditional power. Management neither trusts workers to be more productive for these concessions, nor does it feel a pressing *need to share power.*

Now, there are genuine exceptions to this with phenomenal results. Some organizations have, in fact, created this type of climate. H. Ross Perot, founder of Electronic Data Systems Corporation (EDS), attempted for years to *wake up America* to the needs of workers and their potential for contribution, seeing *all* workers as professionals, establishing the following credo at EDS:

First feed the troops, then the officers. (Not only does he see the bonus system as ludicrous, but self-serving.)

The running of the corporation belongs to the workers. (He does not see it belonging to 'custodial power,' or management.)

If there is to be a bonus rule, the same rule should apply to the workers and managers alike when it comes to special compensation. (EDS has had gain-sharing for years.)

Management, believing it holds the 'Keys to the Kingdom,' gives itself 'Nobel Prize-like' awards, while giving the troops 'baubles and beads.' (Perot considers this not only senseless, but poor business.)

Management, as a word, should be eliminated: inventories can be managed... people led. [20]

We need leaders, not managers; and we need professional workers to become self-managers in the full sense of the word. And we need to 'live' the words by rewarding those that do.

Ever irascible, Perot took on General Motors as a project worthy of rehabilitation. This premier American firm commits most of the sins of this discussion, and in mega-numbers, while operating, according to Perot, "in a blanket of fog." For his trouble, General Motors dumped him off its Board of Directors with a payoff of $700 million for his stock and resignation.

So, generally speaking, management has not been willing to 'step up to the bar' and face reality. It has not been willing to cross a new frontier. Naively, it clings to the *psychology of inertia* as we sink deeper into this incomprehensible abyss.

Remedial Considerations:
Phasing Out & Phasing In

There are no magic answers to this dilemma. Ultimately, if it is to be resolved the workers must find the *will* and create the *opportunity*. Management will resolutely hold its ground until it is convinced that *real change* is both necessary and inevitable. Until that time, it is solely up to the professional workers *to predict their future by creating it.* The talent and energy are there. What is in question is the resolve and resourcefulness.

Eric Hoffer is fond of reminding his readers in such works as *Working and Thinking on the Waterfront* (1969) and *The Ordeal of Change* (1963) that you can find the talent in skid row to build a modern city. Dregs of society on the ash heap of disenchantment represent America's blessedness and how dismal its vision.

To bring back *purposeful performance* requires removing some barriers and constructing new bridges. These may help American workers rediscover their *will* and recreate the *way*.

Figure 6-13: Purposeful Performance Motivation Triangle.

Phasing Out Middle Management & Putting a Cap on MBAs

Middle Management has already died and is ready for burial. This was true a quarter century ago, and at that time, we didn't have the ubiquitous laptop, mobiles with hundreds of Aps complete with cameras, audio recorders, instant messaging, and the omniscient source of information, the Internet, to connect us to work and to each other. They are common to us all now. The function which is being deceptively retained by the *MBA brigade* with the argument that MBAs as middle managers make for good candidates for top management. No, the whole mystique of *middle management* and *MBAs* is wrong. Middle managers and MBAs are mechanics, dedicated to 'cipher management.' Leadership requires more, much more.

Phasing In Visionary Management

Visionary management is a creative response to what the organization is, what it has to sell, and then going into the marketplace and educating the public to see how 'it' fulfills its needs.

Leadership is visionary management in the same sense that Ford and Edison practiced it by creating their markets through 'Imagineering.' Ford did it with the $5 work day, giving his workers the income to buy his Model A's and Model T's; and Edison by creating the electric utility.

Perhaps the reason American management is so myopic is that it is too busy being served than serving; too busy controlling than looking to the horizon for opportunity. Ford and Edison were known as crotchety, demanding personalities, not easy to work with or for, but no one questioned their vision. They knew people and they built their visions on that knowledge. The reason they knew people was because they took the time to observe them and wonder after those observations. They both had little formal education, and were known as tinkerers since they were little boys. They had a center, and a reliable compass. They had a focus and were results oriented. Has this component been excised from our imagination by our faulty programming?

Phasing Out Crystal Cathedrals

More and more conscientious workers are coming in on the weekends to do their work. They claim to get more done in four hours of a Saturday morning than forty hours during the week. There is absolutely no sense, in this time of telecommunications and computers that workers have to spend two to four hours a day commuting back and forth to 'work.' There is no reason most professionals could not better perform their work at home, or near home in some small work center. 'Flex-time,' obviously, is becoming routine. Soon to follow is 'flex-place,' thanks to the transformation of portable technology.

In California, where some people spend as much time in their cars as they do at work, *techno-vans* are becoming popular. Chupp & Sons, Inc., for one, an Elkhart, Indiana, mobile home maker, is exploring this market, working with van conversion companies to produce these 'techno-vans.' Presently, the high-end conversion includes a desk, two cellular phones, a fax machine and a top-of-the-line Texas Instrument laptop computer.

With this new technology becoming easier to use and more accessible, it makes conventional management and management style totally obsolete. 'Mobility' is part of the American tradition and this technology is adding a new wrinkle. For example, cellular phones, once a curiosity, are now standard equipment for busy field representatives. Harvey Rosen, partner in a Los Angeles law firm, estimates his portable office adds about two hours of productivity to his day. [21]

In that same connection, the clock has little meaning to professionals. Putting them on a forty-hour week and attempting to keep them busy chasing 'action items' makes little sense anymore. True, management has been largely reluctant to allow employees to work away from the office, for fear they may not be working at all. The big problem is trust.

These ivory towers and crystal cathedrals as work centers are tantamount to secular churches and are increasingly dysfunctional. Meanwhile, the so-called 'cottage industry' is an idea whose time has come. Alvin Toffler and others have been writing about it for decades, but it is still largely avoided. The heavy corporate investment in physical facilities is doubtlessly one reason, but 'small is beautiful' and 'mobility is in.'

Phasing In Coaching, Counseling & Mentoring

Coaching is adapting to what a person can and will do. This requires seeing the person 'as they are' and accepting and adapting to that knowledge. *Counseling* is active listening and the dynamics of discussion which it commands. Here the person being helped takes responsibility and control of the process. And *mentoring* is being teacher and demonstrator, consultant and adviser to the neophyte who has not had time to 'learn the ropes' of operations, on the one hand, and is not yet familiar with the complexities of the job, on the other. Experience is the best teacher of these.

The late Red Auerbach of the Boston Celtics performed all these functions with consummate skill. Auerbach created a culture of winning by establishing a 'Celtic family' which was driven by 'Celtic pride.' The Celtic reward system, from the start, was based on performance, not individual statistics, on how the player contributed to the success of the team.

"I don't believe in statistics," Red Auerbach confessed, "You can't measure a ballplayer's heart, his ability to perform in the clutch, his willingness to sacrifice his offense or to play strong defense."

Even more incredible, he admitted, "Most of our players have self-retired. They tell me when they don't think they can play anymore." Continuing on this theme, he added, "The players won't con me because I don't con the players. They don't give me what we call 'false hustle,' when a guy just goes through the motions but he's not really putting out much effort."

"We like our players to play for fun and to be happy rather than afraid," he revealed. "It's like that in business. If you have employees who work through fear, you're not going to get any ingenuity out of them. You're not going to get any employees who will take a gamble or come up with ideas. All you'll have are robots that are going to do their jobs, have a low-key approach, stay out of trouble. They'll put in their hours and go home. But I'd rather have it the other way."[22]

Phasing Out the "Sacred Cows" of the Organization

MBOs should be scrapped. "Management by Objectives work," comments Peter Drucker, "if you know the objectives. Ninety percent of the time you don't."

Strategic and Operational Planning Reviews are excessive. They should be slimmed down to two-page documents or scuttled. All an operation needs to know is the *vision statement* with the operating details of their respective concerns developed 'on line.'

Performance Management Systems (PMS) should concentrate on 'process improvement' only. Otherwise, these are just words within a brochure, another excess of Human Resources.

Performance Appraisal, especially, as part of PMS, should be placed in a time capsule and forgotten forever. Everyone in a function knows who are the performers and who are not. Why is this such a mystery to management?

'Human Resources' should be integrated totally into operations. It simply doesn't work 'as is.' Its charter cannot be accomplished without the entire organization's commitment and involvement. It has failed, not for lack of dedication or determination, but mainly due to a lack of skill, confidence, possibly courage, and a lack of understanding of its function.

[There is a role for Human Resources in terms of things (personnel advertising, recruiting, selecting, processing, tracking, checking references, keeping organizational statistics, tracking health and safety laws, compensation, promotions, demotions, hirings, firings, and organizational personnel needs—things.

People, however, are not things. They need to be assessed in terms of counseling, coaching, mentoring and then assessing these needs against those of the organization.

This requires an organizational development (OD) psychologist who performs as clinician to the organization. He is trained to assess organizational needs and the readiness of personnel to meet those needs in the short and long term.

This is shared with the leadership along with possible interventions, but the decision for action is management's, alone, and not the consultant's.

The role of the OD psychologist is similar to that of the clinical psychologist only for the organization and not the individual.

An OD psychologist is not a personnel administrator, but an internal consultant, independent of management and the work force but consultant to them both.]

Bureaucratic mechanisms were surprisingly suitable when the organization was the domain of *bureaucratic management,* but now is increasingly engaged in turf wars with *technocrats.* Technocrats look on bureaucracy differently than do bureaucrats—they use it as a vehicle for accomplishing their technological ends, whereas bureaucrats covet it as an end in itself. It is their *sacred cow.*

These two groups, which could benefit from each other, are moving toward confrontation, not integration. As yet, it is not clear they appreciate their relative *interdependence.*

Bureaucrats, at the moment, represent the dominant management group. Lacking technological prowess, they compensate by making the bureaucratic system their *end.* Conversely, technocrats, primarily educated in technology, see the bureaucratic system as principally a *means to an end.* With them, nothing is sacred or sacrosanct, except their technology. Bureaucrats, many of whom are actually educated as technologists, are not driven by the wonders of technology. They are more enamored of policies, procedures, standards, objectives and measurable 'results.' And always, they are protectors of the *sacred cows* of the bureaucratic system. An assimilation of their agenda with that of the techno-crats could strengthen any organization.

Phasing in 'Gain Sharing' and Making Everyone an Owner

Special compensation for a few executives, say 50, sharing in the fruits of the labor of say, 4,000, may have once been tolerated, if never accepted. In a certain way, the 'vital few,' at one time, brought in the business to the 'trivial many'—but not anymore.

Management, if anything, has become the 'trivial few,' and the professional-technical staff, the 'vital many.' Education has shifted the fulcrum from management to the professional. There is absolutely no way modern management can keep pace with, much less dictate the true course of organizational activity, given its perspective of limited knowledge and information. Add the critical mass, 'timeliness' and it becomes absurd. Yet, admittedly, there is a reluctance to acknowledge this fact. The hierarchy remains and the few judge the many, even though their criteria may be faulty. It is a matter of *cultural bias*.

'Gain sharing' is actually not a bold step into the future, but a step into the past to climb into the present. It is long overdue. Yet, when it is brought up, such comments as this are common:

"It would only mean a few hundred dollars to each employee and that would hardly motivate them to act differently."

Tolerance for this reasoning is growing more tenuous. Beware! Economics are understood by professional-technical workers, who realize their contributions are significant if not critical to organizational success. Phasing out special compensation for a few would seem most prudent, while phasing in equitable gain sharing most wise.

Phasing In Diverse Work Force

Over the next fifty years, a smaller pool of workers will be forced to meet the socioeconomic demands of a much larger complement of retired persons. More over, we are becoming a society in which 80 percent of the work force will be minorities and females with less than 20 percent white males.

Therefore, it should be clear that female and minority leadership is essential. Incidentally, that does not mean women 'who think like men' or minorities who attempt to model themselves after whites. We have far too many of that type presently. Indeed, it is time Snow White has a black face and Captain Courageous has a feminine sense of humor.

We need desperately to groom and train thousands of women and minorities to take leadership roles in virtually every American industry and institution. It is happening in athletics. Now, we need to make it happen in the classrooms and boardrooms of America as well.

Phasing Out Cultural Biases

There is no crystal ball which tells what the organization of the year 2025 is likely to be. But many of these cultural biases will doubtlessly go to ground:

Performance Appraisal	Working 8 To 5
Weekly Staff Meetings	Managers/Supervisors
Action Registers	Job Descriptions
Special Perks For Executives	Viewgraph Presentations
MBOs	Women As Clericals
Security Badges	White-Male Dominated Operations
Matrix Management	40-Hour Work Week

Edifice Complexes'

Hierarchical Organizations

Paper Being The
Principle Product

Individual Over Group
Recognition

The way to 'phase out' *cultural bias* is tricky because it is so simple. You talk about values and beliefs that aren't working, with the people who are affected by them. You do this by *easing into the process,* not by making provocative statements, waving banners, or calling attention to them. 'Subliminal' is the guiding word.

The *cultural bias story* is tied to pesky, insistent values and not to what management thinks makes for an effective organization. This is illustrated when—

- Talking incessantly about 'promotion' when performance is what is needed;

- Focusing unremittingly on 'pay programs' which actually makes workers feel more like 'loaners' than 'owners';

- Treating 'perks' as special incentives for a few, which further separate employee from employee;

- Giving the edge to authority over contribution whenever they collide with each other.

Clearly, *cultural biases* can be overcome. Consider how the national outlook has changed in recent times on cigarette smoking, the seriousness of drunk driving, physical exercise, casual sex and diet. Admittedly, the more personal the cultural bias the more difficult it is to overcome. Remember, this is *felt knowledge* and the process could take months or years. The talking about it eases the way for change… with no hurry in mind, the process discovers its own momentum.

The Process of Empowerment

This entire discussion has been devoted to empowerment. The word is a strange one. The only way anyone has any power over another person is when that person gives 'power' up to the other person. For one person to be dominant, there must be another willing to be submissive. Otherwise, the dominating person is powerless. Therefore, management or anyone else, for that matter, is incapable of 'empowering' employees to work differently. Management has assumed, falsely, that it has the power. And workers have bought into this obvious false assumption. These workers now must discover, first of all, what they have given up; and then gain some understanding of why they have allowed a *significant other* to dominate them, before they can reclaim their power.

For example, we are conditioned to be managed rather than to manage ourselves. We are conditioned to elect people to public office who, like ourselves, share certain definable traits of the herd, so it should be no surprise when they embarrass us before the world. The same kinds of people ascend the latter of most organizations and then lead us by the nose.

This problem of *empowerment* can be frightening. In the United Kingdom the press related how some sixty 5th-form youths (i.e., sixteen-year-olds), who had been at a roller skating party, were robbed of their money, clothes, and other possessions, as they left the roller skating rink... by five young toughs. They were asked to line up, and those who hesitated were kicked into line. The sixty youths obediently followed. A few dominated many. Were the young toughs' leaders? No. The more interesting question relates to the sixty youths.

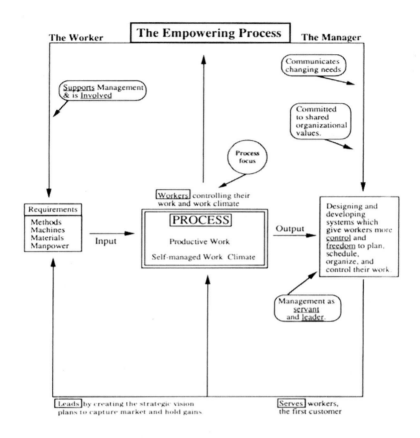

Figure 6-14: The Empowering Process to Organization Health

This event happened in 1987. Great Britain, it appears, is still one of the most repressive societies in Europe with children conditioned to be obedient, to behave, to be 'kicked into line' by the time they are sixteen years of age. Where does that put Americans?

It should put Americans in touch with the simple fact that there is no longer time for hesitation. True as this may be, vested interests will ignore this reality, and continue, 'as is,' in the hopes of a miracle. That is why it has become the time of the *Outsider*.

The *Outsider* is such because, as Colin Wilson puts it, "He stands for Truth." Many of you reading this are *Outsiders* and perhaps are finding it out for the first time. You are *change agents* standing for *truth*. Your time has come to make a difference. This is your day. Wilson spoke of this truth more than three decades ago, and still struggles to make it known:

> "The problem for the 'civilization' is the adoption of a religious attitude that can be assimilated as *objectively* as the headlines of last Sunday's newspapers. But the problem for the individual always will be the opposite of this, the conscious striving *not* to limit the amount of experience seen and touched; the intolerable struggle to expose the sensitive areas of being to what may possibly hurt them; the attempt to see as a whole, although the instinct of *self-preservation* fights against the pain of the internal widening, and all the impulses of spiritual laziness build into waves of sleep with every new effort. The individual begins that long effort as an *Outsider*, he may finish it as a saint." [23]

ENDNOTES

(1)   See Buchholz, Steve, and Thomas Roth, *Creating the High Performance Team*, ed. Karen Hess (New York: John Wiley & Sons, Inc., 1987).

(2)   No accident, there has been a plethora of 'baseball books' in this period of uncertainty, from the crafted prose of George F. Will's *Men At Work: The Croft of Baseball* (New York: Macmillan, 1990) to the scientism of Robert K. Adair's *The Physics of Baseball* (New York: Harper & Row, 1990). Baseball is the architecture of the 'frozen music' of the atavistic American spirit.

(3)   *Logical positivism* is a philosophical position holding that truth of any statement lies in its verification through sensory experience (i.e., based upon experience, observation, or experimentation). Any statement that cannot be verified

through sensory experience, such as metaphysical statements, is held meaningless.

(4)   Capra, Fritjof, *The Turning Point: Science, Society & The Rising Culture* (New York: Simon and Schuster, 1982), p. 453.

(5)   Capra, op. cit. p. 23.

(6)   Sorokin. Pitrim. *The American Sex Revolution* (Boston: Porter Sargent, 1956).

(7)   Economists, for one, readily admit they are operating in a fog. From former Chairman of the Federal Reserve, *Arthur Hunts* ("The rules of economics are not working quite the way they used to.") to *Milton Friedman* ("I believe that we economists in recent years have done vast harm by claiming more than we can deliver."); from former Secretary of Treasury, *Michael Blumenthal* ("I really think the economic profession is close to bankruptcy in understanding the situation, before or after the fact.") to *Juanita Kreps*, former Secretary of Commerce, when asked if she would go back to Duke University upon leaving government ("I wouldn't know what to teach."). Source: Interview: *Washington Post.* November 5, 1979).

(8)   Robert M. Tucker and David C. Hendrickson offer a nostalgic piece which gives substance to this argument in "Thomas Jefferson and American Foreign Policy." *Foreign Affairs*, Spring 1990.

(9)   Cartoon by Bill Day originally appeared in *Detroit Free Press* and in the *International Herald Tribune.* February 24, 1988.

(10)   Judith Bardwick in *The Plateauing Trap* (New York: Chandler Publishing Company, 1986) does a superb job in showing how plateauing can be the beginning, not the end of things.

(11)   Kotter, John P., *The Leadership Factor* (New York: Free Press, 1988). Kotter insists leaders are made, not born. His survey

of 900 U.S. executives indicates 'corpocracy,' the American bureaucratic disease, stifles people from becoming effective leaders.

(12) The Kellogg School of Management, Northwestern University announced a "new program," THE STRATEGY OF LEADERSHIP: Unleashing the Power of Influence— November 17- 19, 2014. I received such invitations all the time, the newest linking old ideas to the virtual reality of the Information Age.

(13) Isaiah Berlin, *Four Essays on Liberty*, Oxford University Press, Oxford, England, 1969, pp 118-172.

(14) See *The Outsider* by Colin Wilson, (Dell Publishing Company, New York, 1956). Wilson was in his twenties when he wrote this explosively popular international "bestseller." He attacked the problem of man's increasing retreat into comfort and the status quo at the expense of his identity and reality.

(15) Wilson, Colin, *Access to Inner Worlds* (London: Rider & Company, Ltd., 1983), p. 125.

(16) A *double bind*, as defined by Bateson, is a situation in which an individual feels they are receiving contradictory messages from a highly significant other person. This happened in one organization when all professionals were asked to take a voluntary *pay cut* across the board, while the CEO and his direct reports were given a 20 percent bonus.

(17) Hayes, Robert H., and William, J. Abernathy, "Managing Our Way to Decline," *Harvard Business Review*, July-August, 1980. This hard hitting article profiling American management's obsession with short term results as a major factor in our economic decline was not disputed. It was almost as if American management was resigned to the fall. A decade later (1990), it is even worse.

(18) Wilson, op. cit. pp. 128-129.

(19) Argyris, Chris, "A Few Words In Advance," *The Failure of Success*, ed. A. J. Marrow (New York: American Management Association, 1972).

(20) Perot, Ross H., in a manifesto article titled, "How I Would Turn Around GM," *Fortune Magazine*, February 15, 1988.

(21) Greene, Jay, "Portable Office: Technology Is Transforming The Workplace," *The Tampa Tribune*, November 24, 1989.

(22) Webber, Alan M., "Red Auerbach on Management," *Harvard Business Review*, March-April, 1987.

(23) Wilson, Colin, *The Outsider* (New York: Dell Publishing Company, 1956), p. 281.

AFTERWORD

"The greatest discovery of my generation is that human beings, by changing the inner attitudes of their minds, can change the outer aspects of their lives. It is too bad that more people will not accept this tremendous discovery and begin living it."

—William James (1842-1910),
American psychologist and philosopher

As WORK WITHOUT Managers began, so it ends. We are in trouble as a nation and as a people. The problem rides on the American organization's inability to manage, motivate and mobilize the professional-technical class of workers to more productive effort. This is America's crucial challenge. But before such a challenge can be met, these workers must first be aware of their power, of their remarkable potential to make a difference. Once sensitive to their power, they must then find the means by which to secure a prehensile grasp of their advantage. Not an easy task, it necessitates embracing their many faceted resistance to this challenge... from cultural to climatic, from societal to management conditioning.

What's more, it demands the organization give professionals' special access to controlling what they do and how they do it. It means treating them as professionals. This requires a fundamental shift for most American organizations as it involves "changing the attitudes of their minds," as American philosopher William James puts it, by literally establishing a foundation of trust.

At this writing, trust is largely a 'word game,' which is seldom played out in organization behavior. As one prominent executive put it, "Organizations don't give a damn about people. They ride and fall on economics. When times are good, people get treated fairly well. When times are bad, they get short shrift. It's the law of the jungle."

That philosophy is a luxury organizations can no longer afford. Hint this is the prevailing norm of the organization and professionals will go underground, literally becoming 'urbane guerrillas.' On the other hand, establish trust as the basis of organization culture, and professionals will explode into purposeful performance, releasing their energies to undreamed of outcomes.

On balance, this compels professionals to become their own managers. The 'authority and responsibility' baton must now be passed from managers to these workers. In the field of "do-what-the-coach-says" runners, American management had the 20th century largely to itself. Professional workers now own the race in the 21st century. The next leg of the race can only be won by professionals who decide and implement the best strategy and actions. For the challenge is not merely to run a fast race, but to close the huge gap in effectiveness that 20th century management has lost to the competition. The transfer process is hindered by the fact that many on the management team are so far off the pace that they have no idea how badly they are losing. Others sense the loss, but refuse to relinquish the baton, convinced that their stumbling effort will be seen as courageous, even valiant. But professionals, full of vigor and spirit, cannot wait to take the baton and close the distance. They feel in their bones, even from far back in the pack, that the race still belongs to them. We shall see.

The Good News—Maybe—
the Burgeoning Professional Class

The explosive growth of the professional-technical working class touches every segment of American enterprise from the service sector of the economy, such as the health care field and the computer industry, to research and development, and manufacturing. According to the *United States Department of Labor Study of White-Collar Employment Growth* (1987), the percentage of nonproduction workers has almost doubled since the end of WWII, going from 15.2 percent of total manufacturing employment to 29.7 percent. The increase is even greater in some industries such as the chemical and allied products industry, for instance, where in 1983 the percentage of nonproduction workers was already 44.5 percent.

The four fastest growing occupations in the next decade, according to the *Bureau of Labor Statistics* (1987) projections, are all white-collar. They are:

The paralegal profession	Computer programmers
Computer systems analysts and	Medical assistants.

At the end of the last century, the United States had 98 percent more paralegal employees, 72 percent more computer programmers, 69 percent more computer systems analysts, and 62 percent more medical assistants.

Indeed, nine out of every ten new jobs created are in such service fields as communications, telecommunications, trade, finance, insurance, real estate, and government, according to the Bureau.

At the same time, the occupations which are declining precipitously are all blue-collar... machine operators and tenders in shoe manufacturing, and blue-collar workers in the iron, steel, glass, and textile industries.

"Some observers," the report states, "are predicting that white-collar workers could jump to 90 percent of the work force by the year 2000." Presently, it is close to this in 2014. Incidentally, the *Census Bureau* (1987) reported that the biggest job growth would continue to be in the executive, administrative and managerial ranks.

These statistics are somewhat disquieting because they could mean we are moving even faster toward 'administrivia.' This is the 'corpocracy disease' that fosters 'non-doing of non-thing things.' Meanwhile, at the other end of the spectrum, we have such a shortage of skilled labor that it may be a more crucial problem for U.S. businesses in the next several decades than the national debt or the U.S. trade deficit.

Currently, more than one million workers are being imported annually to meet our skilled labor needs, according to Richard D. Reinhold, president of the National Association of Temporary Services, [1] If we start running out of skilled workers, Reinhold reflects, "It could cripple us as a competitive global economy."

'Busy work' or administrivia is not the answer, the kind of work that increasingly commands the attention of the organization. Focused skills training of professional workers to become competent paralegals, computer specialists, computer system analysts, and medical specialistsis is a more suitable alternative.

Professionals come into the organization after years in the educational process, but with little application experience. They can be trained to be highly skilled in virtually any discipline, however, providing the opportunity, the inclination, and the climate conducive to such development is available. In fact, given this opportunity to stretch themselves into a discipline other than their academic preparation proves motivating. So, this potential disastrous situation could be turned around to be an opportunity. That is, if these professionals accept the fact that they are essentially untrained, but trainable… uneducated, but educable.

The Bad News—No Doubt—
Productivity Is A Problem

Obviously, the professional-technical working class looks impressive until you look beneath the statistics to the anemic productivity which it masks. While most students of organization have been focusing on management as the core problem and the blue-collar worker as the locus of attack, professional workers have been largely ignored. As a result of this misdirected attention professionals have been dragging their feet, not blue-collar workers.

"If labor productivity in 1977 is equal to 100, by 1985 manufacturing productivity had risen to almost 120 while service-sector productivity had risen to only 107," so states a *U.S. Labor Bureau Report* (1987). Service-sector productivity failed to grow at all, while labor productivity in manufacturing continued to rise a respectable two percent.

The only way America's economy can grow, economists say, is if productivity grows. True, productivity is growing in the blue-collar ranks which, ironically, are disappearing; while productivity is going nowhere with the professional class of workers, who are now the working majority.

The University of Michigan's Institute For Social Research (1987) has noted, "Over long spans of time, differentials of one or two percentage points in productivity growth add up to the difference between our national ability to solve a great many pressing economic, social, and political problems and our ability to do much more than to decry their existence." This suggest we are in a heap of trouble, and it will get worse before it gets better, if we don't do something about professional worker productivity... now as opposed to later.

How To Measure The Productivity of
Professional Workers: The Pundits Are Perplexed

There are many vested interests in the professional working class. These arise partly out of a value system that finds professionals 'investing' in an education largely to 'get a good paying job,' rather than to become educated. Partly out of a belief that they can mortgage their future without risk, pain or inconvenience. Partly out of expectations founded more in fantasy than reality, as they visualize how exciting it will be as 'power brokers' one day. And partly out of a love affair with the socialization aspects of employment, which are endemic to and a fringe benefit of the modern American organization.

Work and America, which have always been synonymous, lately have gotten a bad name. But for professionals, work is still a way of life, and the main avenue to legitimacy. The problem is, because work is now largely counterfeit, it produces little added value to enterprise. Therefore, work today could even be described as primarily a 'movie picture' in the heads of professionals projecting their most private fantasies.

Imagine the shock to their systems when the textbooks are put aside and their careers commence. It is not just the chaos and confusion, the duplicity and politics they encounter, but the fact that their education has prepared them poorly for the transition, which is exacerbated by being given little real work to do in the workplace. As they experience the rites and rituals of enterprise and are inculcated with the organization's culture, these very clever people learn quickly:

- That it is more important to make an impression than a difference;
- That productivity is not a relevant consideration:
- That presentations and salutations count much more;
- That paper... the memo with a copy list to scores... is substituted for information sharing;

- That meetings… which command 60 to 80 percent of time… are surrogate for 'worry beads'; and
- That 'presence' and personality take precedence over performance.

The consequence of this shattering exposure is that professionals, of various disciplines within the organization, are more inclined to fighting with each other than fighting to increase *the organization*'s market share. With the failure of the organization to perform in the business arena, the 'Bean Counting Brigade' has once again taken on the prominence of the 'Spanish Inquisition,' looking for heretics everywhere. This can get quite absurd, albeit with the best of intentions. To wit,

One CEO of a $6 billion corporation boasted how such an inquisition 'saved' the corporation $100,000 in pencils, erasers, paper clips and note pads. What this 'savings' actually produced was a nightmare of high jinx with people guarding their supplies as if it were Fort Knox. Attention moved from being productive to being acquisitive. The pettiness endemic to us all was moved several notches higher. And the cost of this 'savings' in gamesmanship, defeated teamwork ("Get your own supplies!") and malicious obedience ("If they want to play 'chicken shit' games, I can play them, too!"), alone, escalated easily into the six figures.

Such activities routinely sap the strength and motivation out of otherwise well-intentioned workers, discouraging them from doing anything constructive or departing from the arbitrary standards of policies and procedures. It creates the 'petty monsters' that thrive on counterfeit activity. Worse still, it promotes conformity, duplicity, subversive insurgency, and organization counter dependence. It literally spawns and sustains the very culture the organization abhors, the *Culture of Complacency*.

With so many highly educated, but poorly skilled people fighting for their 'territorial imperative,' the customer gets scant, if any attention at all—especially the first customer, co-workers. On the contrary, these irascible performers tend to punish or bulldoze their customers by all sorts of subversive activities... from taking 'their-colleagues-as-customers' for granted to playing on historical precedence of their ultimate customers ("We've been serving you for more than thirty years."); from using their special knowledge against their colleagues to giving their customers deals they cannot refuse ("Let me remind you, we own twenty percent of your voting stock."). Being 'service friendly' never enters such a mindset.

It is indeed, guerrilla warfare, and it is sapping the very strength of America at a time when it has little if any, in reserve. In the face of this, as I've attempted to illustrate throughout *Work Without Managers,* the organization throws money at problems in Research and Development, Training and Development, Production and Control, Quality Management, and other activities... or it frantically, even impulsively, acquires operations to sustain its feeble equity position, only to plummet further. This translates into always looking for the 'miracle'... the miracle strategy, the miracle acquisition, yes, even the miracle worker.

Meanwhile, management attempts to deal with the problem:

With 'strategic and operational planning' review cycles and technical Power Point presentations hoping to have a sense of being on top of the problem when it is clearly buried under it.

Thus, you have this most venerated class of American workers, American management, being the least effective performers and, ironically, setting the performance standards for all other workers to follow. Management takes ownership of the problem when it has little insight into the solution. The results have been just this side of disastrous as *Work Without Managers* has attempted to show.

When Yesterday's Analyses Give Only Yesterday's Solutions

H. Ross Perot is one of the few voices that has challenged the status quo, but he is treated as an *Outsider* and an irritant. Yet, he was not afraid to have an opinion, not afraid to be wrong, not afraid to think. But was anyone listening?

Peter Drucker offers little reassuring guidance. Perhaps this is a generational problem in understanding this new breed of Americans. Perhaps we are too immersed in Newtonian psychology and Cartesian philosophy. As a result, what people like Drucker offer is predictable, but, not helpful. Drucker is right when he says professionals are unmanageable. Yet, he would still have management 'calling the shots,' when clearly only professionals can manage themselves.

Drucker's yardstick is:

"The ratio between the number of units of output (i.e., automobiles made or patient-bed days delivered in a hospital) and the number of white-collar people on the payroll (or white-collar hours worked and paid for)." [2]

Clearly, although not intended, this is a warped authoritarian vision of productivity with workers viewed the same except for having a different colored collar.

"We cannot hope to compete against the vast supply of young, low-wage, blue-collar workers in the developing countries through blue-collar productivity, no matter how much we improve it," he says. "The only competitive advantage the United States—and every other developed country—can have lies in making productive its one abundant resource: people with long years of schooling who are available only for white-collar work." [3]

This is a remarkable statement, yet Drucker's methodology is reminiscent of blue-collar measurement, and therefore absurd.

This is another area in which the Japanese do better, Drucker says. Noting that Japanese auto makers produce more cars per hundred white-collar workers than do U.S. manufacturers, he says, "U.S. car makers do not employ substantially more engineers per car made than the Japanese do. They employ fewer—probably too few—white-collar people to serve dealers and customers. But Detroit does employ many more clerks, clerical supervisors and clerical managers in record keeping, reporting and controlling. It substitutes paper for information." [4] Again, Drucker is comparing apples to oranges. Japan is a group think culture, the United States is individualistic. Japanese management is feudalistic while American management is parternalistic.

Drucker cites three other ways to measure white-collar productivity.

- The length of time it takes to bring a product or service successfully out of development and into the market.

- The number of successful new products and services that have been introduced in a given period, especially as compared with domestic and international competitors.

- The number of supporting staff people and particularly the levels of management needed for a given output. "Ideally both… and especially the levels of management… should not go up with volume at all," Drucker states. "Perhaps in modern organizations both should actually go down… for there is something like an 'information economy of scale' just as there are manufacturing economies of scale."

These 'other ways' of measurement are still quantitative and objective, which is Drucker's orientation, while work is increasingly qualitative and subjective. The emphasis should be placed where the biggest payoff could be derived and that is in *the process*.

Manage the Process and allow the 'psychological climate' to be established—the climate of freedom, control and trust—and true productivity gains are assured. Drucker's criteria, generally speaking, are modest if not simply manipulative. The emphasis is still on the bottom line and not on process. We should have learned by now that an 'output focus' is neither a necessary or sufficient condition to output because unless chronic problems in the system are addressed the results will be consistently disappointing. When you measure productivity in Cartesian terms, as Drucker and others are wont to do, you have a one dimensional approach (i.e., cause/effect/solution) to a multidimensional problem.

This is, quite frankly, embedded in anachronistic thinking suggesting we know the limits to which professionals can perform, which we do not. We let professionals determine, on their own, what their limits are. If Henry Ford or Thomas Edison had been measured and manipulated the way we are attempting to measure and manipulate professional workers today, I don't think we would ever have had the inexpensive automobile or the public utility, at least not from these two individualistic thinking entrepreneurs.

Creative energy is discouraged when you establish limits; when you develop criteria by which professionals are to be measured; when you try to bind their minds with tourniquets of quotas. When you use such methods to measure performance, your biggest products are stress and anxiety, accidents, chemical dependency, and a logarithmic progression in churn and turnover, tardiness and absenteeism. Once this behavior is in place, then, the invisible behaviors take over with the 'Mad Monarchs' spreading their venom. A 'breakdown culture' follows. It is a case of getting what you asked for, but not what you wanted.

Output Versus Outcome

In the final analysis, if you focus on measurement, you get the output you expect. If you focus on process, you realize outcomes well beyond your wildest expectations. It is a matter of focus and emphasis. Here is the irony and paradox:

Workers like to measure themselves against their own criteria and track their progress towards their desired outcomes. It gives them a sense of value added, accomplishment and worth in their work. They want to be 'effective' in what they are doing. But they resent it when they are measured on the basis of how 'efficiently' they perform. 'Effectiveness' is a measure of service, meeting the needs of the users and customers. Being effective is very important to workers. Efficiency, on the other hand, serves the needs of internal auditors and managers, who often use such measurement as a basis for justifying their existence.

'Efficiency experts' are therefore resented as atavistic appendages on the organization. So, the use of efficiency as an arbitrary criteria for performance fosters a sense of resentment, but also self-contempt as professionals think poorly of themselves for compliance with such measurements.

Focusing on efficiency instead of effectiveness promotes competition rather than cooperation, collusion rather than collaboration, individualism rather than collective identity and enterprise.

To illustrate this final point, in a two-year study between 1983 and 1985 *The American Productivity Center* of Houston, Texas, developed a six-phase methodology for measuring white-collar productivity and tested 56 pilot groups in 13 major United States organizations. This approach called for groups of up to 25 professionals to analyze what they did, define their own main services, devise their own measurement systems for their work and recommend what technology would help them (e.g., computers) do a better job. The emphasis was clearly on effectiveness, not efficiency. And the overall results were most outstanding. In every instance productivity gains were realized.

Still, despite such studies, we have not reached the point of acceptance that professionals must have control of their work and the freedom to do it in a trusting environment. Once provided with this climate for productive work, professionals still need bona fide leadership:

- Leaders determine the outcomes that are required to accomplish the organization's mission, while the

- Professionals have the responsibility of managing these processes toward achieving these desired outcomes.

In this manner, a team is formed of working professionals and managing leaders in a common guild. The leadership leads, but does not interfere with the process of achieving such outcomes. Instead, the leadership facilitates the process by providing these workers with the appropriate resources, tools, training and coaching-counseling-mentoring required, along with a climate conducive to doing productive work. These workers, holding up their part, can then focus on organizational effectiveness.

A Final Caveat

Professional workers will not be badgered about and treated like children. They are at the moment trying to handle a "double bind" situation of mixed messages in which they are told to take ownership of what they do, while being given little freedom and control. Don't be fooled by the masks they wear. While showing the face of conformity, their hostility toward the organization grows daily. This is manifested increasingly in what *Work Without Managers* describes as subversive activity with invisible behaviors taking over.

The only way to eliminate these subversive activities is for the organization to 'let go' and take some real risks, starting with being much more trusting of its workers. We need to get back to the basics; to make professional workers *self-managers* and managers *leaders* in the true sense of serving and seeing. It is an immodest agenda, but do we have any other choice?

Endnotes

(1) Szymanski, David, "Skilled-Labor Shortage Ahead, Experts Say," *The Tampa Tribune*, March 25, 1990.
(2) Whitney, op. cit.
(3) Ibid.
(4) Ibid.

SELECTED BIBLIOGRAPHY

These are the books that have influenced me, directly and indirectly, in the writing of *"Work Without Managers"*.

Abramson, Jeffrey B., *Liberation and Its Limits: The Moral and Political Thought of Freud.* New York: Free Press, 1984.

Ackoff, Russell L., and Fred E. Emery, *On Purposeful Systems.* Seaside, CA.: Intersystems Publications, 1972.

Adair, Robert K., *The Physics of Baseball.* New York: Harper & Row, 1990.

Andreasen, Nancy C., *The Broken Brain.* New York: Harper & Row, 1984.

Argyris, Chris, "A Few Words In Advance," *The Failure of Success,* ed. A. J. Marrow. New York: American Management Association, 1972.

—*Integrating the Individual and the Organization.* New York: John Wiley & Sons, Inc., 1964.

Arnold, David O., *The Sociology of Subcultures.* Santa Barbara: University of California Press, 1970.

Ansbacher, Heinz L., and Ansbacher, Rowena R. (eds), *The Individual Psychology of Alfred Adler*, Basic Books, Inc., New York, 1956.

Auerbach, Red, with Joe Fitzgerald, *On and Off the Court,* New York: Macmillan Publishing Co., Inc., 1985.

Baird, Bruce F., *The Technical Manager.* Belmont, CA.: Lifetime Learning Publications, 1983.

Banas, Paul A., "Employee Involvement: A Sustained Labor/Management Initiative at the Ford Motor Company," *Productivity in Organizations,* ed. John P. Campbell, Richard J. Campbell and Associates. San Francisco: Jossey-Bass Publishers, 1988.

Bardwick, Judith, *The Plateauing Trap.* New York: American Management Association, 1986.

Barrett, William, *Irrational Man.* New York: Anchor Books, 1962.

Barrymore, Dianne, *Too Much Too Soon.* New York: Buccaneer Books, 1981. [Reprint of 1961 edition.]

Bateson, Gregory, *Steps to an Ecology of Mind.* New York: Chandler Publishing Co., 1972.

Becker, Ernest, *The Birth and Death of Meaning.* New York: Macmillan Publishing Co., Inc., 1962.
—*The Denial of Death.* New York: Macmillan Publishing Co., Inc., 1975.

Beecher, Willard and Marguerite, *Beyond Success and Failure.* New York: Pocket Books, 1971.

Bellah, Robert N., Richard Madsen, William M. Sullivan, Ann Swidler, and Steven M. Tipton, *Habits of the Heart.* Berkeley and Los Angeles: University of California Press, 1985.

Bellamy, Edward, *Looking Backwards.* New Orleans: River City Press, 1987. [Reprint of 1888 edition.]

Bennis, Warren, *The Unconscious Conspiracy: Why Leaders Can't Lead.* New York: AMACOM, 1976.

Berger, Peter and Brigitte, and Hansfried Kellner, *The Homeless Mind: Modernization and Consciousness.* New York: Random House, Inc., 1973.

Berlin, Isaiah, *Four Essays on Liberty*, Oxford University Press, Oxford, England, 1969.

Birnbach, Lisa, *Going to Work.* New York: Villard Books, 1988.

Blake, Robert R. and Jane S. Mouton, *The Managerial Grid.* Houston: Gulf Publishing, 1964.

Blakeslee, Thomas R., *The Right Brain.* New York: Playboy Paperbacks, 1983.

Blanchard, Kenneth, and Spencer Johnson, *One Minute Manager.* New York; William Morrow and Co., Inc., 1982.

Block, Peter, *The Empowered Manager.* San Francisco: Jossey-Bass Publishers, 1987.

Bloom, Alan, *The Closing of the American Mind.* New York: Simon and Schuster, 1987.

Blumer, Herbert, *Symbolic Interactionism.* Berkeley: University of California Press, 1969.

Briles, Judith, *Woman to Woman: From Sabotage to Support.* New York: New Horizon Press, 1988.

Brill, Naomi I., *Working with People.* New York: J. B. Lippincott Company, 1973.

Buccholz, Steve, and Thomas Roth, *Creating the High Performance Team*, ed. Karen Hess. New York: John Wiley & Sons, 1987.

Burns, James MacGregor, *Leadership.* New York: Harper & Row, 1978.

Burroughs, William S., *The Naked Lunch.* New York: Grove Press, 1969. [Reprint of 1954 edition]

Butcher, Lee, *The Accidental Millionaire: The Rise & Fall of Steve Jobs at Apple Computer.* New York: Paragon House, 1987.

Cammer, Leonard, *Freedom from Compulsion.* New York: Pocket Books, 1977.

Camus, Albert, *The Plague.* New York: Alfred A. Knopf, 1948.

Capote, Truman, *In Cold Blood.* New York: Random House, 1967.

Capra, Fritjof, *The Tao of Physics; An Exploration of the Parallels between Modern Physics and Eastern Mysticism.* Glasgow: Fontana Paperbacks, 1976.

—*The Turning Point: Science, Society & The Rising Culture.* New York: Simon and Schuster, 1982.

Carroll, Lewis, *Alice in Wonderland: Through the Looking Glass.* New York: Random House, 1946.

Carson, Rachel L., *Silent Spring.* Greenwich, CT.: Fawcett Publications, Inc., 1962.

Christopher, Robert C., *The Japanese Mind: The Goliath Explained.* New York: Simon and Schuster, 1983.

Cole, Robert E., *Japanese Blue-Collar.* Berkeley: University of California Press, 1971.

—*Work, Mobility & Participation: A Comparative Study of American and Japanese Industry.* Berkeley: University of California Press, 1979.

Collier, Peter, and David Horowitz, *The Fords: An American Epic.* New York: Summit Books, 1987.

Cousins, Norman, *Modern Man Is Obsolete.* New York: Viking, 1945.

—*Anatomy of an Illness.* New York: Bantam Books, 1981.

—*Human Options.* New York: Berkeley Books, 1986.

Cribbin, James J., *Leadership.* New York: AMACOM, 1981.

Crosby, John F., *Illusion and Disillusion.* Belmont, CA.: Wadsworth Publishing, 1973.

Damasio, Antonio, *Descartes' Error*, Vintage Books, London, 1994.

Dawkins, Richard, *The Selfish Gene.* New York: Oxford University Press, 1976.

Deal, Terrence E., and Allan A. Kennedy, *Corporate Culture.* Reading, MA: Addison-Wesley Publishing Company, Inc., 1982.

Dean, John W., Ill, *Blind Ambition.* New York: Simon and Schuster, 1977.

DeBono, Edward, *Lateral Thinking.* Middlesex, England. Penguin Books, 1970.

—*Po: Beyond Yes and No.* Middlesex, England: Penguin Books, 1972.

Deming, W. Edwards, *Out Of The Crisis.* Boston: Massachusetts Institute of Technology, Center for Advanced Study, 1986.

Dickens, Charles, *A Tale Of Two Cities.* London: Penguin Books, 1988.

Donlevy, J. P., *The Ginger Man.* New York: Dell Publishers, 1970. [Reprint of 1959 edition.]

Douglass, Merrill E., and Donna N. Douglass, *Manage Your Time, Manage Your Work, Manage Yourself.* New York: AMACOM, 1980.

Downs, Anthony, *Inside Bureaucracy.* Boston: Little, Brown and Company, 1967.

Drucker, Peter F., *The New Realities.* New York: Harper & Row, 1989.

Edison, Thomas A., *Diary and Sundry Observations,* ed. D. D. Runes. Westport, CT.: Greenwood Press, Inc., 1968. [Reprint of 1948 edition.]

Ehrlich, Howard J., *The Social Psychology of Prejudice.* New York: John Wiley & Sons, 1973.

Eichenbaum, Luise, and Susie Orbach, *Between Women: Love, Envy, and Competition in Women's Friendships.* New York: The Viking Press, 1988.

Eliot, T. S., *The Waste Land.* New York: Harcourt, Brace & Co., Inc., 1972.

Ellis, Albert, and Robert A. Harper, *A Guide To Rational Living In An Irrational World.* Englewood Cliffs, NJ.: Prentice-Hall, 1961.

Encounter, ed. Arthur Burton. San Francisco: Jossey-Bass Inc., 1970.

Erasmus, Desiderius, *The Praise of Folly.* New York: Farrar, Straus, 1953.

Erikson, Erik H., *Childhood and Society.* New York: W. W. Norton & Company, Inc., 1963.

Etzioni, Amitai, *An Immodest Agenda.* New York: McGraw-Hill, 1983.

Festinger, Leon, *A Theory of Cognitive Dissonance.* Stanford: Stanford University Press, 1957.

Fisher, James R., Jr., *Confident Selling.* Englewood Cliffs, N.J: Prentice-Hall/Simon and Schuster, 1971.

Fitch, Robert Elliot, *Odyssey of the Self Centered Self.* New York: Harcourt, Brace & World, Inc., 1960.

Ford, Henry, with Samuel Crowther, *My Life and Work.* Salem, NH: Ayer Company Publishers, 1973. [1923 edition republished.]

Frankl, Viktor E., *Man's Search for Meaning.* New York: Washington Square Press, 1985.

Freud, Sigmund, *Civilization and Its Discontent.* New York: W. W. Norton & Co., Inc., 1930.

Freudenberger, H. J., *Burn Out: The High Cost of High Achievement.* New York: Doubleday & Co., Inc., 1980.

Fromm, Erich, *Beyond the Chains of Illusion.* New York: Simon and Schuster, 1962.

—*Escape From Freedom* New York: Rinehart & Company, Inc., 1941.

—*The Act of Loving.* London: Unwin Paperback, 1987.

—*The Heart of Man.* New York: Harper & Row, 1964.

—*The Sane Society.* Greenwich, CT.: Fawcett Publications, Inc., 1955.

—*To Have or To Be?* New York: Harper & Row, 1976.

—*On Disobedience and Other Essays.* London: Routledge & Kegan Paul, 1974.

Gabor, Dennis, *Inventing the Future*, Secker & Warburg, London, 1963.

Galbraith, John Kenneth, *The Affluent Society.* Boston: Houghton Mifflin Co., 1984.

—*The Anatomy of Power.* Boston: Houghton Mifflin Co., 1983.

—*The New Industrial State.* New York: The New American Library, Inc., 1968.

—*Economics in Perspective.* Boston: Houghton Mifflin Company, 1987.

Garson, Barbara, *The Electronic Sweatshop: How Compters Are Transforming the Office of the Future into the Factory of the Past,* Simon & Schuster, New York, 1988.

Gary, Romain, *Promise At Dawn.* New York: New Directions Press, 1987.

Gellerman, Saul W., *"Why 'Good' Managers Make Bad Ethical Choices," Leaders of Humanity.* New York: Center for International Leadership (Bell South Management Institute), 1986.

—*Management by Motivation.* New York: AMACOM, 1968.

Gibb, Jack R., *Trust.* Los Angeles: The Guild of Tutors Press, 1978.

Gibran, Kahlil, *The Prophet.* New York: Alfred A. Knopf, 1923.

Ginsberg, Allen, *Reality Sandwiches: Poems: 1953-1960.* San Francisco: City Lights, 1963.

Glasser, William, *Reality Therapy.* New York: Harper & Row, 1975.

Goffman, Erving, *The Presentation of Self in Everyday Life.* New York: Doubleday Anchor Books, 1959.

Goldratt, Eliyahu M., and Jeff Cox, *The Goal: A Process Of Ongoing Improvement.* New York: North River Press, 1986.

Goldwin, Robert A. (ed.), *Toward the Liberally Educated Executive,* Fund for Adult Education, New York, 1962 [Out of Print]

Gordon, Thomas, *Leader Effectiveness Training.* Solana Beach, CA.: Wyden Books, 1977.

Goth-Neuman, Darlene, *Writings.* Anaheim Hills, CA.: Goth Neuman, Inc., 1980.

Gould, Stephen Jay, An *Urchin in the Storm*. New York: W. W. Norton & Co., Inc., 1987.

—*The Mismeasure of Man*. New York: W. W. Norton & Co., Inc., 1985.

Grass, Gunter, *The Tin Drum*. New York: Pantheon Books, 1964.

Greenleaf, Robert K., *Servant Leadership: A Journey Into The Nature of Legitimate Power and Greatness*. New York: Paulist Press, 1977.

"Guilt and Guilt Feelings," *Knowledge of Man, Selected Essays of Martin Buber*, ed. Maurice Friedman. New York: Harper & Row, 1965.

Haas, Eugene J., and Thomas E. Drabek, *Complex Organizations: A Sociological Perspective*. New York: Macmillan Publishing Co., Inc., 1973.

Hall, Douglas T., and Associates, *Career Development in Organizations*. San Francisco: Jossey-Bass, 1986.

Hart, Leslie A., *Human Brain and Human Learning*. White Plains, NY.: Longman, Inc., 1983.

Heilbroner, Robert L., *An Inquiry Into The Human Prospect*. New York: W. W. Norton & Co., Inc., 1974.

Hersey, Paul, and Kenneth Blanchard, *Management of Organizational Behavior*. Englewood Cliffs, NJ.: Prentice Hall, 1972.

Herzberg, Frederick, *Work and the Nature of Man*. New York: World Publishing Company, 1966.

Hickman, Craig R., and Michael A. Silva, *The Future 500*. London: Unwin Hyman, Ltd., 1988.

Hirsch, E. D., Jr., *Cultural Literacy*. Boston: Houghton Mifflin Company, 1987.

Hoffer, Eric, *The True Believer*. New York: Harper & Row, 1951.

—*Working and Thinking on the Waterfront*. New York: Harper & Row, 1969.

—*The Ordeal of Change*. New York: Harper & Row, 1963.

Homans, George C., *The Human Group.* New York: Harcourt, Brace & World, Inc., 1959.

Hugo, Victor, *Les Miserables.* Bungay, Suffolk: Richard Clay (The Chaucer Press) Ltd., 1986.

Huse, Edgar F., *Organization Development and Change.* St. Paul, MN.: West Publishing Company, 1980.

Huston, John, *An Open Book,* New York: Ballantine Books, Inc., 1981.

Iacocca, Lee, with William Novak, *Iacocca: An Autobiography.* New York: Bantam Books, 1984.

Ichheiser, Gustav, *Appearances and Realities: Misunderstanding in Human Relations.* San Francisco: Jossey-Bass, 1970.

Illich, Ivan, *Deschooling Society.* New York: Harper & Row, 1971.

Imai, Masaaki, *Kaizen: The Key to Japan's Competitive Success.* New York: Random House, 1986.

James, William, *Pragmatism: A New Name For Some Old Ways Of Thinking.* Boston: Harvard University Press, 1976. [Reprint of 1907 edition]

Johnson, Julian, *The Path of the Masters.* Punjab, India: Radha Soami Satsang-Beas, 1939.

Jones, James, *From Here To Eternity.* New York: Dell Publishing Co., Inc., 1935.

Jones, Judy, and William Wilson, *An Incomplete Education.* New York: Ballantine Books, Inc., 1987.

Josephson, Matthew, *Edison.* New York: McGraw-Hill, 1959.

Joyce, James, *A Portrait of the Artist as a Young Man.* New York: The Viking Press, Inc., 1982. [Reprint of 1916 edition.]

Kahn, Robert L., et al., *Organizational Stress.* New York: John Wiley & Sons, 1964.

Kennedy, Paul, *The Rise and Fall of the Great Powers.* New York: Random House, 1988.

Kepner, Charles H., and Benjamin B. Tregoe, *The New Rational Manager.* Princeton, N.J.: Princeton Research Press, 1981.

Kerouac, Jack, *On The Road*. New York: Penguin Books, 1979. [Reprint of 1958 edition.]

Kidder, Tracy, *The Soul of a New Machine*. Boston: Little Brown, 1981.

Klapp, Orrin E., *Collective Search for Identity*. New York: Holt, Rinehart and Winston, 1969.

Kotter, John P., *The Leadership Factor*. New York: Free Press, 1988.

Krishnamurti, J., *You Are The World*. New York: Harper & Row, 1972.

Kuhn, Thomas S., *The Structure of Scientific Revolutions*. Chicago: University of Chicago Press, 1962.

Laing, R. D., *The Politics of Experience*. New York: Ballantine Books, 1967.

—*The Politics of the Family*. New York: Pantheon Books, 1969.

Lasch, Christopher, *The Culture of Narcissism: American Life in An Age of Diminishing Expectations*. New York: W. W. Norton & Company, Inc., 1978.

Lesieur, Frederick G. (ed.), *The Scanlon Plan: A Frontier to Labor Management Cooperation*, M.I.T. Press, Boston, 1964.

Levinson, Harry, *The Great Jackass Fallacy*. Boston: Harvard University Press, 1973.

Lewin, Kurt, *Field Theory in Social Science*. New York: Harper & Row, 1951.

Likert, Rensis, *The Human Group: Its Management and Values*. New York: McGraw-Hill, 1967.

Littwin, Susan, *The Postponed Generation: Why American Youth Are Growing Up Later*. New York: William Morrow and Co., Inc., 1986.

Lorenz, Konrad, *Behind the Mirror*. New York: A Harvest Book, 1973.

Lutz, William, *Doublespeak*. New York: Harper & Row, 1989.

Machiavelli, Niccolo, *The Prince*. New York: New American Library, 1980.

Marcuse, Herbert, *One Dimensional Man.* London: Ark Paperbacks, 1980.

Martin, Jay. *Who Am I This Time? Uncovering The Fictive Personality,* New York: W.W. Norton & Company, Inc., 1988.

Maruya, Saiichi, *Singular Rebellion.* New York: Harper & Row, 1986.

Maslow, Abraham, *Motivation and Personality.* New York: Harper & Row, 1970.

Mason, Marilyn, et. al., *Facing Shame: Families in Recovery.* New York: W. W. Norton & Company, Inc., 1987.

May, Rollo, *The Meaning of Anxiety.* New York: W. W. Norton & Company, Inc., 1977.

McClelland, David, et. al., *The Achieving Society.* Princeton, NJ.: D. Van Nostrand Co., Inc., 1961.

McElvaine, Robert S., *Down and Out: Letters from the Forgot ten Man in the Great Depression.* Chapel Hill, NC.: University of North Carolina Press, 1986.

McGregor, Douglas, *The Human Side of Enterprise.* New York: McGraw-Hill Book Company, Inc., 1960.

Melville, Herman, *Billy Budd and Other Tales.* New York: New American Library, 1961.

Modern Organization Theory, ed. Mason Haire. New York: John Wiley & Sons, Inc., 1959.

Morita, Akio, and Shintaro Ishihara, *The Japan That Can Say 'No': The Case for a New U.S. Japan Relationship.* Tokyo: Kobusha Press, 1989.

Morley, John David, *The Case of Thomas N.* New York: The Atlantic Monthly Press, 1987.

Murrow, A.J. (ed.), *The Failure of Success,* American Management Association, New York, 1971.

Nevins, Allan, and F. E. Hill. *Ford: Decline & Rebirth 1933-1962 (III),* (three volumes). Salem, NH: Ayer Company, Publishers, 1965.

—*Ford: Expansion and Challenge* 1915 1933 (II). Salem, NH: Ayer Company, 1957.

—*Ford: The Times, The Man,* The Company (I). Salem, NH.: Ayer Company, 1954.

Nietzsche, Friedrich, *Beyond Good and Evil.* New York: Random House, Inc., 1966.

—*Thus Spoke Zarathustra.* Baltimore: Penguin Books, 1969.

Nisbet, Robert, *The Present Age: Progress and Anarchy in Modern America.* New York: Harper & Row, 1988.

Novak, Michael, *The Experience of Nothingness.* New York: Harper Torchbooks, 1970.

Orwell, George, *Nineteen Eighty Four.* New York: Buccaneer Books, 1982.

Ouchi, William, *Theory Z.* Reading, MA.: Addison-Wesley Publishing Company, 1981.

Ouspensky, P. D., *The Psychology for Man's Possible Evolution.* New York: Vintage Books, 1974.

Packard, Vance, *The Waste Makers.* Boston: Little, Brown and Company [Out of print].

Pasearella, Perry, *The New Achievers.* New York: Free Press, 1984.

Pelletier, Kenneth R., *Mind as Healer, Mind as Slayer.* New York: A Delta Book, 1977.

Peter, Dr. Lawrence J., and Raymond Hull, *The Peter Principle.* New York: William Morrow & Company, Inc., 1969.

Peters, Thomas J., and Robert Waterman, *In Search of Excellence.* New York: Harper & Row, 1982.

Rabkin, Richard, *Inner and Outer Space.* New York: W. W. Norton & Company, Inc., 1970.

Raelin, Joseph A., *The Clash of Cultures: Management & Professionals,* New York: Harper & Row, 1986.

Ralph Waldo Emerson: Essays and Lectures, ed. Joel Porte. New York: The Library of America, 1983. [Reprint of 1844 edition.]

Rand, Ayn, *The Virtue of Selfishness.* New York: The New American Library, 1964.

Rank, Otto, *Psychology and the Soul*. New York: A.S. Barnes & Company, 1961.

Rifkin, Jeremy (with Ted Howard), *Entropy: A New World View*. New York: Bantam Books, 1981.

Rogers, Carl R., *On Becoming A Person*. Boston: Houghton Mifflin Company, 1961.

Rokeach, Milton, *The Nature of Values*. New York: Free Press, 1973.

Salinger, J. D., *The Catcher in the Rye*. New York: Bantam Books, 1977.

Schickel, Richard, *Intimate Strangers: The Culture of Celebrity*. New York: Doubleday & Company, Inc., 1985.

Schlosssstein, Steven, *The End of the American Century*. New York: Congdon and Weed, 1990.

Schulberg, Budd, *What Makes Sammy Run?* Cambridge, MA.: Robert Bentley, Inc., 1979.

Schweitzer, Albert, *Pilgrimage to Humanity*. New York: Philosophical Paperbacks, 1983.
—*Reverence for Life*. New York: Irvington, 1969.

Sculley, John, and John A. Byrne, *Odyssey: Pepsi to Apple*. New York: Harper & Row, 1987.

Seabury, David, *The Art of Selfishness*. New York: Pocket Books, 1974.

Selye, Hans, *Stress Without Distress*. New York: New American Library, 1974.

Shakespeare, William, *The Tragedy of Othello, The Moor of Venice*. New Haven, CT.: Yale University Press, 1961.

Sinetar, Marsha, *Do What You Love, The Money Will Follow*. New York: Dell Trade Paperback, 1987.

Slater, Philip, *The Pursuit of Loneliness*. Boston: Beacon Press, 1971.

Sloan, Alfred, *My Years With General Motors*. New York: Doubleday & Company, Inc., 1972.

Smith, M. Brewster, *Social Psychology and Human Values.* Chicago: Aldine Publishing Company, 1969.

Smith, Page, *Killing the Spirit.* New York: The Viking Press, 1990.

Smith, Robert P., *Where Did You Go? "Out" What Did You Do? "Nothing."* San Francisco: Lexikos Publishing, 1974.

Snow, C. P. *Two Cultures*, Cambridge University Press, London, 1959.

Sorokin, Pitrim, A *Crisis of Our Age.* New York: E. P. Dutton & Co., Inc., 1941.

—*The Ways and Power of Love.* Boston: Beacon Press, 1954.

—*Social And Cultural Dynamics.* Boston: Porter Sargent Publisher, 1957.

—*The American Sex Revolution.* Boston: Porter Sargent, Publisher, 1956.

Springer, Sally P., and Georg Deutsch, *Left Brain, Right Brain.* San Francisco: W. H. Freeman and Company, 1981.

Steinbeck, John, *The Grapes of Wrath.* New York: The Viking Press, 19:39.

Strohmeyer, John, *Crisis in Bethlehem.* Bethesda, MD.: Adler & Adler, 1986.

Suarez, Rick, Roger C. Mills, and Darlene Stewart, *Sanity, Insanity and Common Sense.* New York: Fawcett Columbine, 1987.

Szasz, Thomas, *The Second Sin.* New York: Anchor Books, 1974.

Tannenbaum, Arnold S., *Social Psychology of the Work Organization.* Belmont, CA.: Brooks/Cole Publishing Company, 1966.

Tarrant, John J., *Drucker: The Man Who Invented The Corporate Society.* New York: Warner Books, 1976. [Out of print]

Taylor, Frederick Winslow, *The Principles of Scientific Management.* New York: W. W. Norton & Company, Inc., 1967. [Reprint of 1911 edition.]

Terkel, Studs, *Working.* New York: Pantheon, 1971.

Tocqueville, Alexis de, *Democracy in America,* Volumes I and II. New York: Alfred A. Knopf, 1945. [Reprint of 1835 edition.]

Toffler, Alvin, *Future Shock*. New York: Random House, Inc., 1970.

—*The Third Wave*. New York: William Morrow and Co., Inc., 1980.

Valentine, Alan, *The Age of Conformity*. Chicago: Henry Regnery Company, 1954.

Ward, Barbara, Lopsided World, W. W. Norton & Co., New York, 1968.

Warner, Samuel, *Self-Realization and Self- Defeat*, New York: Grove Press, 1966.

Watts, Alan W., *The Wisdom of Insecurity*. New York: Random House, Inc., 1951.

—*Psychotherapy East and West*, New York: Ballantine Books, 1961.

White, Theodore, *America In Search of Itself: The Making of the President 1956-1980*. New York: Harper & Row, 1982.

Whitman, Walt, *Leaves of Grass*. Ithaca, NY.: Cornell University Press, 1961.

Whyte, William H., Jr., *The Organization Man*. New York: Simon and Schuster, 1956.

Wilcock, Keith, *The Corporate Tribe*. New York: Warner Books, Inc., 1985.

Will, George F., *Men at Work: The Craft of Baseball*. New York: Macmillan, 1990.

Wills, Garry, *Reagan's America: Innocents At Home*. New York: Doubleday & Company, Inc., 1987.

Wilson, Colin, *Access to Inner Worlds*. London: Rider & Company, Ltd., 1983.

—*The Outsider*. New York: Dell Publishing Co., Inc., 1956.

Wilson, Sloan, *The Man In The Gray Flannel Suit*, New York: Arbor House Publishing Co., 1983.

Witcover, Jules, *The Resurrection of Richard Nixon*. New York: Putnam, 1970.

Wolfe, Thomas, *Look Homeward, Angel,* New York: Charles Scribner's Sons, 1929.

Wolff, Kurt H., *The Sociology of Georg Simmel.* New York: Free Press, 1950.

Wood, Allen, *Karl Marx.* New York: Routledge & Kegan Paul, 1981.

Woodcock, Alexander, and Monte Davis, *Catastrophe Theory: A Revolutionary Way of Understanding How Things Change.* Middlesex, England: Penguin Books, 1978.

Yankelovich, Daniel, *New Rules: Searching For Self Fulfillment In A World Turned Upside Down,* New York: Random House, 1981.

Yeats, William Butler, *Collected Poems of William Butler Yeats.* New York: Macmillan Company, 1950.

Zilbergeld, Bernie, *The Shrinking of America: Myths of Psychological Change.* Boston: Little, Brown and Company, 1983.

INDEX

F

factors contributing to this
 dilemma 54
Fairness Issue is generally
 viewed in terms of 258
Fall From Grace 91
family once meant 73
Fatiguing Preoccupation
 With The Negative
schematic 182
FDR declared war on 94
final solution 307
First Machine Age
 closed system 30
Fisher, James R., Jr.,
 "America is dead! Long live
 America! - essay 301
Fisher, James R., Jr. (quote) 1, 4
flower children 90
followers - safe hires - 70% 156
Ford
 only grammar school edu-
 cation 138
Ford created
 $5 work day 137
Fortune 100 company
 case study 66
Frederick Herzberg's
 Work and the Nature of
 Man - book 240
Frederick Winslow Taylor-
 quote 112
freedom, control and trust 348
free lunch mentality 41, 307

French Revolution 102
French say 331
Friedrich Nietzsche 38
Friedrich Nietzsche asserted 38
Fringe Benefits and
 Entitlement 253
Fritjof Capra 11
Fromm, Erich 207
 To Have and To Be - book 301
Fully Developed Human
 Being 136
fun to be at work 282

G

Garten, Jeffrey E. 130
Gary Hart: Inside Outsider
 reckless abandon games 164
Gellerman, Saul W. 209
General Motors assembly plant
 Van Nuys, Los Angeles 196
George F. Will's
 Men at Work - book 379
George Washington 324
Gestalt therapy 244
giving false information 198
GM Van Nuys assemblers see
 team concept as a joke 197
Goethe - quote 133
Good News
 professional workforce 385
Goth Neuman, Darlene 303
grand strategies now are
 reactions to 92
Great American Dream
 when it explodes 87

ABOUT THE AUTHOR

D R. JAMES R. Fisher, Jr. is an industrial and organizational development psychologist with a diverse work experience. He writes from this background spelling out what he thinks needs to be done to get senior managers, midlevel managers, and workers off the dime and on the same page. What is unusual about his approach is that he examines work, workers, and the workplace from the perspective of workers in the trenches. This finds him as objectively diagnostic of workers as of management. He sees them both guilty of self-deception and self-delusion. Dr. Fisher has been a laborer at Standards Brands, Inc., during five summers while earning degrees at the University of Iowa, a bench chemist at Standard Brands upon graduation, then a chemical sales engineer, field sales manager, and an international corporate executive with Nalco Chemical Company. At this point, he took a sabbatical and went back to school and earned a Ph.D. in industrial and organizational psychology. Consulting Fortune 500 companies followed, then a stint with Honeywell, Inc. as a management psychologist, and finally Director of Human Resources for Planning & Development for Honeywell Europe, Ltd. Dr. Fisher has worked and lived on four continents. In addition he has found time to be an adjunct professor, fiction and nonfiction author, lecturer, and consultant. This is one in a series of books in the genre of industrial psychology and organizational development. He resides in Tampa, Florida with his wife, Betty. He may be reached for keynote speaking at this e-mail address: TheDeltaGrpFL@cs.com. Check out his website: www.fisherofideas.com where you will find all his books and essays on a diverse repertoire of subjects.